VIVIENNE KNIGHT left fashion journalism for films in 1942 when she was invited to join Britain's most innovative team of film-makers — Michael Powell and Emeric Pressburger.

As their Public Relations Officer she had the pleasure of promoting such films as *A Matter of Life and Death* (U.S. title *A Stairway to Heaven*), *Black Narcissus*, *The Red Shoes* and *The Tales of Hoffman*.

In 1952 she went to Sir Michael Balcon's Ealing Studios where she became an Associate Producer in 1954.

In 1956 she became an independent scriptwriter for films and television, often working in collaboration with her late husband, Patrick Campbell — the 3rd Baron Glenavy.

She lives mainly in the South of France and has written this biography at the request of the late Trevor Howard and his wife, Helen Cherry.

TREVOR HOWARD

A GENTLEMAN AND A PLAYER

Vivienne Knight

SPHERE BOOKS LIMITED

To Paddy...
also for Kate and Emily

SPHERE BOOKS LTD

Published by the Penguin Group
27 Wrights Lane, London W8 5TZ, England
Viking Penguin Inc., 40 West 23rd Street, New York, New York 10010, USA
Penguin Books Australia Ltd, Ringwood, Victoria, Australia
Penguin Books Canada Ltd, 2801 John Street, Markham, Ontario, Canada L3R 1B4
Penguin Books (NZ) Ltd, 182–190 Wairau Road, Auckland 10, New Zealand

Penguin Books Ltd, Registered Offices: Harmondsworth, Middlesex, England

First published by Muller, Blond and White Ltd 1986
Published by Sphere Books Ltd 1988

'War Poet' by Sidney Keyes, which appears on page 36, is taken from *The Collected Poems of Sidney Keyes*, edited by Michael Meyer (1962), and is reproduced by kind permission of Routledge & Kegan Paul plc. The extract on pages 132–3 from *Clinging to the Wreckage* by John Mortimer is reproduced by kind permission of Weidenfeld & Nicolson.

Printed and bound in Great Britain by
Richard Clay Ltd, Bungay, Suffolk
Set in 10/11pt Monophoto Palatino

PICTURE CREDITS

The publisher has endeavoured to acknowledge all copyright holders of the pictures reproduced in this book. However, in view of the complexity of securing copyright information, should any photographs be wrongly attributed, the publisher will make any appropriate changes in future editions of this book.

Stills from the films *The Way to the Stars* and *Brief Encounter* by courtesy of the Rank Organization plc and the National Film Archive, London. Photograph from *The Taming of the Shrew* by courtesy of the Royal Victoria Hall Foundation. Stills from the films *The Third Man* and *The Heart of the Matter* by courtesy of EMI Screen Entertainment Limited and the National Film Archive, London. Still from *Sons and Lovers* © 1960 Twentieth Century Fox Film Corporation. Still from *Mutiny on the Bounty* © 1962 Metro-Goldwyn-Mayer Inc. Still from *Ryan's Daughter* © 1970 Metro-Goldwyn-Mayer Inc. Still from *Hedda Gabler* copyright BBC (Enterprises) 1962. Cartoon strips by Flook reproduced by kind permission of the *Daily Mail*. Still from *Catholics* by courtesy of Hemisphere Productions and Granada TV. Still from *Staying On* by courtesy of Granada TV. Still from *Sir Henry at Rawlinson End* by courtesy of Blue Dolphin Film Distributors Limited. Still from *No Country for Old Men* by courtesy of Derek Evans. Still from *Dust* by courtesy of Eric Vauthier. Family photographs contributed by Trevor Howard and his sister, Merla Lagière.

Acknowledgements

My first debt must be to Trevor Howard and Helen Cherry who invited me to write this book. I am deeply grateful to them for a completely absorbing experience and I very much hope that the result does not fall too short of their trustful expectations. They have both given so generously of their time, hospitality and help.

My fondest thanks are due to Hayley Francis for all her aid and for her unflagging enthusiasm for the work in hand, also to Irene Josephy for her staunch support and encouragement.

I am also most beholden to the following who have consented to be interviewed, quoted or rendered assistance in many other ways. Any errors or omissions in this list are mine alone and for any such I beg forgiveness.

Stewart Andrews, Sir Richard Attenborough CBE, Ossie Bates, Marie Burke, Patricia Burke, Gladys Barnes, Mrs Bodinacoda, Jack Cardiff, Adrienne Corri, Theo Cowan, Jack Davies, Daniel Farson, Dulcie Gray, Sir Alec Guinness CBE, Graham Greene CH, OM, Jane Greer, Marge Guterman, Martin Hardcastle, Sir Anthony Havelock-Allan, Dame Wendy Hiller OBE, George G. Jameson, Sybil Kerisson, Bernard Kimble, Merla Lagière, Danny Lavezzo, Sir David Lean CBE, Christopher Lee, Jack Lee, Euan Lloyd, Michael Meyer, Keith McConnell, Anthony Mendleson, Sir Ewen Montagu CBE, John Mortimer QC, Ronald Neame, Major G. Norton (RTD), Tony Palmer, Lorene Polanski, Venetia Pollock, Dilys Powell CBE, Douglas Roberts, Brigadier J. S. Ryder (RTD), The Duke of St Albans OBE, George Schaefer, James Sharkey, Douglas Slocombe, Lt. Colonel J. R. Stephenson OBE, Gilly Stone, Margaret Unsworth, Philip Wrack, Raymond Young.

V.K.

CHAPTER ONE

'Child overboard!'

Passengers rushed to the liner's rails, bells rang, whistles blew and speaking tubes from bridge to engine room and elsewhere hummed with urgent commands.

A young mother, who had been happily swinging her small daughter on deck, rushed to the side and seeing the little body floating in a sailor suit; fainted. While the small daughter cried and sal volatile was administered to the young mother, the thrum of the engine room gradually ceased and then was silent. Topsides, sailors were swiftly lowering a boat and anxious observers eyed the distance between the pitiful body in the sea and the rescue boat as it hit the water. Strong rowers pulled away, watched from every deck, porthole and, most acutely, by the Captain on the bridge. The rowers came abreast of the body and quick hands reached out to lift it into the boat. As it rose, the sea drained away and the sailors discovered that they had rescued not a child but an uninhabited white sailor suit.

On board, passengers reacted in the customary fashion to sudden relief from anxiety: they cheered, laughed, and chattered rather more loudly than usual. On the bridge, the Captain probably expressed himself more quietly, but much more forcibly. Captains of liners do not care to stop the ship to pick up the laundry.

Only our young mother, now restored to activity, spared no time for rejoicing. She was too busy searching the ship for the owner of the sailor suit because he happened to be her son. He was certainly not on any deck, neither was he in their stateroom, none of the stewards had seen him, and so the search went on. Meanwhile, the rescue boat returned alongside and was hoisted back onto its davits, a different verse of whistles and bells sounded, and the engines began to slide into life again.

And there he was.

A stark naked little boy crouching in the engine room, totally entranced by the huge world of greased metal around him. A helpful engineer took him out of his trance, and the engine room, to restore him to his mother.

It was Trevor Howard's first contribution to drama. At the time he was five years old and his name was Trevor Wallace Howard-Smith.

This was Trevor's second sea voyage. He had been born in Cliftonville, England, on 29 September 1916 and shortly afterwards sailed to Ceylon with his parents. His father, Arthur Howard-Smith, held an office in Colombo for Lloyd's of London. Sadly, there are now no traces or recollections of him in Colombo. His former office on the harbour is no longer a concern of Lloyd's and the Grand Oriental Hotel, where he lived for some time before returning to England, is now the Hotel Taprobane. The hotel can have changed little since his time: the lift is still worked by a pulley and the whole, vast building has all the charm of another age.

Indeed, little is known about Trevor's father except that he was born in the middle of a family of seven and was a dedicated philatelist. While he was working in Colombo he returned to England on home leave just once every three years, more like a favourite uncle than a regular father. Merla Lagière, Trevor's younger sister who was born in Colombo, remembers him best. However, both children were sent to schools abroad at an early age so childhood memories are few. Trevor could not travel to Ceylon during the school holidays as the sea voyage was too long to be worthwhile. Therefore, by the time his father returned to England in the late thirties it was too late to regard him as a father. He was called Dad and was loved and respected, but the parental ties were loose.

Mother emerges as a much more positive character and as a remarkable woman. She was born Mabel Wallace, the youngest child of ten, to a Scots-Canadian family. At an early age she decided to leave Canada and become a nurse. By the rather unusual process of advancing her age by a few years she entered a training hospital in America, a country favoured by several of her brothers and sisters for the furtherance of their careers. Once trained, she left hospital routine behind her and became something of a specialist as a private nurse. Then, as now, an attendant private nurse was a prerequisite of the rich and from their ranks came Mabel Wallace's patients. They were not only rich but many of them travelled widely, taking her with them. In view of the tenacity of purpose and resourcefulness that she exhibited later in life, it can be assumed that she chose her patients with one eye on their luggage. A trunk without evidence of travel held no interest for her. She wanted to see the world, and she did.

Trevor thinks that his parents met on board ship, but Merla is almost sure that they met in Ceylon. Either is possible. They were certainly married in England but spent much of their married life in Ceylon.

In the hot weather Mabel took the children up in the hills to N'Eliya where Trevor has a dim recollection of going to kindergarten. His clearest memory of early childhood is a visit to the Buddhist Temple at Kandy during a religious festival, where elephants carried the sacred tooth of Buddha. The most sacred elephant did not touch the ground, but walked on a red carpet. Trevor recalls this as his first experience of grandeur. It might also have been the beginning of his deep affection for elephants.

According to the very slim, but invaluable, collection of notes left by his mother, N'Eliya boasted one of the finest golf courses in the world. The professional golfer in residence at the time fashioned a miniature set of clubs for young Trevor and taught him to play. By the time he was five he was playing with a local caddie who was not much bigger than himself. Interestingly enough, golf is the only game that Trevor never played again. Neither was he to see Ceylon again for many years because he was soon to take that second sea voyage.

When Arthur Howard-Smith saw his family off on an American liner out of Colombo he was not to see any of them again for nearly two years, and it would be rather longer before he was reunited with Trevor. Today, with the convenience of air travel, such a long separation seems inhuman; then it was almost commonplace. Added to this, it would seem that Mabel Howard-Smith's thirst for travel had not abated with marriage. Her itinerary on this occasion, accompanied by two young children, would have daunted most mothers — but not Mabel.

The liner was bound for San Francisco, stopping over at a

variety of ports: Singapore, Japan and the Philippines. Between the latter and Honolulu she suffered a storm at sea which nearly wrecked her. Personal belongings and clothes were washed overboard and the damage done to the ship kept her in harbour at Honolulu for a month to be refitted.

Of all adventures, it might be supposed that two young children would remember this as greatly exciting, but both Trevor and his sister seem to have taken it all as a matter of course. Neither, it seems, did Trevor fail to live up to his early promise on board. His mother notes that, 'During that long voyage from Colombo, Trevor was once put in irons on the deck by orders of the Captain – for having climbed to the crow's next.' It boggles the mind. Well might the Captain have wearied of the antics of young Trevor, as skipper next to God he'd had troubles enough, but 'put in irons'? It must have been done, at least in part, as a game but there is a trace of the long shadow of Captain Bligh.

After refitting at Honolulu the ship proceeded to San Francisco and from there the Howard-Smith family went on to Los Angeles. This was to be a long visit to Mabel's best friend. They had known one another since girlhood and Mabel had been the maid of honour at her friend's wedding in 1906. On 18 April of the same year the San Francisco earthquake had struck and Mabel had immediately left Los Angeles for San Francisco to offer her nursing services. Many years later, his mother told Trevor about her experiences in the San Francisco earthquake. He listened politely but could not believe it was all true: he thought she was romancing and had gone a little too far. It was only after her death that he found the story was documented.

While in Los Angeles, Trevor remembers that they stayed in a house on Hermosa Beach for six months, which he didn't altogether enjoy. During this time he thinks he attended school, which might account for his disenchantment.

Again the long shadow fell when Trevor was taken to watch Mary Pickford and Douglas Fairbanks filming on the beach. Merla thinks this was around Christmas time because Trevor was talking about Father Christmas and was overheard by Mary Pickford, who thought the nomenclature cute; to her that legendary figure was Santa Claus. In later years Trevor was told by his mother that he had actually appeared in a film called *Bubbles* with Mary

Pickford. In fact his mother notes that, 'They talked to Trevor and offered to put him in the picture, but we were just about ready to leave for Canada.' Trevor's hour for stardom had not yet struck.

So they left for Canada by train, travelling through the Rockies where Trevor saw snow for the first time: naturally he stayed out in the observation car until he was covered with it. En route they stopped off at Colorado Springs and Chicago, where Al Capone's distinguished career was already flourishing and licking Prohibition was the order of the day.

An entire year was spent in Canada visiting the many members of the Wallace clan in Ottawa, Toronto and Brantford, Ontario. Again a certain amount of schooling must have been endured but the holidays saw the tireless Mrs Howard-Smith on the move with her brood of two once more.

Next they travelled south to New York to stay at the Pennsylvania Hotel from which they sallied forth to see the sights, the greatest of these being that new wonder of the world the Empire State Building. Trevor's later passion for jazz must have already been in embryonic form as his mother records that he requested the bands in the different restaurants they visited to play his favourite pieces. It's as well that Merla remembers that he looked so engaging that 'nobody could refuse him anything'. *Plus ça change* . . . She also remembers that he took command of every hotel lift in sight.

During this visit Trevor met one relative who was to have a great effect on his life some years later, his Aunt Margaret. Another dauntless member of the Wallace family, she was already the Superintendent of the General Hospital in Passaic, New Jersey, and rapidly became Number One Favourite to Merla and Trevor. As Merla puts it, she was *the* one.

The last lap of this long voyage around the world was across the Atlantic to England. Here, after a personal refitting, Trevor was to begin his education proper at Clifton College, Bristol, a seat of learning famed for educating and safeguarding the sons of British gentlemen abroad and boys of other nationalities whose parents wished them to have an English schooling.

Trevor was not yet eight years of age and his mother and sister were on their way back to Ceylon. Life might have looked rather bleak to him at the time but he remembers no great unhappiness as he was absorbed into the Junior School. He was a lively, friendly little boy who enjoyed the companionship of other boys and delighted in all the games. Holidays became his only problem. While Merla remembers their mother returning to England for Christmas and summer holidays every year, Trevor dwells on time spent with seaside landladies, one of whom locked him out during the day leaving him to amuse himself by taking donkey rides on the sands of Weston-super-Mare. It's the not uncommon case of sibling memory at total variance and the facts most likely lie somewhere between the two. Their mother notes that, 'Some of the masters always looked after him during the holidays.' This became true, but not for some time.

Trevor certainly remembers a Christmas being spent at the Lancaster Gate Hotel in London because he recalls going to theatres and films. Merla remembers that he took her all the way to the Dominion Cinema in Tottenham Court Road by underground. As they emerged from the cinema Trevor nudged his sister, 'Do you know how far we are from home? We're ever so far. This is Tottenham Court Road and it's *miles* from Lancaster Gate.'

When they returned to the hotel, having had a lovely afternoon at the cinema, they encountered two elderly sisters who were permanent residents. They were the Misses Playfair and reflected the Edwardian age with their high-boned collars and piled bird's nest hair. They both took a great interest in the children, one tending to favour Merla while her sister was captivated by the angelic-looking Trevor.

Trevor's admirer bent over him, 'Did you see a nice film?' Off came his cap and he gazed at Miss Playfair through blond curls.

'*The Sin Flood*,' he replied.

Summer holidays, when Mother came to England, were passed in hotels at a variety of South Coast resorts. During this part of their childhood Merla and Trevor were very close, despite long separations. When Merla was newly born Trevor had wanted to know whether she could whistle, probably because he was struggling to achieve that accomplishment himself. On being told that she was a bit too young to whistle, he decreed that she should be called Bontoy. Only Trevor knew why he had chosen the name and he has long forgotten, but it stuck – in the form of Bonnie – until Merla rebelled often enough to reclaim her baptismal rights. But during those holidays she was Bonnie, and Bonnie's first holiday task was to sit and memorize all the names of Trevor's cricket teams. Not surprisingly, Merla's interest in cricket is now very slight. 'Boring? Of course it was boring. But I thought he was a god. I didn't mind doing it for him because it pleased him.'

Later, when Merla was at school in Switzerland, there were occasional skiing holidays with Mother and Merla. Trevor had learnt to ski and skate in Canada and he continued to enjoy both pursuits for many years.

But the London and seaside hotel holidays with Mother and Merla – and Father, if it happened to be his year – didn't fill all those long weeks when school was out – not every year.

At Clifton College Martin Hardcastle was then a young master in the Junior School. Although he was not connected with Trevor's house, he had taught Trevor in his early days at the school and knew him quite well. He was horrified to discover that the boy spent many holidays alone in a seaside boarding house and told his mother. She was equally horrified and promptly invited Trevor to stay. Martin Hardcastle's father was the Archdeacon of Canterbury and Trevor found himself staying in a very old house in the Cathedral precincts, with a complete family: parents, Martin and four sisters. For the first time since leaving Ceylon, Trevor enjoyed family life in a family home. He not only loved every minute of it but he fitted in extremely well and Mrs Hardcastle became very fond of him. She was deeply upset when his first visit came to an end and he cried on leaving. He would have been about eleven.

He was to return to Canterbury for at least part of the holidays for the next two or three years. Often there were other boys in a similar state to his own, King's School was nearby and games were played. Even the cathedral was a great source of joy because they could climb up on to the roof. There was always something going on and Christmas was a marvellous time there. Trevor enjoyed at least two Christmases in Canterbury.

Trevor's adaptability and ease of manner when visiting Canterbury made a great impression on the Hardcastles. Trevor had beautiful manners, he went to all the parties and generally revelled in the way of life furnished by the Archdeacon and his lovely family. 'There were never any problems. He never put a foot wrong, which was remarkable in a boy of his age.' But it is allowed that the lad was rather more rumbustious at school than he was at Canterbury, thus showing sensitivity and wisdom well beyond his years: he was not about to blot his copy-book in Paradise.

At school Mr Hardcastle remembers that Trevor's sole interests were to be found on the sports fields or in the boxing ring. A natural games player, he played cricket and rugby, and boxed for the College. 'He was not an aggressive player but was an extrovert.' When Martin Hardcastle started a Scout Troop, Trevor was among the first to join, but although he enjoyed scouting and the controlled freedom of going on camping expeditions, his first and for-all-time love was for sports. Certainly he was not a scholar, either when young or as he grew older. It is unlikely that this was due to lack of ability as he was quick and bright enough: he just didn't care and didn't work.

Although Martin Hardcastle followed Trevor to the Upper School when Trevor was about fourteen, they had little to do with one another at school as Trevor became more adult. But their friendship continued way beyond school years. Trevor has always kept in touch with Martin Hardcastle, although sometimes many years have passed between meetings. But, to his old friend, Trevor's voice and manner, his solidity of character, are all easily recognizable no matter how many years pass. Even his walk, particularly on the cricket field, is 'Exactly the same, exactly the same.' Mr Hardcastle calls to mind a post-war cricket match when Trevor went down with the MCC to play Clifton. The college was out in force and there was a breathless hush as Trevor went out to bat. The walk was the same but, most unfortunately, Trevor was run out before he could touch the ball at all. 'A frightful tragedy.' Martin Hardcastle remembers taking one of his sisters to Brighton to see Trevor in a play. Trevor had not seen the sister for about twelve years and, 'He was so delighted to see her. He might have seen her only two weeks before so immediate was the warmth, the great warmth.'

Martin Hardcastle is still puzzled by Trevor's emergence as an actor. As far as he can determine, nobody ever saw him act at school. He just might have taken part in an end-of-term house play, but that would have been the absolute limit of Trevor's theatrical experience while at Clifton. On the other hand, Michael Redgrave's starry career was entirely understandable. He was a notable boy actor when at Clifton, where acting was far from discouraged.

Close as he was to Trevor, Martin Hardcastle knew him best at school during his pre- and early teens when it was highly unlikely that Trevor saw himself as a latter-day David Garrick – C. B. Fry for emulation, maybe, but surely the bat before the boards.

'A novel boy. If he was theatrical at all it came out slightly on the playing fields. Yes, a little flamboyant on the field. He also tended to put on a bit of an act when boxing.'

Clifton enjoyed a rather unusual classroom tradition which, it must be supposed, has since fallen into disuse, if not disgrace. If a master took his place in class more than fifteen minutes late a 'cut' was called, leaving the boys the rest of the hour free from lessons. A few of the masters were famous for 'cuts', which could only have made them very popular. One such was Richard Prescott Keigwin. He was a dedicated sportsman who had more Blues than any other master at Clifton, or practically anywhere else. He was also Trevor's housemaster.

With Mr Keigwin for housemaster, a good all-round sportsman had it made; flunk exams, but score the runs, get the goals and win the pots. Another master of the time, and of the 'cuts', was Mr Garrett. His field was English Literature and he seems to have had a particular feeling for the works of Shakespeare. He did not have the daily control of the housemaster, but he later proved to be reliable in other ways. For a boy totally devoted to sports, devoid of any interest in lessons and far from fond of any discipline beyond that demanded by playing games well, Trevor had fallen into ideal hands. Well might Trevor Howard believe in his Guardian Angel. It is, at least, a more spiritual notion than being just plain dipped in luck.

CHAPTER TWO

The years between fourteen and sixteen tend to separate the boys from the potential men. Trevor Howard was no exception. He began his onward path by growing a moustache, an adornment for which he was supposed to ask permission at school, but being a self-styled rebel, he failed to apply that particular rule to himself and got away with it. A good all-round sportsman is forgiven much in relatively small matters and the moustache was relatively small. However, it became extremely useful. Suddenly, plans for the coming holidays took a dramatically wide and upward swing that was to affect Trevor, in part, for the rest of his life.

To his joy and amazement his favourite Aunt Margaret invited him to holiday in America with his rather older cousins. The visit was to be passage paid, a matter Trevor believes to have cost between thirty and forty pounds at the time, travelling by ocean liner, the *Samaria*.

The very smell of New York was a delight in spite of Prohibition, or perhaps because of it. Although the idea of Prohibition would hardly have affected Trevor's pleasure then as it might now, he was quickly made privy to the open secrets of a dry nation where suppression of liquor had given birth to warring bootleggers and speakeasies. Had he been visiting Chicago, through which he had passed as a child, he might have found the massacres in the streets altogether too exciting. New York was relatively free of public executions in the Al Capone manner.

But, in the company of his older cousins, he certainly saw the speakeasies where his intake was probably limited to the small beer of the time. Even now Trevor retains a sense of wonderment that he was never barred from, or thrown out of, so many establishments for which he was far too young. Presumably, since young collegiates were prime clients in all the dives, that useful moustache helped him to 'pass'. If, that is, anybody cared at all when the money was right.

10

Either way it mattered little. For Trevor the most important and lasting discovery of that holiday was jazz.

In 1916, jazz had escaped from the South. Emanating mainly from New Orleans, it had paused briefly in Chicago and then swept America. By the Twenties it had swung into Europe: jazz players became the Pied Pipers of the post-war world. But, as yet, nowhere was it better played than in its country of origin. Trevor listened and loved. His cousins were equally besotted: the tidal wave of that sound having long carried them into every jazz club they could find – and now they took Trevor. At the Cotton Club they heard many of the best, Duke Ellington and Louis Armstrong being choice examples. Bix Beiderbecke was a special hero. He had taught himself on church organs, graduated to the cornet and, later, the trumpet. In the Twenties, Beiderbecke was one of the very few jazz 'greats' who also happened to be white. His appearance with a black band was either unique or very close to it. In 1949 a film was made called *Young Man with a Horn*, based on the life of Bix Beiderbecke. Trevor Howard yearned to play Bix but the role went to Kirk Douglas.

As well as the smaller jazz combos, there were the big bands. One of these was being run by Rudy Vallee at the Old Pennsylvania Hotel – the scene of Trevor's many lift operations as a child. At this time Rudy Vallee was the flavour of the month on every housewife's shopping list. He may not have stimulated mass hysteria, which was a phenomenon yet to come, but he had won their hearts. As far as Trevor was concerned, listening to Rudy Vallee and his band was an experience he could take or leave alone. Even then he knew that the big band sound was not his preferred listening and nothing has changed. But he does admit to having sung 'Sweet and Lovely' from time to time.

By one of those coincidences that are so commonplace in the film business, more than twenty years later Trevor Howard starred with Jane Greer in *Run for the Sun*. Jane Greer was once Mrs Rudy Vallee.

Finally, the star-studded holiday was over, having made its indelible mark. Now every time Trevor is in New York he follows the same pattern, doing the rounds of the jazz clubs. Speakeasies have gone the way of all stop-gaps, but there is always P. J. Clarke's bar on Third Avenue, where Trevor no longer drinks small beer. Many jazz highspots of earlier years have gone, such as the Metropole on Broadway, but Trevor noses out fresh venues on every visit. Down the years many of the players have become his beloved friends.

Returning to Clifton College after such a liberated holiday felt, not unnaturally, very strange but, although it was 'school', it was also Trevor's home to a large degree and he was extremely happy there. However, his imagination had been stretched by his experiences, and the sight and sound of the inventive freedom exhibited by great jazz musicians had lit a personal fuse, a performer's fuse. Obviously Trevor wanted to play jazz and, equally obviously, he chose to have a crack at the drums. Drummers, by the very nature of the multifarious instruments that go to make a set, are frequently extrovert and very physical. Trevor was both but, by his own testimony, he wasn't a very good drummer. This honest personal assessment did not altogether hinder his ambition to play drums; he has been known to sit in and have a go in various places around the world.

Trevor's personal fuse burned brightly and suddenly in Mr Garrett's class one day. The assembled students had been told to pick any Shakespearean play of their choice and to read it to themselves. Mr Garrett might have had some private matter of his own that required attention and he had chosen to have a quiet time in class rather than arrive fifteen minutes late and give them a 'cut'. When a fair part of his hour of non-teaching had passed, Mr Garrett thought to call for readers.

One by one the lads rose and mumbled lines from the plays of their choice until invited to desist and sit down. When Trevor was called upon he got up and *acted* Marullus's very long speech from *Julius Caesar*: 'Wherefore rejoice? What conquest brings he home? . . .'

Mr Garrett regarded him thoughtfully and the rest of the class roared with unrestrained laughter. Trevor was furious, 'Because that was the only way you could really learn it and I vowed to myself that I'd show the buggers.'

He certainly did, but it took time. Meanwhile, he gave them more of the same when he read the lesson in chapel.

In those days, Frank Benson's Company was on tour and often

played in Bristol. As discreetly as possible, Trevor took to nipping out of his dormitory by a rather difficult window and making his way into Bristol to watch Frank Benson and his company at work. He also became a patron of any other company that passed through. These sorties into the night could well have led to expulsion but Trevor had his Guardian Angel, his moustache and his housemaster, Mr Keigwin, on his side. There was never any doubt in Trevor's mind that Mr Keigwin knew exactly what was going on, but since it didn't interfere with Trevor's prowess on the sports field, the housemaster was blind to other pursuits.

As Trevor got his theatrical eye in, he became something of a critic. If, he said to himself, this is the best they can do, I might as well become an actor. But nobody knew about that reflection except Trevor. With the sharp cruelty of youth he was dismissing the considerable talents of Frank Benson at a time when that gentleman was possibly past his best – but still going.

If Trevor had seriously begun to consider the theatre in terms of his future, at no time did he think to pursue this goal by taking an interest in school plays. That would have encroached on spare time and every minute of that commodity was used strictly for cricket, rugby or boxing in their respective seasons. The theatre was an interest rather than an obsession, but it was there and it remained guarded. This was a sign of the man to be: private to the point of secrecy.

At about this time Trevor began to experience other signs of private manliness. It had long been accepted, by everybody concerned, that Trevor was far from being a scholar and that any glory he might bring to the College would be in the line of sportsmanship. That being acknowledged, no man was unduly bothered by the amount of time that Trevor managed to spend in the sick-room. This was not the more serious school 'san' but a room in the house used for minor illnesses, such as loitering.

Without pushing his luck too far, Trevor managed to spend quite a bit of time in this refuge: 'Getting away from work and ready for cricket.' As those suffering from such minor illnesses as a disinclination to work were not expected to starve, a rather pretty young maid used to serve trays of food at the bedside. A lusty young man had to be far more ill than Trevor ever was to overcome such a temptation. Neither was the young lady averse to outdoor sports so, when the sick-room was otherwise engaged, she would lead him through yet another window and out by the fire escape.

Much later in life, when in Calcutta making *Sea Wolves*, Trevor was most surprised to receive a letter from an ex-officer in the Calcutta Light Horse who wrote to tell him how thrilled all the younger boys in his dormitory used to be when Trevor read to them before lights out and before he 'nipped out of that window with the pretty maid'. This had been one of the rare times that the private and secret man had slipped up. Trevor was so sure he had been super-discreet that his secret was safe. But 'the boys all knew!'

I spite of the faint patina of sophistication created by New York, the theatre and sex, Trevor was far from worldly enough to escape all the social miseries of adolescence. When visiting the Hardcastles at Canterbury he had been completely at ease, but it was the ease of childhood when good manners and a desire to please suffice; distinctions of class and wealth rarely affect children. Trevor's lack of home roots and the remoteness of his family put him in an even more vulnerable position in society than many young men of his age. But at fifteen or so, signs of position and wealth are clearly visible. They invite comparison, subsequent shyness and, often, unhappiness.

Howard Marion Crawford, also to become an actor, was at Clifton with Trevor and was known as Boney. Although he was older than Trevor, they had a mutual bond and so became friends. This bond was their hopelessness as students. Apart from that, Trevor played cricket, rugby and boxed for the College – and Boney had a Lagonda. They were men to be reckoned with inside the confines of Clifton.

Boney's stepfather was a colonel and a gentleman of some substance. He had a fine country house in Chiddingfold and an elegant town house in Kensington. Boney's lifestyle, outside Clifton, was therefore worlds apart from that of Trevor – who could hardly be said to have had one at all. Trevor was invited to Chiddingfold where, in spite of all kindness, he immediately felt the pangs of inferior status. It was a way of life he had never seen and had never shared before. The large and gracious house, the gardens, the paddocks, the stables, the staff: it was all there and to Trevor it was completely overwhelming. But he was determined to conjoin with this privileged world. He was going to do whatever Boney did, and so when he was asked which horse he would care to ride, he invited his host to choose a mount that would suit him. Since he had never been on a horse in his life, he promptly fell off and cracked his head open against a tree: 'Everyone was awfully sorry for me and they were so kind. But why the hell didn't I say, "I don't ride"?'

Whatever Trevor's sense of social inadequacy may have been in relation to Boney's family, it was not, apparently, a feeling that they shared. He was next invited to the London house. Again, the elegance and aura of status and wealth caused Trevor to lose his equilibrium. One evening at dinner the colonel, in all kindness, asked Trevor what his father had done during the War. Trevor had no idea at all, nothing came to mind, but he thought he had better say something so he blurted out, 'I think he was a colonel in Colombo, sir.' Then, fearing that there had been no such thing, he added, 'Or maybe he was a private.' For the rest of the evening, and long after, Trevor suffered internal hell. 'I didn't know what my father did. I barely knew who he was. And they were being so kind and so polite.' The misery was intense and Boney couldn't help. When Trevor referred to this occasion to Boney in later years, he didn't even remember it.

It seems incredible that there should have been such a lack of curiosity and communication between Trevor and his family. His mother had told him that his father was with Lloyd's in Colombo and he received a weekly letter from him without fail. But the line was drawn too fine for questions and confidences. For a boy who sees his father once every three years, if that, it must have seemed an impertinence, ungentlemanly, to question his way of life, his past history or future hopes. There was no common ground and, since Trevor left Colombo at the age of five, there never had been.

Had Trevor been a different boy he might have pressed for more knowledge of his father, but he was too private himself for that, even then. For as long as he could remember, his life had been bound up in Clifton, which he loved.

As school-leaving time draws near, the inevitable question of a future career concentrates the mind – if only from time to time. Trevor had already passed through the phase of wanting to become a professional cricketer. Then it was the turn of the relatively new and most exciting of all the Services, the Royal Air Force. At some point Trevor tried for Cranwell, but failed the medical – or so the story has it, although it's hard to believe. The failure was due to one bloodshot eye, '. . . and I think I had a boil on the bum'. Whatever the cause, the Guardian Angel was right there, on parade. For a young man who has consistently regarded his own personal discipline as being the only one that counts, any kind of Service career would have been fatal – possibly for all concerned, and certainly for Trevor.

Martin Hardcastle helped with introductions. One possibility was with Clark's of Street, the distinguished shoe manufacturing family firm. An appointment had been arranged and Trevor was to travel by bus to Glastonbury to be interviewed. He missed the bus and nothing further was done about that.

The next entrée was to Harrods where Trevor actually managed to go. His first task was to write an essay on some aspect of the store. He cast a cold eye at the Children's Department and devoted his essay to describing how terrible he found it. For this he won ten pounds, an astonishing sum at the time. He also won an interview with Harrods' Chairman, Sir Richard Burbidge. Although Trevor displayed patent disinterest in Harrods, and all to do with it, at the interview he was offered a job in the Argentine, at Harrods' Buenos Aires branch.

'I was supposed to go and sell umbrellas, but I didn't think it rained there so saw no future in it.'

This is Trevor Howard's recollection of his non-career with Harrods and it has been widely quoted. His mother's notes have a slightly more piquant flavour: 'One Christmas holiday he won a prize at Harrods for the best letter describing what he saw on a tour through the different departments. When Sir Richard Burbidge sent his prize – a cheque for ten pounds – he asked him if, when he was ready to leave Clifton, he would care to come to him and take a course to fit him to become a buyer for one of their foreign departments.

'Trevor wrote and thanked him for the cheque and his suggestion. At present he wanted to be a professional cricketer but he thought he was a bit young to decide his future career and would Sir Richard please write to him in a few years' time. Meanwhile he would order all his tuck from Harrods.'

A poll taken among Trevor's friends would most likely opt for mother's version.

Trevor's last summer holiday from Clifton was far removed from the excitement of New York or the rich life with Boney. He cycled up through France to the Haute-Savoie with a schoolfriend he called 'The Baron'. They were aiming for Le Petit Bornand-les-Glières where the Baron had been before: he thought it would be more fun if they made the journey together. Trevor's log of the trip is still extant, crisped brown by age but just about decipherable.

The following two excerpts record the last two days of a twelve day journey during which the boys cycled four hundred and sixty-five miles:

Saturday August 5th
Very good night. Woke at 7.5. Set out for Hautecour where we walked thro' a living room to a café in the back and had coffee, bread and cheese — 4 frs. Then on in pouring rain, to climb and climb, then descended to beer. We climbed thro' and above the clouds and could look back over them and across an enormous valley to the hills we had crossed. It was queer to see what appeared to be lumps of floating earth, sailing at anchor — quite apart, apparently, from the mainland of a hill below the clouds. I could understand the exhilaration felt by airmen at seeing great billows of foaming cloud beneath them, like the froth of beer! We came out into sunshine and I saw pale yellow bells like snapdragons, crimson thistles and the eternal poppies. A prickly bush was the chief thing where the land was not cultivated for roots, corn or pasture. We had beer at Nurieux after a long coast down — 4 frs. Two photos of Ain River and valley.

Then we had a flat run to Nantua along the edge of a green lake, with the huge pine-fir and bushy covered hills rising high on each side and little fishing stages stuck out in the lake with 6 or 7 rods on them. We had seen bullock transport for some time now. Lunched in Nantua on bread, cheese and beer. On to climb up and then descend along Valley de la Vonte to Châtillon and then to Bellegarde where it poured again and we had coffee and rum in a pub.

We decided to carry on and eventually arrived from the Juras via La Fort de l'Écluse where photography was *Verboten*. Then it rained again and we struggled on across the Rhône to Valleiry where we stopped to have dinner at the Hotel of a shifty old devil. Rain still pelting down. We stopped to put Baron's crank straight just above Châtillon, after he'd slipped on wet tar. Two gendarmes pulled up and gave us useless advice, looking at our papers, which were O.K. and asking if we were brothers – after reading out both our names! (French, of course.)

Dinner good. Coffee, rum, bread, vin rouge, sauçissons, ham, runner beans, beef, lettuce, cheese omelette – 40 frs.

On a little way to camp in a wood-clearing where we kept comparatively dry, although it was a very wet night.

Sunday August 6th
Decided to finish the Expedition and cycled through rain after breakfast at Viry on chocolate and coffee. Then to St Julien en Genevois in drizzling rain and on to Collonges. Beer 4frs. Then via Annemasse to Bonneville. Beer 2.25 frs. Cut straight south up to Petit Bornand by a huge climb through stupendous scenery of rock, gorge and cascade. Heavy clouds and rain in progress.

Arrived at Hotel Terminus to be greeted with open arms and a Pernod by 'M. Jon et sa famille'. A little chat and then changed and ate gigantic lunch, afterwards feeling pleasantly replete.

Their meticulous records of food eaten, money spent and miles travelled indicated a solid set of values. By the time they reached England again they had cycled 1,060 miles and spent a grand total of £8.16.0 between them. In 1932, the pound sterling was exchanged for ninety French francs. Those were the days.

Returning to school in their final term the young gentlemen were allowed to give a party, the guest list being entirely of their own choice. Notwithstanding their options, virtually every boy used to invite the same people: the housemaster, the house tutor, the art master and so forth, all drawn from within the College. Trevor paid little attention to what was customary and cast his net wider. He invited Jimmy the gardener because he'd been invited to his house in Bristol and had been well entertained. Those who looked after the cricket pitch and other sports fields were on his list together with anyone else whose daily work around the College had contributed to his pleasure in being at the school.

Astonishingly, and ungratefully, he did hot invite his housemaster, Mr Keigwin. He knew he was safe from authority because it was a rule that the boys could invite the people they chose – so he invited all the people that nobody else had ever recognized. 'It was really expressing respect for the individuals outside the daily run.'

Before leaving Clifton College, Trevor played cricket for his school against Tonbridge at Lord's. His mother was in England at the time and watching the match she found herself seated beside Mr Garrett. In the course of play the question of Trevor's future was raised, and it must have been a fairly gloomy subject for a lovely day at Lord's. Trevor had vouchsafed no particular interest in any career, either to his mother or at school. If his parents had discussed the matter between themselves, it's possible, as has been suggested in later interviews, that the Army might have provided an answer.

If this was suggested to Mr Garrett, it found no favour at all. He knew Trevor far better than did his absentee parents. His own rather astonishing idea was that Mrs Howard-Smith should send her son to the Royal Academy of Dramatic Art. Even more astonishingly, she agreed.

Clifton's match against Tonbridge was rained out that day but as Trevor's Guardian Angel was in the stands, it hardly mattered. Without a word to anyone, Trevor had got what he wanted. It's possible that this stroke of luck encouraged the habit of retaining certain areas of silence that has remained with Trevor Howard. Unlike almost every other actor, he never talks about himself or his work when outside the theatre or off the film set. It's so rare a habit as to be disconcerting.

CHAPTER THREE

Entering RADA was no trouble at all for Trevor Howard. 'They never refused men. There were five men to twenty-five girls.' In his first term he studied two plays: one was *Much Ado About Nothing* through which passed seven Beatrices. Since the men were in such a minority, they were all able to enjoy the big roles and make the most of the experience – and the girls. Trevor believes that many of the girls were not really serious about acting. RADA training gave them confidence and taught them how to move but the great advantage lay in having a justifiable reason for leaving home. It was an ideal climate for romantic attachments and doubtless many were forged, but not by Trevor, according to his own testimony. Some of the girls were 'easy', but failed to win his heart. 'I was really only in love with my game – the work. Anything that came my way was really only incidental to that interest.'

Trevor's own dedication never wavered; no idea that he was training for a precarious profession ever entered his head. There were no second thoughts or second strings. He was as committed to being an actor then as he is today; quietly and without fuss he had found his niche and he loved it, nor was he a prey to fears of failure. In an insouciant fashion he just *knew* he had chosen the right game.

The acting style of the early Thirties still had a whiff of the declamatory actor-manager: the strokes were sometimes broad, both physically and vocally. But Trevor had been an avid student of the theatre for quite a while. When other lads were at the pantomime, he was watching the legitimate stars of his day, including Gerald du Maurier, whom he thought had got it about right. Indeed, his acting was so subtle and realistic that he was often dismissed by the old school as not acting at all, just 'being himself'. Trevor thought that, whatever he was doing, he was bloody good, and held to his course, believing that: 'Acting had to be easier than everyone makes it out to be because du Maurier never acted – which was rubbish, because of course he did.' They never met but if Trevor Howard can be said to have had a mentor it was Gerald du Maurier. Trevor believes that he was the only student of his time who, without working it out, behaved as if he was actually in the drawing-room – or whatever setting the play had – when he was acting: 'And that's what du Maurier did. He was realistic.'

When scholarship tests for new students were set in Trevor's second term he was given a modern play by John van Druten, *London Wall*. He played naturalistically in the face of a certain amount of posturing by the rest of the cast – and won. Elsie Chester, a teacher at RADA, must have disapproved of the outcome since she was famous for throwing her crutch at students who failed to declaim as she required. She must have had a field day aiming at Trevor who continued to take du Maurier as his model, leaving the breast-beating to others.

Having agreed to Trevor's studies at RADA, his mother had arranged for him to stay with a friend of hers called Cassie, in West Acton. Miss Cassie, as Trevor called her, had become a friend of his mother's in Ceylon. She was also a private nurse and through her Trevor met Henry Ainley, who was one of her patients. Frank Benson was another. Trevor remembers going with Miss Cassie to Broadstairs where Ainley was 'having a dry-out' and hearing him sing 'Little Brown Jug' while in the bath. On one occasion Trevor had taken his work with him and was walking in the gardens learning his lines when he came upon Ainley. 'You've been out here, spouting your lines,' said Ainley. 'You'd better be an actor.'

With that end in mind, Trevor cast about for holiday work and landed his very first part at the Gate Theatre in Villiers Street, which was run by Peter Godfrey. He played the Second Boy in *Revolt in a Reformatory* – a title he still finds apt and quite personal. It was written by Peter Martin Lampel and produced by Peter Godfrey in May 1933. Admittedly Trevor had no lines, but he was up there on the boards. He also had the pleasure of working with that masterly actor, Alastair Sim. Bruno Barnaby and W. E. C. Jenkins were also in the cast and the play ran for about a month. Trevor Howard's name was not yet in lights, but it featured in a bona fide theatre programme.

He was to continue with his studies for nearly a year before it happened again.

That year, Mrs Howard-Smith returned from Ceylon to stay. Her husband was not to join her for several years but Merla's schooling — in Switzerland, Germany and England — was now finished and her mother probably thought it better for the young girl to remain in England than to join her parents in Ceylon. While it was fine for Trevor to stay with Miss Cassie and study at RADA, it was more correct for Merla to be with her mother. An additional factor might have been Mrs Howard-Smith's increasing dislike of the Ceylonese climate: if she was obliged to take to the hills in Ceylon, she might just as well settle in England. With Miss Cassie's help she found a house to rent, a few doors away from Miss Cassie, and settled in with Merla and Trevor. For the first time since leaving Ceylon, Trevor had a family home, a base.

He also had someone to hear his lines and give him his cues. Merla remembers the pleasure it gave them all, and fun they had when Trevor, once word perfect, would play with Shakespeare's words, substituting outrageous phrases — but always keeping to the metre.

Then there was the excitement of watching Trevor play at RADA. In particular, Merla recalls him 'ranting and raging' as Capulet. This might have been the beginning of the bull moose roar for which Trevor is famous, and rightly so; it can be heard across two counties. Another family amusement was listening to Trevor sing. Since he couldn't play the piano, he mimed at it, imitating jazz singers he had seen at the Palladium. Cab Calloway was one favourite with 'Minnie the Moocher' and a softer note was struck for 'I'm Going to Sit Right Down and Write Myself and Letter'. He made them laugh and he entertained them, but Trevor always resented his inability to play the piano. He had a true ear but it was Merla who could read music, playing effortlessly and well; it was a talent that enraged her brother.

Quite independently of her brother, Merla was totally stage-struck. She studied at the Webber Douglas School and did very well. After training, she played for Robert Atkins' Open Air Theatre in Regent's Park with Gladys Cooper and Ellen Pollock in *Lysistrata*, and understudied in a rather ill-fated production of

Floodtide. With the advent of war she joined the WRNS and afterwards felt that too much time had passed to continue with a theatrical future. Instead she became a tutor of English and French.

Since he was living at home with his family, Trevor met many of Merla's girlfriends and several were very attractive: 'But nothing happened. We were so different then. When we were young it was an age of terrific secrecy – and shames. We belonged to the Victorian age, really. If one had been a Lothario one would have gone around the corner on a borrowed bike and done something about it – but never did. I do remember one rather romantic bike ride, but nothing much came of it. I never wanted to go where they were going.'

The chances are that some of them might have been prepared to change direction, but Trevor was very much a young man of his time as far as girls were concerned. What might have been 'easy' at RADA didn't apply to young ladies found in the bosom of his family. It's as hard to think of such fine lines of distinction being drawn now as it is to think of today's young buck going courting on a bicycle.

Although true love was not yet for Trevor, another play was. He was given the part of Schwenck in *The Drums Begin* by Howard Irving Young. It was produced at the Embassy Theatre, Swiss Cottage, by John Fernald – who also taught at RADA – and ran for sixteen performances. Since RADA students were unlikely to have had agents it must be assumed that Robert Atkins was out front during the run, because Trevor's next chance was in a minor role for Atkins' production of *Androcles and the Lion* at the Winter Garden Theatre. This gave him twenty-eight performances.

For a young student, Trevor was packing in quite a lot of invaluable experience: studying by day, apart from rehearsal calls, and playing by night whenever possible. At the end of 1934 he won roles in two end-of-term plays for RADA. They were staged at the Westminster Theatre and each played four times. The first was John Masefield's *The Faithful*, which was produced by Norman Page. The second was Sydney Howard's *Alien Corn*, produced by Beatrice Wilson, in which Trevor played Harry Conway. These productions served as excellent showcases for young players and Trevor reaped the benefit.

The following February Dennis Robert's needed a replacement at the Q Theatre for Captain Absolute in *The Rivals* and Trevor Howard came to mind. As he had played the part at RADA, Trevor knew the lines and so was able to step into his predecessor's shoes at once and literally, since he also wore his clothes. But Trevor was rather more heavily built and during one of the performances his breeches split up the back like a burst zip. Safety pins were hastily assembled and applied and Trevor played on, quite unruffled. 'What had I got to lose? We had such a nice life, you see. We didn't really have amibition in those days.' Then, as now, Trevor Howard doesn't equate working as something you love doing *and* get paid to do, with being ambitious. Acting to him is an essential part of life, his everything. He would as soon deem it ambitious to continue to breathe.

Trevor's last roles before leaving RADA, in February 1935, were for John Fernald at the Embassy Theatre, where he played the Coachman and Dmitri in Gaston Baty's *Crime and Punishment*.

There was an American in London at the time called Donovan Pedelty who was a talent scout for Paramount Pictures. Having seen Trevor Howard at work, he offered him a screen test. Trevor thought it a bit of a joke but agreed to do the test. However, unlike many another, he did not remain at home waiting for the golden call, he went to the Royal Court Theatre to play Willie Tatham in Frederick Lonsdale's *Aren't We All* with Marie Lohr. He was called for the screen test and given the orangey-yellow face that was routine for the cine-cameras at that time. Leichner numbers five and nine. Afterwards he returned to the Royal Court where he walked on-stage just in time, still wearing the orangey-yellow make-up. Nobody seemed to notice but later Trevor felt that it was 'very unprofessional, in some ways'. It was, but a young actor might be forgiven if he gave the rest of the cast a hint as to how his day had been spent.

The run of the play was over by the time Trevor heard from Paramount, who offered him a five-year contract. Without hesitation he turned it down flat. This was quite a brisk decision to make. Paramount was a prestigious company making a number of quality films at a time when the comparatively new challenge of sound had arrived to stay. They had Cary Grant and Ray

Milland under contract indicating, apart from all else, that British voices served the sound-track well — but not Trevor Howard's. 'I couldn't bear the idea of going to Hollywood and leading the kind of life I'd heard about. I wanted to be an *actor*.'

Even then he felt there was a difference although, considering his future career, his reasoning might be examined. For years there was more than a hint of snobbism among legitimate stage actors when films were mooted. To work for the cinema was slightly *déclassé*, although one or two experimental forays were fine. The early days of television brought the same reaction; it was a long time before first-rate artistes accepted the new showcase for their talents. As for the 'kind of life' to be found in Hollywood, although Trevor has subsequently made films in, and for, Hollywood, he still cannot enjoy the 'lifestyle pattern' there.

Ten years were to pass before Trevor appeared in his first film. Meanwhile, as far as he was concerned, acting meant the theatre.

In the theatre of the time there was often a strange dichotomy between the age of the leading lady and that of the leading man. This was a splendid way of keeping production costs down since the male juvenile was paid five pounds a week to play the lead and to understudy. It was an immutable salary that Trevor Howard was to earn for several years to come, and very happy he was to do so; a fiver went a long way in 1935.

This being Jubilee Year, Leon M. Lion mounted a Galsworthy Festival at the Playhouse Theatre. His first production was *Justice* in which Trevor played Walter How and Wooder with the immensely promising young actor, Stephen Haggard, playing the Prisoner. *The Skin Game* followed with Trevor playing opposite Olga Lindo; believed by Trevor to be older than his mother. By the same token, the younger brother was played by an actor far older than Trevor. Later that year, Trevor played opposite Phyllis Neilson Terry in *Lady Patricia* at the Westminster Theatre. She was not only much older than he, but considerably larger. One evening she invited him to her flat to 'go through the lines'. The scene in question was played in a tree and Trevor found he had a previous, pressing engagement.

The last play in the Galsworthy Festival was *A Family Man* which gave Trevor the small part of the journalist in the third act. Now he was to play with a remarkable actor whom Trevor, among many others, was to revere for the rest of his life: the unique Wilfrid Lawson. It is said that Donald Pleasence once found himself in the same underground carriage as Wilfrid Lawson and travelled on for six stations beyond his destination because he just wanted to *look* at him.

During one matinée of *A Family Man*, Trevor noticed that Lawson was still in his dressing room when he should have been on-stage. Trevor raced down interminable stairs to the dressing room calling 'Mr Lawson! Mr Lawson!' Lawson emerged from his dressing room showing no haste and patted Trevor on the shoulder, 'Never hurry, dear boy. Never hurry.' He then walked up to the stage very slowly. On-stage, in total silence, waited Patricia Hilliard and Yvonne Rorie. They didn't ad lib, they didn't do anything – they just waited for Wilfrid Lawson's arrival and for the play to continue. When Trevor made his entrance in the third act, it was from the opposite side to Lawson. As he took a prop card from his pocket he said, 'Mr Lawson, Mr Lawson,' but the character's name was Mr Builder. Lawson cocked an eye, as only he could, and got a laugh.

After the previous evening's performance, Leon M. Lion had given notes to the cast; encouraging some, chastening others. Following this somewhat shaky matinée, he announced that the performances were much better. It was very obvious that he hadn't seen it.

'But it was all bloody good experience,' says Trevor. 'I was learning the trade. My game.'

Another place to learn the game was in Sunday night repertory. These presentations were given largely for the benefit of the managers and new playwrights: the hope being that even if the managers didn't buy the parcel, they might buy the play. A lot of work went into these one night stands but Trevor loved them. 'It was a hobby. We'd have got bored to death doing nothing.'

After the Galsworthy Festival, and *Lady Patricia*, Trevor played Lucullus in *Timon of Athens* at the Westminster and was subsequently invited to join the Stratford Memorial Theatre Company in the 1936 season of Shakespeare.

Trevor Howard is almost vehement in his belief that the study and playing of Shakespeare should be the basis of all tuition for the stage – or for acting in general – and that such experience should come before embarking on a lengthy career: 'Then they have it in them. Just as a man has soldiering in him if he chooses a career in the Army. If an actor goes into-Shakespeare later, when he's established, he won't have the grounding or confidence. Also you learn how to move.' Considering Trevor's own superb work down the years, he is probably right.

During the 1936 Stratford season he was mainly called upon to understudy, thereby increasing his range and furthering his experience. Among other roles, he understudied Petruchio in *The Taming of the Shrew*, which he was to play some years later with the Old Vic Company.

Members of the 1936 company included Alec Clunes, John Laurie, Vivienne Bennett and Donald Wolfit. The remarkable Robert Atkins was the guiding directorial light, occasionally giving way to Komisarjevsky, who was a seasonal visiting director. As far as Trevor was concerned, Randall Ayrton's *Lear* was the treat of the season.

After his first Stratford season closed, Trevor had little time to brood or wonder. He was asked to visit A. D. Peters, who was Terence Rattigan's agent. It's quite unusual for literary agents to become involved in casting and the interview seemed not to be about much at the time, but the next voice Trevor heard was from the office of the impresario Bronson Albery, offering him a part in Rattigan's *French Without Tears*. It was a much smaller part than Trevor had been used to either at RADA or on engagements, neither was it very demanding – but it was a job and it was a West End engagement. It was also a smash hit and ran for two years. During that time Trevor was never off for a single performance, and for the first time in his fairly short career in the theatre he became somewhat bored. However, he made two lasting friendships, with Rex Harrison and Roland Culver.

Two years is a long run and it didn't give Trevor much of a taste for them. He recognized the dangers of getting bored and stale, at the expense of the audience, and has never played one since. Years later, he was asked to play Professor Higgins in *My Fair Lady* and, scenting an unending run, turned it down: a

28

decision that did quite a favour to his friend Rex Harrison. It was a decision Trevor never regretted.

During *French Without Tears*, Trevor's father, now retired, returned from Ceylon and settled in with his family. For the first time since he was a baby, Trevor shared a home with his father, his mother and his sister. But he was now twenty-one and busy with his own, full life. His father was also absorbed in his abiding passion, philately, on which he was something of an authority. Although they were a fond and considerate family, the lines of communication had been drawn too fine to encourage great intimacy. Trevor and Merla were both deeply involved in the theatre, a world which their self-affacing father could hardly enter, no matter how proud he might have been of his children for being part of it. As for their mother, there seems to be no doubt that it was her strength and energy that bound the whole family together and kept the ship afloat.

When *French Without Tears* closed, Trevor was again invited to Stratford, for the 1939 season. As far as work was concerned the mixture was much the same as before: some minor roles but mainly understudying. He did play Benedict in *Much Ado About Nothing* once or twice, in place of Alec Clunes.

It has been said that casting for Stratford had as much to do with prowess on the cricket field as on the boards. True or false, Trevor captained the Stratford Festival Players that year. Among other fixtures, they played Birmingham and Wolverhampton Rep, and the Malvern Festival Players: actor against actor all over the field. Trevor Howard, John McCullum, Michael Goodliffe and Richard Wordsworth were handy players for Stratford while Anthony Bushell, for Malvern, made a hundred and twelve not out against them, covering himself with glory. The match was a tie and Trevor made ninety.

The Whitsun weekend was a holiday from the theatre so Trevor, Alec Clunes and Richard Wordsworth decided to take canoes up the river to Tewkesbury, which was quite a long paddle. Richard Wordsworth got stuck at the first weir, when they were barely under starter's orders, so he dropped out. The other two pressed on. Trevor remembers that they slept under bridges in pouring rain, 'We were mad. Quite mad.' But the sharpest memory of all is of a Lucullan feast at a riverside inn; a seven-course dinner with champagne followed by a bill for five pounds – for two!

It was a lovely summer which was to end in tears. On the fateful morning of Sunday, 3 September, many members of the company were gathered on the terrace of the Dirty Duck – as the Black Swan is inevitably called – in Stratford. There they heard Neville Chamberlain's announcement that war had been declared.

CHAPTER FOUR

On returning to London, Trevor volunteered for the RAF and was turned down. This was no reflection on him, or indeed on anyone else who had the same experience. In the early days of the War, the Forces lacked the administrative strength and the necessary centres to deploy the numbers of eager young men who queued to join up. The Services had their own reservists who were at least partially trained and therefore given priority, so the Army also rejected Trevor's first application. Neither was he sorry to have to wait his turn. In spite of volunteering, his feeling about going to war wasn't even ambivalent; he loathed the whole idea of Service life, the waste of time that was valuable to him as a striving actor, and the apparent futility of killing or being killed. He has even said that, given the courage, he might have become a conscientious objector.

One of the unusual features of Trevor's theatrical career up to 1939 was that he had never joined a repertory company or worked with an actor-manager both being the norm by which young actors required experience. He had never been aboard that train which could be seen in the sidings at Crewe labelled 'Fish and Actors'. Yet there existed some very distinguished repertory companies. One was at Liverpool, run by Willie Armstrong, and another, Barry Jackson's company at Birmingham, was regarded as a theatrical Mecca by the young. But Trevor hadn't tried for either – he didn't want to go into rep. 'My Guardian Angel again, you see. I grew up and worked in London from the beginning. I was rather a joke, I think . . . just a playboy.'

Maybe so, but he had been a very busy, fully stretched one in the years since he left RADA, and none too idle during his time there. But now that conditions of war had put him on a back burner, he thought that work with a repertory company was the way to wait; back-to-front and typically Trevor.

He became partly responsible, with Bob Digby, for the establish-

31

ment of Colchester Rep, where he stayed for about three months. Derek Bond was also in the company and one of their productions was Noël Coward's *Private Lives*. When pantomime time came around it was decided to do *Cinderella*, and Derek Bond plumped for the part of Principal Boy. The fact that the smallest child knew that the Principal Boy was always a girl only added to the fun. Not to be outdone, Trevor demanded to play the Demon King. The same children also knew that there is no Demon King in *Cinderella*, but there was one that Christmas — because Bob Digby wrote him in.

There could have been no possible connection between the two events, but now the Harrogate White Rose Players beckoned and Trevor followed. This was a well-established company run by two ladies, Mrs Peacock and Miss Marie Blanche. They were very serious about their work and had a few future stars with them, including Brenda de Banzie, Sonia Dresdel and Dulcie Gray. There was an RAF camp in the area, providing highly receptive audiences, and for Trevor there was a bonus. A fellow lodger at his digs was Michael Flome, the conductor of the band at the Majestic Hotel, and a band was to Trevor as a magnet to a steel filing. After the show he was frequently at the Majestic, singing and swinging with the band and devising new and naughty lyrics for the tunes then current and choice.

Trevor has always favoured friendships outside show business and, through Michael Flome, he made a number of interesting friends in Harrogate including Mrs Greenwood and her sons of the Gainsborough Dairy, where he and Michael were royally entertained.

Dulcie Gray joined the company just after Trevor. She was already married to Michael Denison and he, by good fortune, was stationed with the Royal Signals nearby. On her arrival the company lined up on stage to meet her but she saw few smiles and felt at once that she had not joined a very happy ship. But Trevor was kind to her and she still regards his friendship as a saving grace during her time there.

'Trevor is such a wonderful companion. We spent occasional evenings together in pure friendship, which is marvellously rare when one is young.' Most weekends, Dulcie was able to join her husband while Trevor had a girlfriend who used to visit him in Harrogate. Much later, Michael Denison noted in his biography that there was an actor in Harrogate who used to take Dulcie to the Majestic Hotel to dance. Trevor was quite shocked by what he computed to be a suggestion of none-too-honourable behaviour with another man's wife. 'I thought it read as if I was up to something and, of course, I wasn't.' And he wasn't. Indeed, although he enjoyed an affair or so, his emotional involvements were slight or brief. It always came to the same conclusion: 'I was in love with my work. That was all that mattered.' So much for the playboy.

Although the company worked as an *ensemble*, Dulcie and Trevor played together in *The Importance of Being Earnest* and also in a rare-sounding piece, the title of which has been forgotten – most fortuitously. In it Trevor played a clergyman and Dulcie a woman who experienced a deep tragedy. In rep the act has to be got together very quickly and Dulcie was very worried about her role – and how to play it – because the cause of her misery was that she had thrown her baby on the fire, and this she had to tell to the clergyman. The part carried with it no explanation as to why she had taken this novel step so she was fairly sure that she would get a laugh.

She confided in Trevor her fears of getting a laugh eight times a week with this astounding revelation. How could she tell him of her tragedy without having them rolling in the aisles?

'If you really want to know, I'll tell you,' said Trevor. 'When I ask what the cause of your unhappiness is, you begin to cry and turn your back on the audience, so the only word they really hear is "fire" – which you say tragically.'

'And it worked! It was absolutely brilliant of Trevor – but I don't think the play has ever been performed again.'

It is nice to feel that there has been no cry for revival of a piece which sounds to have all the allure of a badly-rinsed version of *Desire Under the Elms*.

Apart from Trevor's invaluable help over that mossy stile, Dulcie recognized other qualities in him. 'Although he was young, he was a marvellous actor even then. He had real star quality and tremendous charm.'

*

The day inevitably came when Trevor's call-up papers arrived, but he wasn't to learn of it. Mrs Peacock and Miss Marie Blanche were so loathe to lose him that they destroyed the papers. The ladies were not very young, they lived for their theatre and could have had no notion of how great was their little crime. That, at least, is the charitable view.

Some time after his employers' self-protective gesture, Trevor was arrested. He was to go to Fourmark Hall, in Derbyshire, to be inducted into the Army. But they didn't get him as easily as that. 'I've got to go home and see my Mum and change my clothes,' he said, and took off. He was late getting to his posting and, once there, found himself in uniform in double-quick time. The Army must have become pretty tired of trying to nail Howard-Smith, Trevor Wallace, but they finally slotted him into the Royal Corps of Signals on 2 October 1940. His own view of the speed of events was that, once in uniform, you had to salute the officers.

After the initial hurry and bustle, life in the Army became very slow. It reminded Trevor of being a new boy placed in a 'holding' house at school, because all the other houses are full; and it appeared to him that the Army was very full indeed. After he had been in for a short while, he received a letter from the White Rose Players. There were plans to tear down the theatre in Harrogate, and could he get two weeks compassionate leave? Those ladies were nothing if not triers. Even Trevor couldn't claim to be surprised when his application was turned down.

Trevor was far from being a happy soldier. He had originally chosen to spend his war service in the RAF and he was disgruntled to find himself 'in goon skins in the Army'. He couldn't have guessed that the time would come when he would find himself in the Army fairly often in the course of his career. Now the Army was intent upon finding in which field, if any, Trevor could become a useful soldier; a case of trial and error that lasted some time.

He was the soldier that might have broken his mother's heart, but was not going to get away with doing the same for the sergeant-major. Whatever they sent him into, he turned out to be useless and had to be 'Returned to Unit'. They tried him at railway signals – 'Signals were bad enough , but *railway* signals?'

At least three times he was R.T.U. He asked, almost begged, to be transferred to the infantry; at least he knew he could walk. But this was the Army, so he was sent to Coastal Artillery. There he found huge guns, about which he knew nothing at all, and undoubtedly cared even less. It was R.T.U. again after a few months of that.

This time he was sent to Prestatyn in Wales where, largely in desperation, he became even more bloody-minded. Whatever ploys he chose to use, they worked. He was posted to the infantry and sent to an Officer Cadet Training Unit in Dunbar in Scotland. There he began to enjoy Army life. The adjutant was somewhat stage-struck, which suited Trevor very well. In no time at all, Trevor was directing a presentation of the play *Rope*, by Patrick Hamilton, in which both he and the adjutant performed. This not only gave pleasure to one and all, it also got Trevor off one or two difficult courses.

It was at Officer Cadet Training Unit, in Dunbar, that Trevor formed a friendship with the young poet, Sidney Keyes. They shared a billet and it was an association that must have fed the true, serious and sensitive side of Trevor's nature. Irrational though it might have been, there seems little doubt that he was opposed to the discipline and strictures that have forever been an essential part of service life. He could support no other discipline than that which was self-imposed; he preferred to have sole charge of himself and of his life. Thus, as a soldier, he could not but behave out of character.

Although Sidney Keyes was Trevor's junior by six years, he was a dedicated and immensely fruitful writer – of poetry, stories and plays – possessed of great gifts and a remarkable intellect. Trevor remembers him writing constantly, even on guard duty. While others were bored, he was creative, and Trevor remembers him with great affection and respect. Here was a young man of barely twenty years who could channel his repugnance for war into the beauty of his poetry. Like Trevor, he was frantically bored by the Army and felt deeply the futility, destructiveness and emptiness of life as a soldier. But he could write. It's possible that Trevor envied him this solace; he certainly revered it.

Sidney Keyes was commissioned in September 1942 and left England for the Tunisian campaign six months later. After two weeks on active service he was taken prisoner and died 'from unknown causes' on 29 April 1943. He was not yet twenty-one. Twelve years after his death, Michael Meyer edited a collection of his poems — they number ninety-seven.

The early death of Sidney Keyes fuelled Trevor's hatred of war. In 1972 he paid tribute to Keyes in a programme arranged by Julian Jebb for BBC2. The poems he read were selected by Michael Meyer, a personal friend, and one of these says it all:

WAR POET

I am the man who looked for peace and found
My own eyes barbed.
I am the man who groped for words and found
An arrow in my hand.
I am the builder whose firm walls surround
A slipping land.
When I grow sick or mad
Mock me not nor chain me:
When I reach for the wind
Cast me not down:
Though my face is a burnt book
And a wasted town.

During the programme Trevor said, 'In my view Sidney Keyes should never have been in the Army. He put in at the very beginning for the Intelligence Corps. I think nine months later the posting came through, but he was on the boat to Africa by then. It came as no surprise to anybody who knew him to hear of his death ... artists really don't make good soldiers.'

Trevor was no longer in Dunbar when Sidney Keyes was commissioned, he had left on a training course. 'One day a man came along advertising for volunteers for the Airborne Division, the Red Berets — I had my hand up first. This will be a bit of drama, I thought.' He was sent to Hardwick Hall to learn jumping and gliding. It was a stiff course, there was no leave, and Trevor finished it in good order. On 3 October 1942, he was appointed to an emergency commission as 2nd Lieutenant Trevor Wallace Howard-Smith, 2nd South Staffordshire Regiment. He was then posted to Bulford in Wiltshire where he became bored to death. 'I was at least an officer, but I don't think I behaved like one at all.'

One of his few pleasures was to take his commanding officer's letters to the post office, because it was a good excuse to get out of barracks. As the CO's family was then living in Medicine Hat, Alberta, Trevor used to get some sport out of this. It was a truly dire case of absolutely anything for a laugh. Trevor's post-war meeting with his commanding officer was to be of a genuinely humorous nature.

From Bulford, he was posted to Plymouth but change of base changed little. The day came when there was to be an Army competition on motor bikes. Trevor signed up for this because he knew that Clifton College had been moved to Bude for the duration of the war and thought he would visit Martin Hardcastle, whom he hadn't seen for years. He waited for a full moon to enable him to return from Bude overnight, but had no thought of becoming involved with the competition. 'Bugger the competition. I wanted to see Hardcastle.' So he did. Hardcastle's Scouts were out in force, knotting and climbing. Trevor had a splendid time with them and, far from riding through the night, was extremely late returning to barracks.

The Airborne Division was a new, crack force. Its officers and men would be called upon to achieve physical feats that had hitherto only been dreamed of in fiction about supermen, rather than ordinary mortals of flesh and blood. They were sent on assault course after assault course and tested hard. Trevor's group was sent to Watford for examination by Army psychiatrists in civilian dress. They were also given tests for physical fitness that would have sought out the slightest weakness. In Trevor's words, 'They couldn't afford to have new officers in charge of platoons unless they were absolutely first class. If there was any risk . . . you failed the physical.'

And Trevor failed.

He was invalided out of the Army and relinquished his commission on 2 October 1943 – exactly three years after he had joined up.

Although Trevor has never claimed to be other than relieved to be out of the Army, the three years in it had left a mark. It is possible that, along with the relief, he suffered a confusion of emotions: a hatred of war, dislike of regimentation, a deep regret that three years had been wasted to no useful purpose, and a sense of failure. Whatever he felt, he was not prepared to talk about it then, or ever. But silence in show business is like well-tilled soil waiting to be planted and it is never allowed to lie fallow. Helpful guesses take root and flourish. A well-meaning theatre publicist and warmly disposed journalists created a myth of action endured and medals won by a man who was too modest to talk about either. They were good stories and written with all the good will in the world — but the myth haunted him and there remains a nearly submerged sadness in him which might date from that time.

Ironically his later portrayals of British officers were not only beautifully played but the truth in them was perfectly observed. The true pity of those wasted years is that they could, and should, have been put to very good use. While many of Trevor's contemporaries were in the Services and seeing action, many were also making their contribution through work with ENSA, taking plays and other entertainments out to the troops or engaged in making propaganda films which were acknowledged to be a very worthwhile aid to the war effort. Jack Hawkins spent some time with ENSA, co-ordinating companies and concert parties in India. Ralph Richardson and Laurence Olivier were making films. All three were in uniform and had seen some form of routine service in Britain, but they had been put to the work they knew best and which might better serve the general cause. Few would suggest that Olivier's *Henry V* was a waste of time.

Admittedly Trevor was not in the same league as Richardson and Olivier; they were his seniors, they were well-known and much admired, but no film ever made had only one actor in the cast. Of course Trevor had never been seen on the screen, which was a pity. He had felt, with many others, that British films were not really very good — and few were — so having rejected Hollywood, he had stuck firmly to his first love, the theatre.

The exigencies of war proved to be a shot in the arm for British films. The Ministry of Information recognized the value of the medium for propaganda purposes and morale boosting, and gave encouragement to film companies who were prepared to make films which not only entertained but also reflected the mood of the nation. Much of the good work was done by documentary film-makers, particularly those working with the Crown Film Unit. The main target, for commercial and documentary films, was America; their impact was considerable – both before and after Pearl Harbor.

CHAPTER FIVE

Trevor Howard was now a civilian and an out-of-work actor. For the first time – in 1943 – he was obliged to beat on doors in search of a job. One door led to impresario Firth Shepherd, who was mounting productions in London. 'Difficult, old boy,' said Shepherd. 'You see, I have to remember the chaps who've been holding the fort while you lot have been away.' Firth was not to be his 'shepherd', but neither was Trevor to want for long. He soon learnt that Alec Clunes, his old friend from the Stratford seasons, was running the Arts Theatre. They had last met in Harrogate when Clunes was passing through. At the time he was suffering severe financial embarrassment and Trevor had happily given him his weekly stipend of a fiver, a matter that Trevor had long forgotten.

Alec Clunes had a better memory. As soon as he saw Trevor again he yelled, 'I owe you five pounds and how would you like to play opposite a glorious redhead?' Trevor would have played opposite a horse, but a redhead was even better. Her name was Helen Cherry, which meant nothing to Trevor. Helen wasn't too aware of Trevor Howard, either. But she had become friendly with Dulcie Gray through working with her for Robert Atkins in *Twelfth Night*. She told Dulcie about *The Recruiting Officer* and mentioned her co-star. 'You are going to meet the most enchanting of all men,' said Dulcie. When they did meet, at the gathering of the cast, Helen found that Dulcie had not erred; for her it was a virtual *coup de foudre*, but Trevor took a little longer to capitulate. Not that he wasn't entranced, he's just not the man to risk rejection. In an attractive man this touch of humility usually doubles his allure. However the pavane was danced, Helen makes no secret of having made the initial running.

The Recruiting Officer was a success and in it Trevor sang for the first time on stage. Sir Richard Attenborough remembers seeing the play with his wife, Sheila. They were both very young at the time and Attenborough's first job in London had been in

Awake and Sing at the Arts Theatre. He thinks that *The Recruiting Officer* followed his play very closely and is sure that Trevor 'absolutely zonked the West End'. He knows that he and Sheila were both bowled over by an actor called Trevor Howard, who was virtually unknown. *The Recruiting Officer* had a limited run and came off before the end of 1943. For the first time in his life Trevor had been paid a little more than five pounds a week. He was not quite as unknown as he had been, but he still had to fight for work. However, he was as aware as the next actor that British films had grown in stature with such classics as *In Which We Serve* and *Henry V* and hoped he might break new personal ground were he to be accepted for the screen. Carol Reed was making *The Way Ahead*, a semi-documentary about raw recruits with a star-studded cast headed by David Niven. Trevor sent his Army identity photograph to Reed, explaining that he had been in the Army and if there was a small part ... He received no reply so he went to Denham Studios, where the film was being shot. Whatever strategy he used on arrival, he managed to get into the office of a member of the production staff for some kind of interview. While there he noticed his photograph lying on the desk: the director had never seen it. The interview yielded nothing, but Trevor was insistent. He hung about and finally managed to meet Carol Reed. He landed a very small part as an officer on board ship. The part was so small that he wasn't even registered on the cast list – but it was a beginning. It was also the beginning of a warm association with Carol Reed.

Trevor Howard's first moment for the screen was shot at night on the Denham lot. In view of the rigorous black-out then enforced he was astonished to see the arc lamps blazing skywards, apparently inviting enemy action. There was no enemy action and *The Way Ahead* proved to be more than worth any risk taken.

Before the film was shown, Trevor was back in the theatre, at Wyndham's, playing Ronald Vines in Reginald Beckwith's *A Soldier for Christmas*. In it he scored a personal triumph, which brought him to the closer notice of the presenters, Linnit and Dunfee. They were not only occasional impresarios, they were also high-powered agents, and Trevor found himself represented by Eric Goodhead, of their company.

The year of 1944 was quite an active one for Trevor. Apart from his work, he was spending every possible weekend at Stratford where Helen Cherry was the young leading lady of the season. She was playing Portia in *The Merchant of Venice*, Rosalind in *As You Like It*, and other roles of note. She was under the direction of Robert Atkins, with whom she had worked in Regent's Park. He had engaged her on that occasion because she said 'violets' instead of 'vilets', and had expressly taken her for a drink at The Volunteer to explain why he had given her the job. Helen had an amused respect for Robert Atkins, holding him to be much underrated and one of the last theatrical eccentrics. The following season, in which Helen figured in the audience but not in the company, he proved her right.

Claire Luce was then the leading lady and was playing, among other parts, Cleopatra in *Antony and Cleopatra*. The occasional music for this piece was furnished by Arthur Dewley and his Cameo Orchestra, and it proved to be far too tinkly for Robert Atkins. Finally his patience ran out. 'Look, old man,' he urged Mr Dewley, 'Put more cock and cunt in it.' According to Helen, 'He didn't get it, because they hadn't got it – and probably didn't even know what it meant.' Robert Atkins was already under notice from the Flowers family, the famour brewers, whose controlling interest in the theatre gave them that choice. At the end of the season he made a farewell speech in the theatre he had served long and well, his final line was: '. . . and what's more, Flowers' beer is piss.'

For her own season, Helen had chosen to rent a caravan, in which Trevor joined her for weekends. The course of true love had its tricky patches – during one of them Helen threw a bicycle at him. Neither of them can now remember the root cause of this somewhat unusual expression of blind fury. Whatever the cause, the outcome was marriage.

Helen Cherry's background was completely different to Trevor's. She had enjoyed an immensely happy family life with her parents and two brothers. She was born in Worsley, outside Manchester, and had been reared and educated in the patrician manner. The daughters of families such as hers were usually discouraged, if not forbidden, to think of the stage as a career, but her father was ahead of his time. He accepted Helen's determination to go on the stage with the proviso that, by that choice, she could earn her own living. If she were obliged to be subsidized by him, she would no longer be an actress. It was a fair bargain – and the need never arose.

In the course of their courtship, Helen had introduced Trevor to her family; he was instantly loved, and the warm affection was entirely mutual. A similar climate of total acceptance was present in Trevor's home: his parents and Merla were delighted by Helen. Notwithstanding the roars of applause, Trevor and Helen chose to have a quiet and completely private wedding, nipping off to do the deed and spreading the good news after the event. As soon as her Stratford engagement allowed, Helen went up to tell her parents that she was now Trevor's wife.

Her mother would have been less than human had she not been a little tearful. She had, after all, been robbed of a mother's finest hour: the orchestration of a grand wedding for her only daughter. Helen's father was not only delighted, he also thought of the money the happy pair had saved him. As Helen was leaving, her father ran down the drive and halted the taxi. He put his head in the window and said, 'Tell me, darling – what is Trevor's other name?'

A month after they were married, Trevor was back in the Arts Theatre playing a role he has always savoured, Mat Burke in O'Neill's *Anna Christie*. In the interim he had played a small, but telling part in his second film, *The Way to the Stars*. When it was released in 1945, it proved to be one of the best, and most successful, films of its era. Its provenance was excellent – written by Terence Rattigan and directed by Anthony Asquith – and the cast, which included Michael Redgrave and John Mills, was superb. The film also introduced an enchanting young girl called Jean Simmons to an appreciative public. Trevor played the commanding officer of an RAF fighter station and, although he was surrounded by known and seasoned film artistes, he made the part memorable. It was a small performance but in it he proved himself to be as strong and as truthful an actor on the screen as he was on stage. His sister has a nice word for it, 'He had a lovely showy bit before he got killed.' So he did, and although he was unaware of its importance, it was to be his launching pad.

However, before take-off he was in for a salutary disappointment. Carol Reed and Garson Kanin had collaborated on an Anglo-American film, *The True Glory*, a documentary composed of newsreel material taken from D-Day to the fall of Berlin. It was a triumph of conception and compilation and won more plaudits than any film of fiction. Carol Reed asked Trevor to speak the accompanying commentary. Trevor was overjoyed, his admiration for Carol Reed was already deep and he was well aware of the honour such an invitation implied.

He approached the first day's dubbing with high heart and gave it all he'd got – which was too much. As a novice at reading commentaries, he couldn't know that they didn't have to be *acted*, that a good level and unobtrusive voice-over was what was required. Carol Reed was sad, and so was Trevor – but he lost the job.

Helen and Trevor's first marital home was a small flat in, of all unlikely places, Pall Mall. To this prestigious address in the heart of clubland was sent the script of *Brief Encounter*. It came, without much explanation, from Trevor's agent, Eric Goodhead, and before Trevor had a chance to read it he received a telephone call from the producer, Anthony Havelock-Allan. He wanted to know at what time during the afternoon it would be convenient for Trevor to go to the tailor, Leslie Roberts. Trevor and Helen had planned to go to the cinema that afternoon, to see Veronica Lake and Alan Ladd in *I Married a Witch*, so the answer was, 'I'm afraid I can't. I'm taking my wife to the cinema.'

This might have seemed a cavalier approach to the plum role of the year, *if* Trevor had known he had been chosen for it. He had no idea as nobody had bothered to tell him: 'I didn't realize I'd been cast and that it was serious.' Well, it was nearly serious. Failing to get Trevor to the tailor, Anthony Havelock-Allan then arranged to meet him for lunch. Trevor turned up wearing corduroys and a lumber jacket for a rendezvous with an impeccably dressed producer. He still thought he was 'just meeting somebody in films' on the off-chance that something might come of it. It did. He was offered the male lead in *Brief Encounter*, but was urged not to mention the fact. A more seasoned actor might have sniffed the air when bound to secrecy, but Trevor was new to this facet of the game.

The film was to be made by Cineguild whose directors, in company terms, were Anthony Havelock-Allan, Ronald Neame and David Lean. Cineguild was one of a group of individual companies who operated within a parent company called Independent Producers, under the expert chairmanship of George Archibald. The films made by Independent Producers were financed and distributed by the J. Arthur Rank Organisation and made in Rank-owned studios, each separate company enjoying an enviably large degree of independence in the matter of scripts and casting. In this case the script was based on *Still Life*, one of the short plays in a sequence entitled *Tonight at 8.30* by Noël Coward, who carried the whip that spun the top: he had written the script and was to be consulted every foot of the way.

Forty years later, Sir Anthony Havelock-Allan is very clear about the choice of Trevor Howard for the role. He had seen him in *French Without Tears* and met him casually at the time, but only thought of him for *Brief Encounter* after seeing him in rushes of *The Way to the Stars*, which was made at Denham Studios – then the home studio of Independent Producers. Ronnie Neame and David Lean also looked at the rushes and they all felt that Trevor looked just right: 'A nice upper-middle-class Englishman, a steady-going character who seemed to be reliable and dependable.' But Noël Coward had the last word and he was 'darting in and out of the country, entertaining the troops'.

At the fateful lunch, Trevor believes he was asked to keep the lid on his good news because Roger Livesey thought the part was his. Sir Anthony knows that Livesey was never considered, but agrees that Trevor might have been encouraged to think there was another actor up for the part because nobody had yet been able to suggest Trevor Howard to Noël Coward. 'At that time Noël referred to Cineguild as his children, and we were not going to talk about Trevor Howard much until we'd told Daddy.'

Ronnie Neame remembers, too. 'In those days, unlike today, we had complete autonomy over casting, and all else. Dear Uncle Arthur Rank . . . but Noël was a stickler for casting correctly as opposed to casting for names. He was determined we should have Celia Johnson. Then it was a question of finding her opposite number. Somebody mentioned Trevor Howard, who'd been making a film in the same studios. We saw some rushes of *The Way to the Stars* and immediately we all said, "That's him".' Sir David Lean's recollection of the event is much the same – only sharper. 'I first saw Trevor in a rough cut of a reel from *The Way to the Stars.* He had one shot on an aerodrome – and I'll never forget it. A plane came in over the field and did a victory roll. Trevor looked up and said, "Lineshoot". It was wonderful. Just on that one word, the way he said it and the way he looked. I said "That's him", and went to Noël.'

They had to see 'how Noël felt', and luckily he felt fine. He even remembered liking Trevor in *French Without Tears.* They ran the same footage for him and he said, 'Don't let's look any further.'

So, in a curious way, Trevor's first gut feeling was right; his casting wasn't sure or 'serious' until Noël Coward agreed some time later. Only then did Trevor Howard find himself playing the lead in a film that became an evergreen classic.

Because of the extraordinary and continuous success of the film, its production history is worth a glance. Noël Coward's original work for the theatre was comprised of twelve one act plays, each with its own title, the whole cycle being known as *Tonight at 8.30.* The rights to all twelve plays had been acquired by MGM, who had a habit of stockpiling properties in case somebody else developed them to advantage. By negotiations that must have been of a fascinating nature, the British producer, Sydney Box, persuaded MGM to sell the lot to him. He in turn sold them, one by one, to the Rank Organisation. When Cineguild became interested in the rights to *Still Life*, hand in hand with its author, they were obliged to pay the Rank Organisation £60,000 for them – which was a lot of money at the time.

The final cost of *Brief Encounter* lay between £260,000 and £270,000. Of that figure Celia Johnson received £1,000 and Trevor Howard £500. By today's multi-noughted standards, those figures look like taxi fares. 'And the horrific thing is that it has been playing somewhere in the world for forty years, with very little profit to the makers. Somebody is making a fortune out of it still.' Sir Anthony has every reason to be slightly choleric on the ground of television revenue alone. At the time film-makers were prone to think that, if they didn't look, television would go away. Unfortunately, agents seemed to agree with them, so no contract carried any clause protecting the makers of the film or the artistes from unpaid exposure on the box. For many years 'old' films were sold outright for release on television, often at absurdly low figures. No matter how often they were shown, there were no residuals for anybody concerned.

There is a scene in *Brief Encounter* which has always puzzled Trevor Howard, and some others. It takes place in the borrowed flat of his friend, Stephen Lynn, played by Valentine Dyall. Lynn returns unexpectedly, rupturing what could have been an idyll for the lovers. Laura – Celia Johnson – has flown but left her scarf behind. Finding it and realizing its implications, Lynn rounds on his friend in one of the ugliest scenes of its kind ever filmed. Viewed today, it is open to a variety of interpretations and even the film-makers themselves seem unsure of the original intention.

Sir Anthony takes the broad view. 'That's right, the owner of the flat comes back unexpectedly. That must have happened to most of us at some time or another. What doesn't make sense is his extraordinarily censorious attitude.' Exactly. Or, as Trevor says, 'What the hell do people lend their flats *for*?' Maybe Lynn suspects his doctor friend is having an affair with a patient, but that would be more a matter for the British Medical Council than for a friend. One thing Sir Anthony is sure about: Valentine Dyall was cast for his disapproving face, his angry face – a Puritan who doesn't approve of doctors having affairs with *anybody*.

Sir David had only vague memories of the scene at first; he hadn't seen the film for years. Then he remembered that the scene in its entirety, from Laura's arrival, had been a problem. She comes in out of the rain and there is some stilted dialogue about her wet coat, the fact that the fire isn't burning properly because of damp wood for which Alec/Trevor apologizes – all of which Trevor found incomprehensible. 'David, I don't understand this scene at all. Why the hell am I talking about the wood being damp? For Christ's sake, I want to bed her and here she is. What am I doing messing about?'

Being an older and wiser man, the director explained that

when a couple who wish to make love, but morally should not, finally find themselves alone, the change of atmosphere, the implicitness, can create a shyness that only banalities can bridge. It was a living experience unknown to Trevor then: 'I must say, you are a funny chap.' Funny chap or not, that was how the scene was played, and Sir David remembers it as being one of the only real differences he ever had with Trevor. He also remembered more of the intention of the scene: 'The Valentine Dyall character is not sympathetic at all – it's all coming back to me – it's part of the whole thing, I think. That flat's really a hostile place, uncosy, unwelcoming. It's all to do with guilt. If the flat had been different it would have taken away a whole colour. I don't think the audience should have thought – well, come on. Now you're alone. They're not alone. The husband's there as far as she's concerned. And guilt is all over the place.'

His view of Valentine Dyall's ugly fury is quite revealing: 'You know, men can be terribly hostile to other men whom they think are a success with women – they want to punish. I think Dyall suddenly saw red because there had been a woman there, although he must have known what was going to happen. And remember the times, remember the times . . . that scene contained the horror of discovery, the overlay of guilt, the lot. It should have ended in ugliness.' It certainly did and the director is entitled to the last word about the motivation of any scene in one of his pictures.

When the shooting of *Brief Encounter* came to an end, Trevor thought 'it would be bloody good', but nobody can ever tell for sure before a film has met an audience. Sneak previews were invented to give film-makers some idea of audience reaction. As Cineguild was then based in Rochester starting on exteriors for *Great Expectations*, it was decided to sneak *Brief Encounter* right there, in dockland. It was a rough audience for a rather tender subject and the showing suffered; laughter at the love scenes led to more laughter and yet more derision. When the lovers were interrupted before Celia Johnson had time to take off her hat the audience groaned with simulated frustration: 'Isn't 'e ever goin' to 'ave it orf with 'er?'

Sir Anthony believes that the laughter was not *at* the film but of embarrassment. This is more than possible but it didn't sound like heavenly music, either to him or David Lean. The latter recalls going back to his hotel just outside Rochester and lying awake all night wondering how he could break into Denham Laboratories to burn the negative of what appeared to be a total disaster. Fortunately, he arrived at no viable plan.

The next hurdle for a new film is the press show – to which Trevor Howard was not invited. Whether this omission was born of oversight, design or plain inefficiency will never be known. But he went, as the guest of his agent, Eric Goodhead, 'because nobody could stop me'. Eric Goodhead was further incensed on Trevor's behalf when he learnt that he hadn't even been invited to the reception that followed the showing. Once inside the cinema he seized one of the organizers and told him so. 'I think it's a bloody disgrace. You've got a press reception across the road at the Café Royal and you haven't told my client!' So they both went to the reception, to the pleasure of many critics. In Trevor Howard they recognized a future star and wanted to meet him, as it was proper that they should.

If the preview had been a traumatic experience for David Lean, the press show was worse. His shoulders were virtually leaning on the knees of James Agate who, throughout the running of the film, gave a precise and detailed criticism of it to his companion. His voice was fairly loud and his total loathing for *Brief Encounter* quite apparent. That was the director's second public viewing of his film: 'Then it came out and I think it got fairly good notices. I can't remember.' He was brainwashed early on.

The film received excellent notices and opened at the New Gallery on 26 November 1945. Trevor and Helen attended the première, where Noël Coward failed to recognize his leading man. Celia Johnson was obliged to introduce them. This was strange because the previous June, having seen a rough-cut of the film, Noël Coward had noted in his dairy, 'Delighted with it. Celia quite wonderful; Trevor Howard fine and obviously a new star'. When it came to talent, the Master was seldom wrong – even if he failed to recognize it in person.

Few major studios, anywhere, accepted a single-picture contract with a new artiste who might lay a golden egg, and the Rank Organisation was no exception. Seven years of servitude was the norm. While this might feel like security, it also placed the players neatly in Morgan's fork. Either they accepted any part the parent studio chose for them, or they risked being lent out at a fee far beyond their own for a picture they really didn't want to make. There was a third possibility: a reputation for being recalcitrant. Only the very, very few golden egg layers were allowed a script approval.

When Trevor Howard signed for *Brief Encounter*, he refused the seven-year clause. Obedience to any organization was never in his scheme of things and he was a successful stage actor. He saw no pleasure in being obliged to have to seek permission to return to the theatre, so one and all settled for a contract that gave Rank one picture a year for five years. This fairly unusual compromise might account for a lacklustre interest in Trevor when *Brief Encounter* was shown. It was short-sighted, but organizations often are, and Trevor didn't relish being treated shabbily. 'They weren't kind, you know. This was my first important picture – but they never tried to make stars. I used to go to the studio dressed in a lumber jacket – looking rather as I do now, no better – a bit worse, perhaps. I stayed in the studios for the night sometimes. One day a minion was sent to my dressing room from the chief production office. Apparently Eric Portman had an appointment at Watford Town Hall, to open or shut something, but he wasn't on call and would I go in his place. I told them I couldn't go as I was, it was a public occasion. I asked for a suit – which I could only have brought back on me – and they refused to let me have one. So I went as I was, which couldn't possibly have done me any good. That's pretty well how it was in those days.'

Celia Johnson, who was not under contract to Rank, went on a promotional tour with the picture. Trevor Howard, a contracted picture-a-year, new leading man, was kept under wraps. No attempts were made to promote him at all.

This attitude to publicity was to change with the creation of the nauseatingly-named Rank Charm School, with pretty pictures of Brylcreemed young men and embarrassingly bad cheesecake pictures of girls, all in pale imitation of the Hollywood system.

Whatever the Front Office did, or failed to do, for Trevor Howard when *Brief Encounter* opened at the New Gallery he was an instant star. Seen again, forty years on, Trevor's immense success at the time is quite remarkable because his role, although essential to the story, is almost shadowy. He is there because he has to be, but he is in no way favoured. The camera rests on Celia Johnson; it is entirely her picture. Sir Anthony says, 'Celia's picture? Naturally, because originally it was Noël playing the doctor and handing the play to Gertie Lawrence. It's a little like ballet, it's very rare – unless it's a solo that hits the roof – that the man who supports the woman gets the biggest hand. And we know so much more about her, the background; her husband and family life.'

A rather surprised Sir David: 'It's a jolly good part, you know – whatever you say. Everything hinges, doesn't it? Bill Holden once said, "I don't look at the size of a part, I look at how good I think the film is going to be – and how good and true the part is".'

All very valid, and all the more credit to a virtually unknown Trevor Howard for his creation of a loved and memorable character. Mention Trevor Howard's name anywhere and the response is immediate, 'Ah, *Brief Encounter*.' Recognition, not infrequently followed by the question, 'Who played the woman?' This is no slight on a superb actress; Celia Johnson just made fewer films. Another question is 'Where *was* that railway station?' The set was a shell built round the existing buffet at Carnforth station in the Lake District and it was chosen because railway officials had time to give a warning to douse the lights in case of an air raid.

This almost passionate interest is most frequently expressed by the young, who hadn't even been born when the film was made. It is an enthusiasm that, in later years, drives Trevor Howard mad – he *has* made other films.

The financial success of any film made in a small country, like Britain, depends very largely on overseas distribution. *Brief Encounter* was shown in Turin – and taken off after four days, because the audience was much the same as it was in Rochester. Even so ... David Lean asked a friend in Rome what went wrong and learnt that, to the Italians, Trevor was *brutto*, meaning, among other things, ugly. Lean found that very strange.

France was reluctant to buy – until it won an award at the Cannes Film Festival. Dilys Powell was present at the showing in

Cannes: 'The French were delighted with it. They thought it so charming that a woman could be loved wearing a hat like that!' Following the film's success at Cannes, Gaumont reluctantly agreed to give it a limited release; it is still playing and was recently shown again on French television.

Dilys Powell has several reservations about *Brief Encounter* but admires Trevor Howard wholeheartedly. She had already noticed him in *The Way Ahead* and *The Way to the Stars*. 'Two small performances but one always noticed him, I think. He was an actor who would do anything that would use his great gifts, and of course you can never take your eyes off him.

'*Brief Encounter* made his name, which was nice. I suppose it's a film that many people remember him in most, but it certainly wasn't his best performance, although there were some things in it that I liked. It's not a film I like terribly but it won a lot of prizes and a lot of praise.'

Another distinguished film critic, Bosley Crowther of the *New York Times*, wrote 'Trevor Howard, who has none of the aspects of a cut-out movie star, makes a thoroughly credible partner in this small and pathetic romance.'

CHAPTER SIX

Before *Brief Encounter* was out of the cutting room, Trevor Howard was cast in another picture. Frank Launder and Sidney Gilliat were also members of Independent Producers, with a company called Individual Pictures, and they offered Trevor the lead in *I See a Dark Stranger*, opposite Deborah Kerr.

Much of the film was shot in Ireland, around Wexford. Although it was the end of the war, it was far from being the end of privations in Britain so the unit found themselves in a veritable land of milk and honey, not to mention unrationed clothes, meat and booze. Trevor thinks of it as a very happy film and is sure that, on the return train journey from Holyhead, they all looked like well-dressed smugglers. He was wearing a Galway tweed suit that was 'absolutely hideous' and all luggage was filled with contraband. At the station the Customs officials waited, and searched. They did a thorough job on Trevor – 'I must have looked as if I was impersonating Sid Field in his act' – and found his trophies, including some bottles, but took no action. Trevor still doesn't think they recognized him. It's a modest thought, if unlikely to be founded on fact.

I See a Dark Stranger was a popular enough comedy-thriller which got a showing in America, under the title *The Adventuress*. Bosley Crowther described Trevor Howard's performance as 'keenly sensitive and shrewd'.

His next film was *Green for Danger*, also for Launder and Gilliat, with Alastair Sim. In it Trevor again played a doctor, and his view of it today is that 'it wouldn't have been worth making without Alastair'. Probably the film's greatest claim to fame is that it was the first production to be completed in the newly reopened Pinewood Studies. This was to be home for Independent Producers for as long as the group existed, which was not for long.

The medical profession had not yet finished with Trevor Howard: this time he was to play a drunken doctor in *So Well*

Remembered for Adrian Scott, directed by Edward Dmytryk. The film broke no new exciting ground, unless the fact that Trevor had never played a dissolute drunk before can be counted.

Trevor hardly had time to get out of his near-white coat before he started again in a somewhat squalid thriller, *They Made Me a Fugitive*. This was directed by Alberto Cavalcanti and the film was enlivened, at least off-screen, by his first admonition, 'Now remember everybody – no acting.'

By now, Trevor Howard had made five films at a gallop and only one, *Brief Encounter*, showed any real distinction. In all the films he had been well-received and nobody doubted that he was an actor not only of great talent, but also one who brought a new quality to acting for the cinema. Sir Richard Attenborough expresses it very well: 'I think the remarkable thing about Trevor Howard is that we tend to think that the style of acting in the British cinema really changed with the emergence of Peter O'Toole, Albert Finney, Alan Bates and so on. In fact, one of the real forerunners was Trevor. Before the war the majority of movie actors in Britain came from the theatre, where the word was the prime factor.

'What so many of them never grasped was that the camera can photograph what you are thinking and certainly what you are feeling – but what you are thinking beyond anything that you say – and Trevor Howard already had this ability in *The Way to the Stars*, from which Noël Coward chose him for *Brief Encounter*. In that film particularly, he demonstrated this quality, as did Celia Johnson. They both set a new standard of cinema acting which had rarely been witnessed on the British screen. After *In Which We Serve*, Noël Coward told me, "You will make a film actor because you know how to listen." Trevor Howard epitomizes that. In the cinema the silent moments are very often the much more poignant, and somehow Trevor knew it. He really changed attitudes. He was to us, to my generation, sublime, because he brought a new style to the cinema. Previously it was the Americans who gave us truth on screen. People like Spencer Tracy, Gary Cooper and Humphrey Bogart; and Trevor had that quality instinctively. He is very significant in British cinema not only because of that, but because of his standards. What Gerald du Maurier did for the theatre, Trevor Howard did for the British screen: total realism in depth. That's why Noël thought he was so wonderful – Noël's hero in the theatre was du Maurier.

'*Brief Encounter* was a wonderfully brave movie. It did so much for actors, film makers and writers. It showed that you did not have to conform or repeat to make a film which was artistically superior while being commercially viable. For years it was, 'What about *Brief Encounter*?' when anyone tried to do something out of the general rut. It was a landmark and touchstone; a fresh view of comparatively ordinary people.'

So it comes back to *Brief Encounter*. Unfortunately there was little sign that many writers and film makers were taking advantage of the new horizons offered to them by the overwhelming success of that one film; those that did aimed even higher with considerable success. Cineguild's *Great Expectations* and *Oliver Twist* confirmed David Lean's place in the first rank of British directors. The most innovative members of Independent Producers, the Archers, produced *Black Narcissus* and *The Red Shoes*, over the unique credit; 'Written, Produced and Directed by Michael Powell and Emeric Pressburger.'

Another distinguished director, Carol Reed, had a nice one with *Odd Man Out*. All these were feathers in the cap of Rank's ever proliferating empire. Elsewhere, another titan, Sir Alexander Korda, suffered from some expensive mistakes which lost a vast amount of money. Ealing Studios, however, showed promise with *Hue and Cry*, the first of a long line of successful and intelligent comedies.

But for the most part British producers were turning out capably made, well-intentioned and basically dull movies, such as those in which Trevor Howard appeared and which used no talent to the full.

Helen was working as hard as Trevor, both for the screen and in the theatre. They changed apartments several times and, during a spell in Leinster Gardens, were once obliged to hide behind the door because they hadn't got the rent. 'Just think of it,' says Helen, 'and Trevor was already a star!'

In the post-war euphrasy, money could be spent on things other than rent. If Helen was in the theatre and Trevor was filming, there were inevitably some long evenings for Trevor to fill. And vice versa. Helen had many outside interests, including opera and ballet, Trevor had work and cricket, and has never been a loner. Neither has he ever put himself about to be seen in the right places to meet the right people. Table-hopping and black-slapping were never for him. Rather a favourite bar and the camaraderie of people he enjoys, with whom he is at ease. In the early days, it was a choice between a glass of beer or a packet of cigarettes, but now the rent could safely wait.

Studio bars were a great lure for everybody after a day's work. If the day had gone well, it could be celebrated, if difficult, relaxation was imperative. Friends abounded and gossip was exchanged, there was much laughter and general bonhomie. Not infrequently an evening so begun went on elsewhere, if there were no other pressing engagements.

Such evenings might have laid the foundation of Trevor's future reputation as a hell-raiser. He was never late on call, he usually satisfied the director with one take and, in all, was a complete professional. But he had reached the top very quickly and jealousy can beget odious labels. Trevor saw no harm in it. He enjoyed celebrating a good day's work and, since he never brought anything but his best to it, he had plenty to celebrate.

Trevor was invited to join the Old Vic Company for the 1947 season. As their own theatre had been bombed, the Old Vic were playing at the New Theatre where the company, led by Laurence Olivier and Ralph Richardson, had been an immense success. Now Olivier was taking a touring company to Australia with Vivien Leigh, and Richardson was going to America. The director, John Burrell, remained in London. Among others in the company were Alec Guinness, Harry Andrews and — for a Shakespearean first — Patricia Burke.

Although Patricia Burke was a known and loved figure as Principal Boy in pantomime and other entertaining roles, she had never been associated with works by the Bard. When John Burrell was casting for his season, Patricia Burke was playing at Wyndham's, an adjacent theatre, in *Clutterbuck* with Constance Cummings, Basil Radford and Naunton Wayne. She remembers it well: 'It was such a happy show. I'd never been happier in my life so I must have been mental to want to leave it. But I had a clause in my contrast allowing me to leave after six months, which were nearly up, and I was devoured with this desire to play Shakespeare – I'd never played it. So I walked across to the New for an appointment with John Burrell and said, "I want to play Shakespeare." "Oh, you do?" he said, "have you ever played it before?" No. "Oh, I see. Will you audition for me?" I'd been refusing to audition for quite a time before then, but not this time. John Burrell said, "Take this home, learn it and come back." So I did and auditioned the last speech of the Shrew. "Would you like to play the Shrew?" I was bowled over. Then when they said that Trevor Howard was to play Petruchio I couldn't believe my luck.

'We started rehearsals and I think I had to go to the osteopath every other week because John Burrell devised a move where Trevor lifted me up in his arms – and then dropped me. We worked it out that I came down holding the back of his leg, but obviously you can't always break a fall like that – so I was bruised all over. But it was an exciting move and when we started playing you could hear the audience catch their breath when he dropped me. And that's worth everything. Trevor had this red beard and red hair and he was wicked and marvellous and he sparked – and I hope I sparked back. He was the best Petruchio I've ever seen – if you can call it seeing when you're playing with him.'

When a role calls for facial hair, Trevor prefers to grow his own so he grew his own beard for Petruchio and it grew, at that time, a lively shade of red, so he was equipped with a wig to match and, he remembers, a mustard-coloured shirt ... 'a very attractive costume'. He was lucky not only with his costume, but with a classic production. Trevor isn't one to search for something extra in Shakespeare holding that there's not much the matter with the original, if you can master it. Neither can he gaze with enthusiasm at the works of the Bard in modern dress, 'It's like reducing the Bible to words of not more than two syllables. Think of Shylock in a loud pin-striped suit. I'm sure *somebody* has done *that*.'

Marie Burke, distinguished artiste and mother of Patricia, remembers the 1947 production of *The Taming of the Shrew*. 'I just want to say that James Agate wrote that he had never heard

Katharina's last speech spoken so beautifully as it was by Patricia Burke.

'Now, I worked with Trevor Howard a long time ago. We did *Reunion in Vienna* for television. I liked working with him very much because he was amusing. I played Frau Loucha. She was a loud person who smoked cigars and he used to smack her bottom, you know? I told the television people I wanted to wear bombazine and when the piece was shown one critic wrote, 'Marie Burke plays a fine bombazine character' – and I was delighted. It was very interesting working with Trevor. He's a marvellous actor – and Helen Cherry was in it, playing with him. Lovely woman. Beautiful to look at and a very good actress. I don't remember who else was in it – I am ninety you know.'

Marie Burke was also in *Odette* with Trevor Howard, 'Yes, I worked with him in *Odette* – well, just. I had a small part because I could speak French you see. I tell you what I loved him in – *Brief Encounter*, I thought he was lovely in that film and wished I'd been in it.' Marie Burke is a truly great lady and her admiration is not easily won.

The Shrew opened in Edinburgh, for the first Festival, and toured the main cities before playing for a week in Brussels. During the tour they played Oxford where Trevor had an enlivening encounter. He was approaching the stage door before a matinée when he realized he was being pursued by a young man who was running like hell to catch him before he entered the theatre. Trevor paused and the young man arrived panting, 'and wearing all the colours of the rainbow in different positions.'

'Are you free tonight?' he gasped at Trevor. 'Please come – we're going to have a wine party and bring anyone you like. Just like to tell you now – we'll talk about it later – that was the laziest performance I've ever seen.' And he panted off. Trevor pondered on that comment quite a lot but, 'Of course we've found out since that it was a compliment.' Indeed it was, the printed version includes, '. . . these quizzical gifts carry him through Petruchio with absolute, even priggish conviction. In spite of its astonishing laziness, this is a brilliant performance, with charm and phlegm in equal measure.'

The writer was the young Kenneth Tynan, then a brilliant Oxford scholar, as well as being one of its most colourful. At the time nobody could foresee that he was to become a dazzling and perceptive theatre critic – or that he would be the first person to say 'F-fuck' on television.

Trevor loved Tynan's keenness and the way he pontificated then, telling Trevor that he just had to play *Macbeth*, which was the last thing Trevor wanted to do. Neither can Trevor elaborate on the 'laziness' of his performance as Petruchio. Today he says, 'You choose, if you have a choice, to play people you think you understand.' He would have understood Petruchio since he himself doesn't actually bully women, but he does tease.

When the production came into the New Theatre, London, it was a resounding success. *The Times* recorded, 'Mr Trevor Howard lets hints of a genuine and growing affection appear beneath the brutality. We can remember no better Petruchio.'

Sadly, *The Taming of the Shrew* was to be Trevor Howard's last Shakespearean appearance. But he had been schooled in the works of the Bard and still maintains such schooling to be invaluable to any actor and absolutely essential to one who plays Shakespeare. He is also sure that it is better to learn the long speeches in bits: 'It gives you a chance to digest them. You get to the heart of the matter. If you sit down and learn a whole lot at once you don't get the same result. It becomes mindless and less concentrated – like schoolboy learning.'

Trevor once asked David Niven whether he had done much work in the theatre and Niven looked horrified, 'Absolutely terrifies me, old boy. And as for Shakespeare, I wouldn't know how to walk or use my hands.'

Although Sir Alec Guinness was in the same company, he and Trevor were never in the same production. Sir Alec writes: 'I hardly know Trevor (whom I admire greatly). We boxed and coxed, using the same dressing room during the Old Vic season at the New Theatre in 1947, but our paths rarely crossed as we were in different productions. His Petruchio in *The Taming of the Shrew* was the best I've ever seen and made that unpleasant play not only bearable but charming.'

Trevor's most lasting memory of the season is the sudden appearance of his father in the dressing room after an evening performance. His arrival was a complete and delightful surprise. He had expressed no wish to see the play and Trevor asked whether he had actually been out front. He had. He had been up in the gallery. A simple telephone call to his son would have placed him in one of the best seats in the house, but that was not his way. He had quietly made his own arrangements and bothered no one. A few months later, in February 1948, he died; loved and revered by his son — but for all human purposes unknown to him.

Trevor Howard had enjoyed a great personal success as Petruchio, but there was no other leading role for him during the season and his contract with Rank gave him a chance to accept another film for Cineguild. This was to be based on H. G. Wells' novel *The Passionate Friends*, with Ann Todd and Claude Rains. The production went through various backstage traumas before getting into rhythm under David Lean's direction. Again, although it was a well-made film and stylishly directed, it was hardly a landmark.

The strength of the Rank Organisation was beginning to fail. Independent Producers, as a free-running group, was on the verge of disintegration, and new voices calling for lower budgets and less imagination were being appointed to control production at Pinewood Studios. There was a flight of talent which was welcomed by Alexander Korda's London Films. Carol Reed was already there and fortunately neither the Guardian Angel nor Carol Reed had forgotten Trevor Howard. He was approached by Carol to play in *The Third Man*, possibly the best film he was ever in. A little-known and fairly bizarre fact about *The Third Man* is that at one time Trevor Howard was asked to play Harry Lime, because nobody could find Orson Welles. Happily he finally came to hand. Trevor himself doubts that he would have been nearly as good in the part 'and neither would Orson Welles have made a very good British officer, whilst he was absolutely perfect as Harry Lime. But he was an awfully naughty man.'

Trevor also had a bout of naughtiness, albeit unwittingly. Carol Reed was shooting a night scene in the International Zone, involving officers of all four Forces. Later he was to require Trevor Howard, but saw no reason to keep him waiting around until called. Trevor had seen lights nearby and heard music, both indications of a jolly nightclub, so he pointed the establishment out to Carol and told him he would be there when needed. He was already dressed for his part, as an Army major, so off he went.

To Trevor, a band is not something to sit and listen to, it's something to join and enjoy, which he proceeded to do. He conducted the band and sang along with it, lark-happy – until he was arrested.

A serving British officer in the club had reported him to the Military Police; his crime being that he was disporting himself while in British uniform to which, as a civilian, he had no right. He didn't exactly go quietly, properly insisting that Carol Reed should be informed as he would shortly be needed in front of the camera.

Sybil Kerisson remembers that night very well. She was with the Allied Commission for Austria, as part of the British Information Services, and was on duty that night – a routine roster in case of need. She received a report from an Army sergeant that an Englishman in major's uniform, who said he was a film actor, had been taken in charge. Her reaction was automatic: 'That's okay. It must be Trevor Howard.' The hell-raising reputation had journeyed with him to Vienna.

Naturally the report had him going from bar to bar but didn't say, in so many words, that he was drunk. Neither was he, since he was waiting to work. Trevor Howard would never have presented himself to Carol Reed in an unfit state to be directed by him, no matter how bad a name had been given to the dog.

Eventually the production manager, Hugh Percival, obtained Trevor's release in time for the show to go on. The following morning, Hugh Percival suggested to Trevor that a personal apology to the British brigadier in charge might be in order. Trevor fully agreed and went off, in civilian clothes, to make his peace with the British Army. To his amazement the brigadier was none other than Trevor's former commanding officer at Bulford. The brigadier did not have instant recall, but he got there in the end:

'Ah, yes. Actor chappie. What do you do, juggling or rough stuff?'

'Films, sir.'

'Ah, yes. People have been telling me. You did that thing in a railway station. Tell me, why did you let that filly go?'

The Duke of St Albans, then Colonel Charles Beauclerc, also remembers the occasion well, but in the cool light of logic: 'Trevor Howard was arrested for the simple enough reason that he was in uniform in a public place, and making himself pretty public too. That's all it was. And if the snooping character hadn't turned him in, nobody would have been any the wiser.'

In London sometime later Trevor met 'the snooping character', while enjoying a quiet glass in a pub called The Anglesey. He was amazed to be slapped on the back by an Army officer he had never met who appeared to be convulsed with laughter at some inner joke. 'I was the chap that reported you in Vienna,' he cried joyously. Trevor shared none of his amusement but did ask where he was serving. 'He was on guard duty at the Tower of London. Well, bully for him.'

The British Information Services attached to the Allied Commission covered a lot of ground. As well as dealing with press material, their film section prepared a weekly newsreel, arranged distribution of British films and dealt with the de-Nazification of other productions, in conjunction with the Allies. They naturally helped with any film being made in the area and thus had much to do with *The Third Man*.

One of their contributions to the film involved the sewers. The Viennese had every right to be proud of their sewers, whose odour was so un-sewage-like that sandwich lunches could be served in them while the film was being made. But there were no rats, and the script required rats. The local populace was not best pleased by the suggestion that their sewers should be polluted by rodents but Carol Reed wanted rats and so rats were specially introduced into the system. 'Unfortunately,' says Sybil Kerisson, 'they were the wrong kind of rats – they were not water rats, just plain rats.' It was unlikely that future audiences could spot the difference and Trevor Howard was amused to share his sandwiches with them.

Off-duty entertainments were also arranged for the film unit, mainly by Colonel Beauclerc's deputy, Ross Williamson. They were introduced to a *Weinstube* in Grinzing, known in that district as a *Heurige*, where new, cloudy and very intoxicating wine was served. There were also other, more sober, treats. Pleasant as it was to have the benefit of such courtesies, they were not Trevor Howard's style; he nosed out corners of interest in a new city before anyone else had unpacked, and in the encouraging company of Bernard Lee he had long discovered the *Heurige* at Grinzing. They had also found one at Hietzing where an itinerant musician played hauntingly on an unusual instrument. Trevor fell in love with the sound. One evening Trevor talked to Carol about his musician, feeling that it was the perfect sound for the film. Few directors are overly concerned about the music until the film is finished – and Carol Reed was no exception. Later, at Shepperton Studios, the matter of music became all-important so Trevor reminded Carol of the man at Hietzing. He urged Carol to go back and find him, even offering to go with him. In the event Carol went alone and returned with Anton Karas and his zither. The rest is film-music history. Anton Karas found fame and fortune and years after, when Trevor Howard was once again in Vienna, he was delighted to find that his discovery now owned the restaurant outside which he used to play.

A number of people, including Sybil Kerisson, believe that Anton Karas was discovered by strangely fortuitous chance. Ross Williamson had organized a party for the film unit to visit Grinzing but the restaurant happened to be closed that evening so the venue was switched to Hietzing where they all heard Karas playing his Austrian zither. It seemed magical that such a casual rearrangement should alter the life and fortune of a street musician, making the name Anton Karas world renowned. It was a fairly romantic story anyway, even if Trevor Howard got there first.

The Third Man was applauded and awarded. The cameraman, Robert Krasker, won an Oscar and Carol Reed an Academy Award nomination. Bosley Crowther smiled upon Trevor Howard 'as a British police major, a beautifully crisp and seasoned gent'.

The Third Man was a co-production shared by David O. Selznick and Alexander Korda, written by Graham Greene, and based on his own original idea. Vienna at that time was under the control of the Allied Commission: British, French, Russian and American Forces, each controlling a separate Zone – Vienna itself being an International Zone. When Graham Greene went to Vienna to research he was greatly helped by Colonel Charles Beauclerc, who was then Controller of Information Services, Allied Commission for Austria. He recalls that pink champagne was one necessity and a rather sordid background another. He managed to supply the first, with some difficulty, and took Graham Greene down into the sewers, which satisfied the second requirement.

After three weeks researching in Vienna, Graham Greene left for Italy to write a treatment. His next visit was with Carol Reed, to show him the location and to work on the script. They stayed in the same hotel and Graham Greene wrote in the morning then lunched with Carol Reed and argued about the script in the afternoon. Although Graham Greene remembers, with some amusement, that 'Carol lay in bed while I worked', it must have been an excellent system because this was late 1948 and the film was finished and released in 1949.

The author was not in Vienna during the shooting of the film – 'Otherwise perhaps I might have supplied the missing line – instead of the cuckoo clock. They needed an extra line for timing. As it was, Orson did it.' But he was pleased with the finished picture. He thought Trevor Howard was excellent and rather regrets that Orson Welles practically stole the picture and the reviews, on the grounds that Trevor's performance was just as good. So it was, but Harry Lime was the more flamboyant role – and Orson Welles was born to steal pictures.

CHAPTER SEVEN

Fresh from success in a truly great film, Trevor Howard was offered a routine piece of hokum called *The Golden Salamander*, to be directed by Ronald Neame. At first he turned it down. In spite of his passion for work he must have felt strongly about lowering his standards so far after *The Third Man*. These many years later Ronald Neame admits that nobody really loved the project, but he badly wanted to direct and this was his first real chance. Whether it was Neame's ability to persuade or the lure of a Tunisian location, Trevor finally agreed. It's possible that Trevor has inherited his mother's wanderlust, for he loves the sight, smell and sound of a new country and it wasn't the only time he was lured into a dubious film by a far-flung location.

His leading lady was Anouk Aimée, very young and very pretty. Her young and equally pretty mother went on location as her chaperone, but inexplicably stayed in a different hotel to her daughter, somewhat reducing the validity of her role, while Anouk stayed in the same hotel as Trevor and other members of the cast. A close friendship between leading man and leading lady is the oldest cliché in show business – particularly when on the road or on location – and the resulting team work usually benefits. Certainly Neame found that Trevor and Anouk worked extremely well together and if the film had been in the upper echelons it might have mattered.

One of the best scenes on location was, Neame recalls, unfortunately not for the picture. Shooting was taking place in the open market place of a native village which was filthy, squalid and filled with Arabs buying and selling fly-covered local produce: a nice natural scene with thousands of free extras. The script called for Trevor Howard to work his way through the crowd in the market place. The camera was set up, creating a stir in itself since none of the locals had ever seen one before. Then came a loud hailer emitting interpreted pleas to the crowd to behave quite normally and naturally, just as though the camera wasn't there and, this above all, 'Please don't look at the camera.' It was a crane shot and there could be no rehearsal.

It was all set. Ronnie Neame lifted his megaphone, shouted 'Action!' and all hell was let loose: the Arabs started to fight, stalls were knocked over and a number of participants were knocked out. In the middle of it all Trevor Howard struggled with shock, amazement and other people.

When, with some difficulty, a degree of order was restored and Arab had stopped tearing into Arab, it transpired that the word 'action' had triggered off something they had either seen in films, or thought should happen in films: action equalled fighting. But Ronnie Neame found that, once they got the hang of it, many of the voluntary extras were quite good. So, up to a point, was the film. At least it has recognizable characters and a comprehensible plot.

As naturally as water flows downhill, news of the close friendship between leading lady and leading man travelled to England. The fourth estate could hardly be blamed for enjoying something so toothsome emerging from such an unlikely source.

Although Trevor and Helen shared an attitude to personal freedom within marriage that was quite unusual at that, or any, time, they were both discreet and both knew that nothing and nobody could seriously disrupt their marriage. However, dalliance made public always hurts, especially when discussed with overt pleasure by the best of friends. It was the major storm in their marriage but it passed, as did any subsequent small squalls. Indeed, it gave rise to a pleasing fantasy of Helen's; she was sure that every three years a memo appeared on some Fleet Street desk detailing a journalist to find out whether the Howards had parted yet. Certainly telephone enquiries have been made down the years and on one occasion, at least, Helen answered the telephone to be asked whether Trevor Howard had left her. 'Why don't you ask him yourself?' she said. 'He's just here, lying in bed beside me.'

As Trevor enjoys a selective memory to the full, he dimisses any question of infidelities on his part with a vocal flourish. Even so, Helen once overheard him say to another man, 'I never chase, old boy, but if I see a green light – I go.'

*

By the end of 1949, nine films in which Trevor Howard appeared had been released and a further three were due for release the following year: *The Golden Salamander*, *Odette*, and *The Clouded Yellow*. They were all worthy, bread-and-butter films of the kind that dulls the senses but, through them, Trevor became a very popular star. In 1950 his contract with the Rank Organisation was at an end, not that the contract had been onerous; he had never been forced to make a film against his will or taste. Also, following the lassitude shown after *Brief Encounter*, he had been much in demand for Personal Appearances – exercises which include a variety of public events from 'being seen' at lush premières to opening garden fêtes.

Theo Cowan, who is probably the best public relations man in show business, was usually his guide, accomplice and friend during Trevor's early years on the PA circuit. He loved working with Trevor and, much more to the point, understood him: 'Anything that is normal with someone else is always somewhat strange with Trevor.' A fair example was the opening of a super Sports Day and Fête for Courtaulds, a company with more than a passing interest in films, since they were investors. This very special occasion was to take place in Flint, just inside the Welsh border near Chester.

Trevor was agreeable: they were to travel by train and Theo arranged to pick him up at 7.15 am to take him to the station. Theo arrived in the usual chauffeur-driven, discreet black saloon. Alf Riglin, the chauffeur, wearing the routine blue uniform with peaked cap, parked around a nearby corner while Theo rang the bell. The door opened instantly and Trevor was ready and waiting. Then he remembered he must take a clean shirt as it was going to be a long day, off he rushed and returned carrying a naked clean shirt. They set off for the car, followed courteously by the blue-uniformed Alf Riglin. Suddenly Trevor glanced round and saw him: 'Christ! The police!' he shouted and started to run. Theo raced after him trying to explain that it was not the police but their driver. It didn't take. 'Bloody police everywhere – don't like the police.' By this time the clean shirt was crumpled into a ball in Trevor's hands.

When Theo finally persuaded Trevor into the car, Trevor was

in jovial mood with Alf Riglin and seemed amazed that he had mistaken him for the police.

By the time they were settled in the train, Theo was hoping for a good breakfast and Trevor was looking for a lager. Suddenly Trevor thought breakfast was a good idea: 'How long have we got – about fifty minutes?' Theo was surprised. 'No. It's about three hours.'

'What? To Fleet? It can't be. I often go to Fleet for the week-end.'

'Yes. But we're going to Flint.'

'*I'm* not going to Flint!' But he was – because the train was moving.

They were met at Chester by an executive of Courtaulds and they finally arrived at the factory buildings to be greeted by the Mayor, all the company executives and a variety of citizens of import. They were led into a huge canteen for lunch and Trevor was being absolutely charming to everyone. Suddenly he said, 'It's the Test – what's the Test score?' This was addressed to a little Welsh lady, who didn't know. 'Well, please find out.' She scurried away and returned with a set of numbers which might have led to a winning streak at Monte Carlo but could have had nothing at all to do with cricket. Trevor gave her a warmish smile: 'No. You've got it wrong. Please find out and get it right.' Theo maintains that there was no rudeness on Trevor's part in this interchange, it was just urgent for him to know. The lady returned with what sounded more like a cricket score, Trevor beamed at her and she was delighted.

Trevor's passion for cricket began at school and it was a game in which he excelled. It was also a game he could continue to play later, hand in hand with work and study. As his prowess grew so did his interest and, since he had no other hobbies or concern outside his work, it became obsessional.

In the train returning to London, Trevor was very mellow and happy; they were met by the 'police' driver and driven back to Selwood Terrace, where Trevor and Helen were staying with a friend. By this time it had been a hard day for both of them, and especially for the 'minder'. Trevor flicked the light switch in the hall and nothing happened – no light. Quite calmly Trevor said: 'The fuse has gone. Let's go to an hotel.'

'But it's only a fuse!'

'I can't mend bloody fuses. Come on.'

So Trevor was left at a small hotel, which he knew — and that was Fleet, or Flint.

Trevor Howard also became a favourite choice for film festivals; either as chairman of the jury, a member of the jury or as a distinguished British actor waving the flag. Down the years he must have attended every one, from Cannes to Cartegena. Theo Cowan remembers meeting him at Northolt after one such occasion. He watched the British travellers come through from the relevant flight, but there was no sign of Trevor. He was beginning to fear that his quarry had missed the plane when he heard the famous roar — Trevor Howard had found his way into the aliens queue. He was swiftly winkled out by an airport official and turned over to Theo. Trevor looked at him pitiably: 'They put me in the aliens' pen! Why do these things happen to me when I'm so simple and easy to get on with?' As rhetorical questions go, that was an ace.

Apart from Helen, Theo Cowan is probably more qualified than anyone else to assess Trevor Howard's public persona, because he has known him and worked with him, for so long, out in the open, where it shows.

'People do love him and they welcome him. Whatever the event, if you say Trevor Howard is going to be there the reaction is always, "Oh, good — he's a smashing fellow." But he does cringe away from anything that looks self-congratulatory — and he is shy. If you see him in a pub, roaring away, it's easy to think, "If he's shy, I'm a Chinaman", but he is. He had a great sense of occasion. For example, at a royal line-up he is very diffident and always anxious not to put a foot wrong.' It follows that, being shy, he is always pleased to see other actors; they are members of the same club, there are easy lines of communication. Theo has never heard a bad word about Trevor from other actors, if they are in a film with him they are happy: 'It'll be all right.' Neither does Trevor bitch about other actors. 'He is generous at work, he has stature, he stands out among his peers but doesn't stand out for the sake of it. He's just different, more civilized.'

Theo finds that one of Trevor's most refreshing characteristics is that he is not chameleon-like. At home, or abroad, he remains the same, all his reactions being human and very direct: if he is ever angry, he is angry for a very good reason. Another rare bonus for Theo is that Trevor has never consciously put him in a difficult or embarrassing situation. He has never pulled star rank, never complained that a car was too small, 'or any of the other kinds of bullshit that have been known. He's very un-actory, but knows how to play his role.'

Organized press interviews can be hazardous to those in charge of public relations. The interviewees can either say too much or too little, and nobody can write their script. Trevor offers more of a third dimension than most actors, his interests are wider and he doesn't elaborate on how and why he had played any part because such explanations are not only alien to his nature, they are beyond him.

Like Martin Hardcastle, at Clifton, Theo Cowan is most interested in why Trevor Howard became an actor — because he's such an unlikely one: 'He could be a successful farmer, a vet or a doctor — most actors you don't think of as being anything else. In an ordinary pub you wouldn't say, "Who's that odd chap?" The oddness, or difference, comes from his personality, his values. Trevor doesn't make efforts, his courtesy just happens. The private character that comes out in Trevor is much more interesting than the actor. In most cases, when an actor takes off his make-up he takes off his personality. Trevor Howard doesn't.'

From his own professional point of view, Theo cannot think of a more rewarding actor: 'That smile of Trevor's — his face crumples into it and it's so warm, people feel, "This man may not know me, but he seems terribly pleased to see me." In all, a testimony as glowing as this from such a wise and long-experienced hand as Theo Cowan, might equal a couple of Oscars to any sentient artiste.

Public parades can also deal a healthy come-uppance to those who take immediate recognition for granted. Helen remembers with joy being on parade with Trevor and Theo when one excited observer yelled, 'Look! It's Leslie Howard and Ellen Terry!' Apart from personal appearances, making films and looking for a new house, Trevor had begun to snatch what time he could during the summer months to play cricket. His aim was to qualify for playing membership of the MCC. This was not only the most interesting approach to membership for a good cricketer, it was also the quickest. According to reliable information from Lieutenant-Colonel J. R. Stephenson OBE of the Cricket Office, the waiting time for ordinary membership in the Fifties was thirty years. Trevor Howard does not have that kind of patience.

To become a playing member, Trevor Howard had to do rather more than present himself with bat, ball and an enthusiastic smile at Lord's. First he had to be proposed and seconded by current MCC members, then put in a further application to become a probationary cricket candidate giving details of his previous cricketing career, such as School 1st XI and the Stratford team. When playing for Clifton against Liverpool Club he is recorded in Whitaker as having taken six wickets in two overs before lunch after the club had already made two hundred. He had also made an excellent showing as captain of the Stratford XI.

He was accepted by the Committee as a probationary candidate and then had to play at least ten days' cricket for the MCC during the next two seasons in the club's out-matches against other clubs and also schools. There were match managers who organized the teams and to them Trevor had to make his availability known.

In order to play his qualifying matches, Trevor had to be mobile and although he carries the aura of a man who might be a car fanatic, this is misleading. Early in their married life Helen's mother had given them a Wolseley. Later Trevor bought himself a Ford, but tended to forget that it needed water as well as petrol. His first 'good' car was an Alvis, bought at the time of *The Golden Salamander*, and in it he swept the country, playing cricket.

When he had played the necessary matches, his record was considered by the MCC Committee and he was found worthy of playing membership, thus advancing entry into the only club he ever wished to join by some twenty-eight years.

During the summer of 1950 Trevor and Helen spent a weekend in Arkley, Hertfordshire with friends, and Trevor fell in love with the village at once. It felt like the country but was close to London and to several film studios. When Trevor told his hosts that it was exactly the kind of place in which he would like to live he was told there was a house nearby for sale. At once the tape was up and Helen and Trevor were off. Although it was Sunday they had the good fortune to find the gardener who had the keys, they saw the house, loved it and early the next morning Trevor was in the agent's office offering to buy the property.

The agent was delighted and chatted eagerly about arrangements for a mortgage. 'No need for all that,' said Trevor, 'I'll give you cash.' The agent was dumbfounded. He cast a wary eye over Trevor who was growing a beard for his next role and didn't look much like a man of substance or, as Helen puts it, 'the agent couldn't believe he had a tosser'. But the cheque was written and thus the house was seen on Sunday and bought on Monday. Although it is close to film studios they have very rarely been those in which either Helen or Trevor have been required to work. Life isn't like that, but the house is lovely.

At the same time Trevor had every reason to believe that his Guardian Angel had another treat in store: Carol Reed had asked him to play Willems, the white trader, in *An Outcast of the Islands*, with Wendy Hiller, Ralph Richardson, Robert Morley – and the silent Kerima. Even the location seemed portentous: it was Ceylon, the island that Trevor had last seen as a child of five.

Although Helen would have liked to see the land of her husband's childhood, she was too busy nest-making. While Trevor was away on location, Helen could apply herself to realizing the potential of their new house and garden. Like many a lady in other walks of life who have husbands who travel, the husband's suitcases are usually packed when it comes to the nitty gritty of moving house.

Trevor set off for Ceylon in high humour: he was to work with his favourite director, a marvellous cast and a script based on Joseph Conrad's classic novel. He also had the non-hero role of a lifetime before such roles became fashionable or desirable for young leading men. *Look Back in Anger* and *Room at the Top* were still to come. Not that Trevor Howard would have weighed playing an unsympathetic character against working with Carol Reed.

Trevor had long recognized that there are two schools of directors. There are those who like actors, understand them, and often coax from an unlikely one an unusually brilliant performance. They are known as 'Actors' directors', with very good reason. The other school frequently includes highly creative directors who are dedicated and visionary film makers, true *auteurs*. They seek out the best possible cast to flesh out their dream, but *they don't like actors*. There is even a catch-phrase: 'Actors aren't people.' They probably believe in the good old days when actors, or strolling players, were rated with rogues and vagabonds and had to be beyond the city gates by nightfall.

Trevor had passed through the hands of both kinds of director and was to continue to do so, but his preference would always be for the first school – to which Carol Reed firmly belonged.

During the location a number of occurrences boded no good; a tropical house on stilts, in which Trevor was living, was washed away by water from the mountains. Carol Reed sprained his ankle and had to be carried up and down the hills, searching for ideal camera set-ups. Every hill looked better than the one he had been carried up, rather like finding the perfect place for a picnic. The worst happening of all was in Anaradapurra, in the far north of Ceylon. Leigh Ammon, now Lord Marley, was the production manager and he still shudders when he recalls it.

The unit was staying in a guest house in the middle of jungle scrub and night after night they were kept awake by the constant barking of wild dogs. Finally, Carol Reed appealed to Leigh Ammon: 'We must sleep. Can you do something to get rid of the dogs?' Trevor, in the room next to Carol's, was also suffering. Leigh explained the predicament to the guest house manager and the following day they left for their jungle location. When they returned in the evening, the manager announced that they had shot about a hundred and fifty dogs, so the night should be calmer.

When Carol heard about the shooting he was furious. He hadn't asked for the dogs to be shot, just quietened. That night the howling of dogs was greater than ever and in the morning Trevor's shoes and socks had mysteriously disappeared – as had those of Leigh. They were found about half a mile away, in the bushes. No wild dogs were seen or heard again, but the conclusion that dogs had ghosts was generally accepted.

A more pleasant location was in Colombo where Trevor's

father's old office on the quay was used for a sequence. The name above it had to be changed in accordance with the script, but it was 'in'.

Although Carol Reed was incapable of making a bad film, *An Outcast of the Islands* was not an unqualified success. Dame Wendy Hiller, who is a devotee of Conrad's work, is humorously sharp about it: 'It was a mish-mash. I was so entranced with the awfulness of it, I really was.' She believes it to have been an amalgam of two books, *Almayer's Folly* and *Outcast*, although a fresh look at the film and the original book doesn't really bear that opinion out. But Dame Wendy is totally right about her own role as Almayer's wife: that lady was a full-blooded native and the child Nina was a half-caste. Magnificent an actress as Wendy Hiller is, she doesn't immediately spring to mind as the native wife of a white man. 'And it began all wrong. Trevor, this young man with high ideals — weak, yes — but he was down before it started. He was a bright young hopeful out from home, the captain of the cricket team. Then he got that dreadful Conrad disintegration. When does honour seep away, where is the weakness? We didn't embark on the Conrad of the slow loss of values . . .' Neither does Conrad in *An Outcast of the Islands*; Willems has his hand in the till from page one. Neither is he fresh from home nor captain of the cricket team; he has been trained on by Captain Lingard from scruffy boyhood to white trader.

Wendy Hiller's version of the content of the book is exactly how the film *should* have been scripted. For in just one unfortunate part, the film is too true to the author and it's the part that matters most: the character of Willems. If the film had embarked on the Conrad of the 'slow loss of values', the audience would have had somebody to care about. 'Of course, Trevor was too fond of Carol to question him,' says Wendy Hiller. 'We should *all* have questioned him.' When the film was shown, she comments, 'I sat through it and laughed like mad, wondering what we were all doing. They should never have had me in it at all.'

Not all the critics were as rough on the film as Wendy Hiller, but coming from the hands of Carol Reed it did disappoint. However, it was generally agreed that Trevor Howard's performance was outstanding. Dilys Powell says, 'The film wasn't good enough, but Trevor was wonderful as Willems — a very difficult part, a self-sacrificing part – although he was a wretched character. It was a tragic performance, a remarkable performance.' When the film was shown in America in 1952, Bosley Crowther noted, 'Trevor Howard, whose performance of the ne'er-do-well is superb.' Trevor Howard was maintaining his reputation for getting good notices, no matter what the fate of the film under review.

As Willems he had also taken a long jump forward as an actor; if he had been excellent before, now he was showing signs of becoming great. His development of the character from a young, over-confident blackguard, through the insanity of a basically weak passion to self-destruction, betrayal and ultimate despair shone with recognition and comprehension. He invested the human frailties with a tragic truth, culminating in the last scene when his self-pity is flavoured with remorse.

Yet his self-searching about the cause and effect is touchingly simple: 'That's the gut again. It depends how you feel. I was going to be left on the island with this ghastly woman and I think I played the last scene with tears streaming down my face because Lingard was going off and that was the rest of my life. That was my punishment. Then there was Ralphie's last line: "You are my shame." '

The interiors for *An Outcast of the Islands* were shot at Shepperton Studios – as far away as possible from the new home in Arkley, Hertfordshire, which Helen had nearly completed during Trevor's absence on location: 'We didn't have any curtains, so I'd put sheets up at the windows – but I had moved in. Trevor was determined to get back from Shepperton to spend his first night in the new house, in spite of a thick fog. He drove through it with the windscreen down and arrived with a coal-black face.'

The house now has curtains, indeed it has probably had several sets of them during the thirty-five years that Helen and Trevor have lived there. It is the perfect setting for them: large, comfortable, warm and welcoming – but in no way grand. It is as unlike the conventional notion of a film star's house as Helen's true eye and quiet taste could make it. There have been no sudden rages of change to compete with 'At Home with . . .' photographs for glossy magazines. The house has grown with them; a proper home for the two very individual people who live in it.

Helen is the heart of the house, she runs it with apparent ease and daily help as neither she nor Trevor have time in their lives for the live-in couple masquerading as cook and butler. Helen cooks but Trevor doesn't buttle. He is not, in any way, a domesticated gentleman but he is as superb a host as he is a guest. Helen was once asked by an interviewer whether Trevor did anything around the house. 'Yes,' she replied brightly, 'he fills the ashtrays.' Even that task has been abrogated — he no longer smokes.

For those he feels close to, Trevor has his own inimitable brand of pet names, such as the Bontoy he visited upon his sister when a child. For years Helen became Hornchurch, for no apparent reason, later it became Hen or Henny. Nobody should be surprised to be addressed by Trevor as Monkeynut, it's a term of affection. Helen's occasional name for Trevor is Trout, because she can always cause him to rise to verbal bait. Since Trevor has a singularly short fuse when it comes to socializing with those he cannot find it in his heart to love, Helen's favourite ploy is an apparent *fait accompli* involving them: 'Oh, darling — you know I have a meeting with Bernard and Bill on Friday? Well, I've invited Bill and Poppy for lunch so Bill will drive me up to town and Poppy can stay with you until we get back. We shouldn't be late.'

Trevor stares at her, aghast. 'You've done *what*? I don't mind Bill for lunch but I'm not going to spend an *entire afternoon* with Poppy — I can't *stand the sight of her* . . .' He paces and roars. Helen lets the scene play for a few beats then she giggles, 'Trout!'

Trevor, bowled yet again, scuffles like a boy caught scrumping apples. 'Oh, Henny!'

Like many close couples, they have a private language. When one of them feels an urge to leave a party that is less than enjoyable, they mutter, 'Manon?' There is a little nod of agreement. Manon Lescaut — or let's get out of here. They have a beauty with which to confuse the unwary, the inversion of 'love' and 'hate'. If Trevor tells Helen that he hates the clothes she is wearing, he means he loves every stitch of them. If Helen hates a bibelot in a shop window, she means she is potty about it and intends to buy it. An additional ingredient in food or drink is said to give a Prince – or a fillip.

They are all warm and loving games.

Apart from the MCC, Trevor prefers pubs to clubs; he is not a Garrick, Savile or Savage man like many other actors. The Gate, their local pub in Arkley, is enjoyed by both Trevor and Helen and the owners, Rosemary and Harry Poole, have become close friends. When Helen is away from home, Trevor can enjoy his own kind of 'club' life locally as well as anywhere in the heart of London. Having no hobbies, he has little taste for solitude – and a little country walk leads to The Gate, where Harry Poole keeps a protective eye on one of his favourite regulars.

Trevor prefers to drink for joy, to celebrate work well done, and recognizes the danger of drinking when bored, when not working. He doesn't believe that alcohol alleviates sorrow: 'That's the excuse of many people but you can't win by it. It doesn't do what you set out to do by having a few because of sadness. It doesn't solve anything.' He never seeks excuses for personal excesses. Asked why he drinks – which is a stupid question, anyway – he is liable to reply, 'It makes everybody so much nicer. It makes the world a nicer place. Sometimes drink is a necessity – but never a crime.' This is an arguable, and very personal, belief but it is true for him because his nature doesn't change with drink; his famous roar might be in evidence but he remains gentle and joyous. He doesn't pick fights, throw things or become rude in any way to anybody. He is not a greedy drinker or a show off. Jack Lee, a British director now living in Australia, says: 'I can't see anything in that silly word "hell-raiser" they've attached to Trevor Howard. I've rarely seen him drunk, but rarely seen him not drink. He drinks and behaves like an eighteenth-century gentleman.'

CHAPTER EIGHT

The Gift Horse was one of the better war films of the many that were around during the early 1950s, following in the wake of American offerings which depicted America winning the war single-handed with a lot of help from Errol Flynn. Trevor headed a friendly cast which included Richard Attenborough and Bernard Lee. It was the first time Attenborough had worked with Trevor and the combination of Trevor and Bernard Lee delighted him: 'They were similar as actors – both had a fundamental truth beyond what we normally describe as acting. Trevor was marvellous, as he always is. He played the skipper of the ship and I saluted him morning, noon and night, which I would do anyway, on or off the set. He was a wonder to act with, no tricks, no upstaging, no nonsense at all. He always treated it as a slight joke that we should be employed and handsomely paid to do something that we absolutely loved doing.'

The picture did well and Trevor culled his customary good notices. One reviewer, Lynn Fenton, went overboard and deemed the film and Trevor Howard 'worthy of the biggest Oscar that the film world can produce.'

No matter how well it was played, the role of a stiff-upper-lipped naval commander was basically familiar on the screen, but that of Scobie in Graham Green's *The Heart of the Matter* was not. The character Scobie, Deputy Commissioner in Sierra Leone during the war, is finally destroyed by his capacity for pity, his frailty in the face of war and his Catholic conscience. This time, the Guardian Angel had provided a splendid challenge for Trevor Howard – and, indeed, for all concerned. It was a brave choice of subject since it depended almost entirely on emotional content, the grit of character against character. The film was made for Sir Alexander Korda and directed by George More O'Ferrall. Trevor remembers it being a very happy picture, the director was so enthusiastic 'and everything was magical. Every morning, before starting work, you could have a glass of champagne or a bottle of beer – just to say Good Morning. It was a routine that made you feel you were going to have a good day.'

Although much of the picture was shot at Shepperton Studios, there was also a lot of work on location, which was directed by Anthony Squire. Initially, the production office saw no reason for Trevor to go on location, they would use a double and save money. Trevor was outraged, he was making a picture and if he was to be in a scene it was going to be him and not a double; he was not prepared to do the film unless he did it all. He felt that nobody could understand that he wanted to do his job properly and thereby give a better performance. He was even prepared to forgo payment for the location work – but he had to be there: 'Producers take it for granted that actors will hold them to ransom.'

Trevor stood his ground and won.

When he arrived in Freetown, he was met and told that he would be staying with one of the British colonial administrators. Where, he wanted to know, were the other blokes? They were staying in some kind of hotel but orders were that Trevor Howard would be entertained by the British official. It was not Trevor's idea of a new and interesting location but orders were orders. After dinner with the British one evening, when the ladies had left the gentlemen to their port, Trevor was appalled when his host rose, made his way to the open French windows and said, 'Come on. Let's have our pee on Africa.' Trevor has no interest in politics, but he can recognize an unfortunate attitude of mind.

In 1956, while *The Heart of the Matter* was being finalized – that long process between acting and showing – Trevor Howard returned to the theatre.

This was his first appearance on the boards for six years. The play was *The Devil's General* by Carl Zuckmayer, presented by Linnit and Dunfee and directed by Trevor's former tutor, John Fernald. Trevor was to play the title role, General Harras of the Luftwaffe, and a key role – that of the General's batman, Korrianke – had yet to be cast.

Trevor requested Wilfrid Lawson for the part, knowing he would be superb, knowing he would be a joy to work with but, above all, knowing Lawson had not worked for a very long time.

To a vast number of actors he was an idol, but to theatre managements he was a bad risk; he was not only a magnificent actor, he was also a dedicated drinker. Trevor had his persuasive way, Lawson was cast and took second billing to Trevor Howard: 'But he didn't care. Or you never knew whether he cared or not. But he would have cared if anyone had told him that I'd got him the part. That would have done it. He had a terrific pride.'

The piece was set in Berlin, 1941. Although General Harras was a career officer, neither he nor his batman, Korrianke, were members of the Nazi Party. The dangers besetting both of them were obvious, particularly as the planes under the General's command were suspected of being sabotaged. Spying, betrayal and finally suicide, were combined in the plot. The general camouflages his ever-increasing anti-Nazi convictions behind a hard-living, roistering, devil-may-care attitude – until his spectacular self-immolation at the end.

Trevor found the play totally enjoyable. It was fun to do and it was also 'more physical then cerebral.' This suggests that Trevor understood the character; he found the general easy to assimilate. And there was Wilfrid Lawson.

Since Trevor was working at close quarters with an actor he had long admired, even revered, it might be supposed that Trevor became privy to the route Lawson took as an actor, to his *modus operandi*. Nothing could be further from the truth. Lawson was a quiet, excessively shy man who never discussed his work or the theatre in general: 'Willy was secretive to a degree. He arrived on his bicycle, just before curtain-up, wearing plus-fours and a beret. He never said more than "Good afternoon" to anybody. He was never rude, but he didn't want to chat. He had to be free up here.' Trevor taps his head. 'The only thing he could afford to store was the play. Anything that came between him and it was disruptive.'

During rehearsals or on matinée days Lawson took a sandwich and a bottle of Guinness to the theatre and he and Trevor would share a quiet and happy lunch break. During one of them Trevor happened to mutter, 'God, you were marvellous in *The Father*.' Lawson got up and walked away, leaving his Guinness unfinished. 'He couldn't take compliments. But if we had a cheerful disagreement about anything outside the theatre he was marvellous.

Now what is that in a man?' It is the same self-protective, deep, personal privacy that Trevor himself possesses.

Trevor feels that Lawson would have liked to be closer, to have become a good friend, but his shyness created too strong a barrier. But when Lawson had drunk a little more than enough he would often ring Helen, liberated enough to proffer the hand of friendship to and through her. But Trevor says rather sadly, 'I didn't really know him beyond pleasantries. So why I felt I knew him at all, I can't imagine.'

He knew Lawson through his work, which inspired so many actors – certainly those who are old enough to have seen him at it and possibly some who saw him as children. There was something magical about him which defied analysis. 'I can't ever visualize him working to a plan in rehearsal. I think we're both gut people.' That's very true and may be one reason that Trevor Howard has often been likened to Wilfrid Lawson. They also shared the ability, to surprise – giving the audience more than it felt it had any right to expect. But such actors cannot explain themselves, they cannot explain that ability to surprise because it comes from instinct, literally from the gut.

Trevor admired Lawson because he was such a marvellous actor, but he thinks anybody who had asked him how or why he gave such brilliant performances would have been in for a hard time. He knew there was an electric current stretching from Lawson to the audience, but had no words to describe it: 'Whenever you try to explain any art, as the artist, it disappears – it's lost.'

The Devil's General opened at the Edinburgh Festival and did the routine tour, during which Wilfrid Lawson returned to his familiar theatrical digs; he never stayed in hotels. Then the play went to London, to the Savoy Theatre. There, Trevor was cheered on the first night.

Christopher Lee remembers meeting Trevor, during the run of the play, in the Kummel Club in Covent Garden. Trevor was having a snack before the theatre and Christopher Lee joined him. Being another admirer of Wilfrid Lawson, Lee asked how he was doing. It was a fair question, it was known that Lawson drank. Trevor gave him chapter and verse of one astonishing performance.

The scene is set as the general returns after being acquitted by a court of inquiry and finds his batman, Lawson, waiting for him. Lawson then launches into a long impassioned speech, the essence of which is that he knew all along that they wouldn't find his general guilty. Then came the performance in which Lawson was in a world of his own and didn't say his lines at all – just gibberish, waltzing round the stage picking up a bottle here and there, and making noises which *said* everything the speech originally contained, but without using any words. Trevor was absolutely transfixed. He didn't know whether Lawson was going to slip in a line or not – or even give him his cue. Finally the noises stopped, Trevor thought that was his cue and got on with the play. He thought Wilfrid Lawson showed sheer genius, 'He was the only actor I knew where it didn't matter if you didn't understand what he was saying, because you couldn't – not always.'

Many might think it a sign of incipient madness in an actor who can actually praise a performance of gibberish when he has been left cueless. But then, Christopher Lee believes that Trevor Howard *is* possessed of a divine madness.

'He's a master of the unexpected and completely unpredictable. Both as a man and as an actor, that's where the excitement of an actor lies; in unpredictability. He always gives you something to remember. He was inner acting.'

As had Wilfrid Lawson and it is pleasant to record that, after *The Devil's General*, he was once again considered castworthy and went on to play several other roles.

Trevor has always believed that Graham Greene didn't care for the film of *The Heart of the Matter*, but the author gainsays this: 'I didn't like the ending of the film – I don't much like the book, either. But I liked Trevor's performance a great deal. It was one of the better films made out of my books, I think. The trouble was the suicide, we weren't allowed to have a suicide because of censorship.'

Although Graham Greene did not script the film, he was properly consulted about such a difficult problem as the ending: 'I had an idea for how it could be made a little more of a suicide to get around the censorship thing, and Trevor was very generous, very good about it. I think he wrote and said he agreed with me and was quite ready to do the extra work for nothing.'

So it wasn't the film Graham Greene didn't care for — it was the book. He thinks he was rusty when he wrote it and finds it exaggerated now, but it remains the best selling of all his books. Although the film was a critic's delight, the modification of the ending caused not only adverse criticism but won quite a lot of sympathy for the author. They couldn't know that Graham Greene himself had tried to solve the censorship problem.

Dilys Powell had long admired Trevor Howard's work and, having seen *The Heart of the Matter* in Cannes, prior to the London opening, was 'disappointed that Charles Vanel's showy performance in Clouzot's brutish *Salaire de la Peur* should have been placed above Trevor Howard's deeply studied portrait of Graham Greene's hero.' In her review of the film in *The Sunday Times* she was laudatory although she deplored 'the failure of courage at the end ... instead of leaving the tragic issue in doubt, suddenly admits a kind of divine intervention.'

When talking of Trevor Howard many years, and many films later: 'I think the first time I went overboard about him was in *The Heart of the Matter*. Perhaps it wasn't such a marvellous film but his was a marvellous performance. I found it deeply moving and I thought, this is a real actor, not just a — well, a film actor. When I say that it sounds insulting to the cinema and I don't mean it to, but he was not the conventional film actor. It was absolutely beautiful; not just sacrificing his life but also his death. Somehow it captured the very best in him.'

Of Trevor's playing of Scobie, Fred Majdalany wrote in *Time and Tide*, 'This is acting of a spiritual and emotional depth rarely seen on the screen. I can think of no English-speaking actor who could have done it as well.'

The private Trevor Howard had also been at the Cannes Film Festival, where he encountered many friends along the Croisette. As a group they found their way into the casino where Darryl Zanuck was spending most of his time at the tables. Gambling has as much allure for Trevor Howard as a cold bath on a winter's night, so he was not among those who watched over Zanuck's shoulder, fascinated by big-time stakes. He wandered off with Van Johnson to look at a kind of aviary which was part of the decor of the casino at that time. It contained flamingos and a variety of similarly exotic birds.

Trevor chatted up the birds for a while and then noticed that the iron gate which kept them captive was unlocked so, quite unobtrusively, he opened the gate. He then moved on, slowly and casually, muttering to Van Johnson, 'For Christ's sake don't give the game away.' In a very short time the casino was in an uproar and at that hour of the night the regular keepers were hard to locate. Croupiers and players – all more accustomed to birds of a different feather – tried, with little success, to herd the birds back: 'They couldn't let the birds out into the streets and couldn't get them back in the cage. There was a tremendous hullabaloo – disturbed the whole building. And nobody ever found out.' It made Trevor Howard's evening.

1953 also saw Trevor in *The Stranger's Hand* in which he was cast at the suggestion of Graham Greene. The original idea came from a *New Statesman* competition, for the best first paragraph to a novel, which was won by Graham Greene. Mario Soldati suggested that he should continue the story as a film treatment and co-produce the film with John Stafford, while Soldati would direct.

The entire film was shot in Venice and Graham Greene remembers that one day, after a rather good lunch with Trevor, they decided to have a race along the Grand Canal. Trevor won and returned to work, Graham Greene wasn't far behind but he had to return to his hotel to rest. He much admired Trevor's ability to enjoy the lunch, run the race and get on with his work. He also appreciated Trevor's willingness to plan his off-set pleasure according to production requirements: 'Trevor was very co-operative in the sense that you know he likes to go out on the town at least once, and he arranged to have his jolly the night before he played a man lying drugged on a cabin floor. He just had to lie down. There were no problems, he was totally professional, as ever.'

Greene thought Trevor was extremely good in a film that was not bad, but a small film. It was also rather unlucky because, by the time the film was finished, Yugoslavia had come over to the western camp – and the story had to do with Tito as a Communist, before he changed his ways and broke with Stalin. The *New York Times* was less than sympathetic, Bosley Crowther disliked the film and referred to '. . . Mr Howard, looking like a Bowery bum.'

The only event to put something of a crimp into a triumphant year occurred in September when Trevor fell foul of an occupational hazard that had been shaking its spear in the wings for some time. Trevor Wallace Howard was charged with being overtired in charge of a motor vehicle. He was fined fifty pounds and disqualified from driving for twelve months, a term later reduced to six.

In October Trevor was working in New York for the first time. Otto Preminger was directing a sequence of Noël Coward's *To-Night at 8.30* for a television series to be shot, as a 'first', in colour. Martyn Greene was cast in *Red Peppers* and Ginger Rogers was playing all the leading ladies, thus she would play opposite Trevor Howard in *Still Life* – or *Brief Encounter*. He had not been to America since his very early teens, he had never played there and he couldn't wait.

Relations between Trevor and the director got off to a poor start when Otto Preminger told him, 'Forget about the picture you made. Here we have something different – we have Ginger Rogers. You must pick her up with you, take her to the counter for coffee and pinch her ass.' Trevor looked at him for a while and then said, very gently, 'I *think* I know what time the next plane leaves for London.'

Some kind of order was restored and the show went on. In New York years later, Helen and Trevor were dining at Toots Shor's when Otto Preminger appeared. He paused at their table and said to Trevor, 'You don't like me, do you?' With a warm smile Trevor replied, 'You know very well I don't.' Preminger moved on and Trevor looked at Helen, 'And that's exactly what he wanted me to say.'

During his first working visit to New York, Trevor sought out the jazz clubs of his youth as well as those that were newly established. His interest in jazz comes as a surprise to many who hear of it for the first time, most of all when they believe they have known him well for years. Yet classical jazz is a logical taste for an actor; it is a musical form that allows self-expression within a governed framework. The instrumentalists have their turn to 'take it away', to improvise while retaining the discipline of the form. The same is true of an actor's interpretation of a role, the words remain the same but the approach, the understanding, the nuances differ vastly between actors playing the same part.

Jazz is also emotional, invoking pain as well as joy. There is even a Shakespearan flavour in a classical blues, since it is based on a rhymed couplet in iambic pentameter. Leonard Bernstein illustrated this with a *Macbeth Blues*:

> 'I will not be afraid of death or bane,
> I will not be afraid of death or bane
> 'Till Birnam forest come to Dunsinane.'

Trevor delighted in all of it, the sound, the beat, the surprises and the enthusiasm: 'The freedom is alluring and the way the players love you for loving them. It's a way of life that brings out the best in you from a point of view of enjoyment and laughter. I feel so sorry for people who don't have those moments.'

Devotion to jazz also offers mobility. If you buy a ticket to a concert you have to sit there; you won't find an alternative or better oboist across the street. 'In one evening after work in New York you can hear as many jazz players as you can move around.'

While moving around on that visit, he struck up a friendship with a fellow jazz buff who worked for the powerful William Morris Agency. This casual friendship led to an actor-agent situation which was quite chilling, but far from unique. Trevor's London agent, who was no longer Eric Goodhead, was using the William Morris Agency to arrange a labour permit for Trevor, but for the purposes of wheeling and dealing with artistes he had a separate opposite number in New York. His friend in the Morris office sent Trevor the script of a play, *Anastasia*, in which Viveca Lindfors and Eugenie Leontovitch were to appear on Broadway. There was a part in it for Trevor Howard, if he was interested. He was more than interested, he was enthusiastic; a play on Broadway with such a cast was hardly to be turned down out of hand. There was the matter of his availability to be discussed but the producers of the play were amenable to juggling with rehearsal dates in order to secure his services. As far as Trevor knew he was available but suggested that this be checked with his London agent, in case he had been committed to other work in his absence.

The next, and last, news Trevor received relating to his opportunity to appear on Broadway was a letter from London. In it his agent put forth, in letters of fire, his own interpretation of Trevor Howard's reasons for turning down a play he badly wanted to do. In its way it was a masterpiece of double-think, quoting Trevor as saying or feeling things he never said or felt. The writer also expressed the optimistic hope that the enclosed copy of an annihilating letter sent to the William Morris Agency on the matter met with Trevor's approval. It had to: the door had been slammed, locked and barred.

It has to be assumed that this destructive ploy arose from the fear that the William Morris Agency might gain a client. Whatever the cause, the incident left Trevor Howard with the suspicion that agents could be manipulative against, as well as for, their clients and might 'land an up and coming chap into an up or down in his career.' He also reckons that any work he gained in America was more the result of producers or directors asking for him than efforts made on his behalf by any agent.

Whoever was responsible, Trevor Howard made two more television appearances in America in the Fifties: *The Flower of Pride*, with Geraldine Fitzgerald; and *Deception*, with Linda Darnell. A long time afterwards, he received a script from Twentieth Century Fox via Carol Reed. Trevor always reads scripts received as soon as possible and one from Carol Reed got even faster attention. As he read it Trevor realized that he had been there before, this was *Deception* under a new title. He rang Carol and broke the news that he had already played the part for American television. Carol was incredulous – Trevor must be mistaken. 'Well,' said Trevor, 'why not ask Bob Goldstein? He's the head of Fox in London. He must know, or be able to find out.' Doubtless somebody was found out because the project was dropped. Trevor nearly regrets letting the cat loose: 'I might have made another film with Carol.'

*

Trevor sometimes refers, with affectionate nostalgia, to the 'Roaring Fifties' ... as well he might. His reputation as a hell-raiser probably peaked during that decade and held its place throughout the next one. He admits to having rather enjoyed being known as a hell-raiser, and certainly never argued the point – possibly because it set him apart to some degree, and from boyhood he has enjoyed singularity. The term sounds rough and tough, which Trevor Howard is not, so maybe there was an unrecognized need for an alter ego; an identity for the shy and private man within.

Thus Trevor's recollections of certain events tend to assume Baron Munchhausen proportions, on the grounds that 'it makes a better story'. A unique example of what was possible was a visit to Dublin in 1954.

The occasion was a Show of the Stars to promote the film *A Star is Born*. The galaxy of which Trevor was a member consisted of Peggy Cummins, Robert Beatty and Adrienne Corri – none of whom were actually associated with the picture; they were there to present a cabaret before the showing of the film. Trevor's memory of events differs strangely from that of Adrienne Corri.

Trevor remembers being met at Dublin airport by two Irish actors, Eddie Byrne and Noël Purcell, and being borne away to sample a few jars, thereby missing the rehearsal for the evening cabaret. However, when the time came Trevor was onstage doing a jig to the tune of *Phil the Fluter's Ball* for which he received an ovation.

Later that night he was awakened by detectives who wanted to search his room. To his amazement, they unearthed a fair amount of jewellery from under his mattress but, rather oddly, failed to take him in charge 'to help with their enquiries'. They just walked out, leaving him to assess his situation. He did, and feeling in no need of personal publicity involving the nicking of tomfoolery, he decided to catch the first plane back to London.

He arrived at the airport just as the London flight was being called – and had his collar felt again. This time the constabulary were interested in some strange packages which appeared to be part of his luggage. They turned out to be bathroom stools from the Gresham Hotel, hardly, Trevor observes in hurt tones, something he would have tried to take out of Ireland when he was trying to escape unscathed. The plane left for London and Trevor left for Mountjoy Prison to make a statement which, as the Irish say, put the heart across him.

At Mountjoy, with the drinks lined up, were the 'detectives' and his other persecutors; some were real and others might have been actors from the Abbey Theatre. Trevor leans towards being victimized and counts this jolly-up among his collection of 'arrests'.

Adrienne Corri's version is different. She recalls that, during the pre-cabaret afternoon, Trevor was due to make a personal appearance in a danger zone – a Dublin distillery. Having rehearsed their show, Trevor's fellow artistes returned to the Gresham Hotel to find Trevor in sore need of black coffee which Peggy Cummins and Adrienne administered, under the sober and disapproving eye of Robert Beatty.

The show went on, the others did their act successfully and Trevor did his jig to *Phil the Fluter's Ball*, which was much appreciated.

Champagne was served after the show and the party included the Chief of Police, with whom Adrienne fell into conversation. She was pretty relaxed herself by this time and it wasn't very long before the Chief of Police was offering to arrest anybody she cared to name. She named Robert Beatty, on the grounds that he was being stuffy and boring, but even she was hazily amazed when four policemen arrived to arrest the poor man. This little tease was swiftly resolved and hilarity was restored.

The following morning the British contingent was due to fly back to London but by then Trevor was convinced that Ireland was his spiritual home and that was where he belonged. Adrienne is sure that she finally got him on the flight by assuring him that it was going to Paris. When they disembarked she was beating a Guinness tray like a drum and Trevor was telling her that he would never forgive her: 'This is London, isn't it? It's not Paris. You've cheated me. You're not on my side.' That was a serious accusation – not to be on Trevor's side was, and remains, the worst offence of all.

Whatever really happened – and who could know for sure, in view of the abundant hospitality – the venue was definite. It had to be Ireland. Long after, whenever Adrienne and Trevor met he would say jovially, 'You got me arrested in Dublin.' She hadn't and he wasn't, but he clings to this belief. Certainly no other personal appearance by Trevor was ever quite like it.

Adrienne Corri is one of many who align Trevor Howard and Wilfrid Lawson. She worked with the latter at the Old Vic and, more than thirty years later, her observations are interesting and pertinent; 'There's a kind of genealogy which links Wilfrid Lawson and Trevor Howard to a generation of intelligent young actors who realized that these two men had genius and thought that, by drinking, they might acquire it. I've seen many young actors behaving in the way they *thought* Trevor or Wilfrid would behave – and hoping the performance would arrive. They didn't see that drinking got in the way because they didn't realize about the inner discipline. But Trevor and Wilfrid were the models, the idols of those boys. I know that Peter O'Toole worshipped Trevor Howard.'

Trevor Howard was, and remains, unaware of his impact on the younger generation of that time. He would never see himself in the role of a guru, or wish to be one, since his only ambitions have been to work as much and as well as lies in his power – and to enjoy himself thoroughly when possible.

In May 1954 Trevor faced the challenge of playing Chekhov for the first time, as Lopahin in the *The Cherry Orchard*. As he has said since: 'These northern plays are heavy, there's not much to laugh about – it's tight and hard work.' So he was delighted to be directed by John Gielgud whose dedication to his work was immensely admired by Trevor. Of Gielgud he was quoted as saying, 'He lives for the theatre and radiates happiness to all those who work with him.' Apart from Trevor Howard, Gwen Ffrangcon-Davies and Pauline Jameson were among those working with John Gielgud. Noël Coward saw the production and noted in his diary, 'A magical evening in the theatre; every part subtly and perfectly played ... we came away prancing on the tips of our toes and very proud that we belonged to the theatre.'

Trevor Howard's next film was a French production, *The Lovers of Lisbon*, with Daniel Gélin. The film amounted to very little, but working in Paris gave Trevor an opportunity to meet two artistes he greatly admired: Jacques Tati and Jean Gabin.

Daniel Gélin took Trevor to meet Tati at his house outside Paris, and Trevor still bubbles with pleasure when he remembers watching Tati: 'He was playing like a child – with his walk and his hat. We were watching pure invention.' What Trevor describes as Tati's 'un-ordinary ordinariness' made a deep impression on him. Trevor loves a perfectionist, and Tati was nothing if not that.

It would have been worth a few years of life to have watched Jean Gabin and Trevor Howard together. Leaving the difference in age aside, they could have been cast from the same mould and could have interchanged roles. Both have the force on the screen which is a combination of truth and authority which nails attention; both have those indefinable tragic undertones and both could have had any woman in the audience had they cared to step off the screen. Furthermore, they have both cost critics and journalists time and anguish in trying to describe their faces.

To Trevor, meeting Jean Gabin was meeting a great person but, 'You didn't get any depth in there – because he probably didn't want you to have it.' As the man said, it takes one to know one.

For a first-class actor who loved to work, and suffered when he didn't, there was, at this time, little on offer that he could accept in good conscience. It wasn't that he was vehemently protective of his own talent, it was never a question of scripts not being good enough for him: he rejected them on the grounds that they weren't good enough for anybody. Many of his fellow actors envied his steadfastness in turning down dross.

Trevor had been offered a number of roles by Warwick Films, an American company operating in England. Not unnaturally they chose their stars from Hollywood and hoped that Trevor would settle for second or third place. So far he had resisted their offers which always came through their intermediary, Euan Lloyd, who knew Trevor very well. As publicity director for General Film Distributions, Euan Lloyd had learnt that Trevor loved to travel and when possible they had darted all over the world together attending film festivals and special premières, whatever occasion necessitated the showing of the British film flag. Trevor was always willing to go, providing he was not working: 'Trevor has chalked up more miles than some airline pilots.'

Euan Lloyd was now a production assistant with Warwick and he approached Trevor with the script of *Cockleshell Heroes*, which was to star and be directed by Jose Ferrer. He also wanted Trevor Howard. Irving Allen, of Warwick Films, suggested that Trevor should fly with him to Hollywood to meet Jose Ferrer and discuss the project. It was to be a hasty two-day trip – but it was travel and Trevor had never been to Hollywood. Their flight was delayed, giving reporters plenty of time to quiz Trevor. He informed them that he was leaving England and would not be returning. This caused a fine furore. Once again it was assumed that the Howard marriage had broken up and Helen was awakened by telephone calls telling her that her husband was leaving England forever. The first caller got a crisp reaction: 'Can I rely on that?' she asked. Later she explained that her time was already committed to touring the Continent with the Stratford Shakespeare Company – but the marriage was fine. Her husband was an actor who was miserable if he wasn't working and none of the scripts he had been offered recently had been nearly good enough. That was all.

When Trevor was reported as saying that he didn't doubt that the Chancellor of the Exchequer would be interested to learn that he would not be returning, Helen was vastly amused, 'Chancellor of the Exchequer? Trevor? He doesn't even know there is one.' On such occasions Trevor enjoyed teasing the press who, in turn, would have found the truth rather dull.

In Los Angeles Trevor stayed at the Sunset Towers where, in the penthouse above him, Bryan Forbes was rewriting the script for *Cockleshell Heroes*. Trevor remembers that Bryan Forbes had a pink Cadillac and Trevor had a Mustang. He had his meeting with Jose Ferrer and was back in London after two days, having agreed to be in the picture. It was his first American film and was made for Columbia Pictures.

Many of the exteriors for the film were to be shot in Portugal and as Trevor always loved to drive through France, Euan Lloyd suggested they should drive down together in his Austin 10 with his two-year-old daughter in a cot on the back seat. They stopped in Paris overnight and, somewhat to Euan's surprise, Trevor elected to watch over the child until she slept, before joining Euan in the bar.

This became a routine during the journey as they made overnight stops in San Sebastian and then northern Portugal. They arrived in Cascais, near Lisbon, where the film was to be shot and where the unit was now gathered, two days before shooting. Inevitably, the hell-raiser reputation had preceded Trevor Howard, and Irving Allen took Euan aside. 'You got him into the goddam picture and you'd better see that he behaves himself.' The fact that Warwick Films had been angling for the services of Trevor Howard through many scripts had been conveniently forgotten.

Shooting started, all went well and Trevor fell deeply in love with Portugal. As always, his expression of pleasure was the bull moose roar, 'I love this place,' and the place loved him. Euan feels that Trevor's trademark is the roar, 'It's fine for the great outdoors, but, heard at close quarters, people can do strange things – or it does strange things to them.'

Suddenly, Irving Allen announced to Euan that the Portuguese government had decreed that filming in Portugal would have to stop unless the film company guaranteed to make a documentary about Portugal to be shown with *Cockleshell Heroes*. It was a rare stab at blackmail coming from any government, particularly as it must have been obvious that, once the film was sold for distribution, nobody could possibly guarantee that another film would be shown with it. However, Euan Lloyd was not about to argue. He had been deputized to write, produce and direct the documentary; he also got the excellent second unit cameraman, Ted Moore, who later won an Oscar for *A Man For All Seasons*. Trevor Howard volunteered to do the commentary.

The schedule was arranged to give Trevor two free days and the unit of three went off to shoot footage of caves and any other points of interest they could find. They also found the famous fado singer, Amalia Rodriguez, who agreed to sing for the film, which was titled *April in Portugal*.

When both films were shown, Trevor received more of the warm reviews that he never took for granted. Campbell Dixon's enthusiastic notice for *Cockleshell Heroes* in the *Daily Telegraph* included '. . . a magnificent performance by Trevor Howard as the regular officer . . . Even when given nothing to do or say he dominates the screen with effortless authority.'

But it was the two-reeler *April in Portugal* that won awards; one from the Berlin Festival and the other at Mar del Plata. The writer-producer-director, Euan Lloyd, is modest about his success: 'It was largely thanks to Trevor because nobody would have paid much attention to the film without his name on it.' With Trevor Howard, Euan Lloyd travelled to ten or twelve countries with this, his first personal production.

Trevor now had time to travel. He had time to take Helen to Switzerland for a skiing holiday. He had more time than he cared to have. He was no longer working in one film after another and the scripts he was offered continued to be unacceptable. The time would come when, desperate to work, he would feel driven to lower his sights and take the best of a bad bunch, but not yet. Neither was his desperation financial. Trevor Howard is probably the least extravagant actor, let alone film star, throughout the world. By the end of 1955, he had been a top-line star for ten years and both he and Helen were secure. Their mutual financial adviser, Bernard Kimble, has looked after them since the early Fifties and thinks Trevor must be unique among actors in his attitude to money. In fact, he finds it quite frightening, 'Trev is the dearest man in the world but he's just not interested in money. He's interested in working and earning, but as soon as it's translated into pounds and pence, he just doesn't care. When told how much is in the kitty, he all but yawns. He just wants to work.'

Although American producers were encouraged to make films in Britain, the domestic industry was far from healthy and cinema audiences were rapidly dwindling. 1955 saw the beginning of commercial television in London and new stations soon spread over the country. Ealing Studios were sold to the British Broadcasting Corporation for television production, but stars of the larger screen still shrank from the smaller one and television producers were chary of approaching them: they were accustomed to larger fees than television could offer.

Small comedies and war films continued to prove successful at the box office but few producers had anything new or exciting with which to combat the availability of well-made golden oldies on television. The Rank Organisation still had artistes under contract who were automatically at the top of the list when casting was in progress; smaller production companies had their own, tried and tested, favourites. It was a bleak period for serious and talented actors such as Trevor Howard.

With about fifty other 'names' he contributed a cameo to Mike Todd's *Around the World in Eighty Days*, but that was hardly work as he understood it. So when he was asked to appear in *Run for the Sun* with Richard Widmark and Jane Greer, he didn't hesitate. It was an American production being shot in Mexico, at Cuernavaca and Mexico City and, apart from other considerations, Mexico was a new country for Trevor.

He probably didn't know that he was second choice for the part – the first was Leo Genn who was not available – but Jane Greer did. She knew because the producer, Harry Tatelman, had a word with her on what he described as a 'touchy subject'. He explained that they couldn't get Leo Genn and the actor who was replacing him wanted second billing, which would give Jane Greer third billing. Not unreasonably Jane Greer pointed out that it would depend on who the actor was. Trevor Howard. 'Trevor Howard? But he *should* be above the title. How wonderful. He's such a great actor.'

They started shooting in near-jungle in which there was a beaten up hacienda. On the first day, Jane Greer noticed that Trevor was in the hacienda getting ready to work. She sought out a production assistant, 'What's Trevor Howard doing in there? Doesn't he have a dressing room?' It seemed he didn't. There was none available. Jane Greer went to Harry Tatelman, 'Don't you know who Trevor Howard is? What do you mean, there's no dressing room?' After some more of the same, Tatelman agreed that Trevor Howard rated proper treatment. In spite of her anger, Jane Greer realized that 'Harry Tatelman really didn't know what he'd got in Trevor Howard. It was shameful.' It was, particularly as the British director must have known exactly who he'd got, but doubtless Roy Boulting had too much on his mind to worry about the comfort of his stars.

It is notable that Trevor himself never complained, neither was he ever told why he suddenly found himself with a dressing room.

Jane Greer enjoyed working with him. 'The thing about Trevor was that he was so beguiling. He had that mischievous twinkle and could get away with anything – but he was a perfect professional. Always prepared, always a good performance.' Then there was the jollity in the evening. There was a pianist around and Trevor sang his way through Cole Porter, knowing all the words.

During that location, Trevor formed a lasting, loving and completely platonic friendship with Marge Gutterman, who was Jane Greer's stand-in. Marge thinks that she was 'a bit of a lame duck and Trevor felt kind of sorry for me, he watched over me, that really began our friendship. It was a perfectly proper one, too.' But the production office couldn't believe that it was all that proper. By then they had discovered who Trevor Howard was and were treating him with kid gloves – he was not only welcome to a dressing room, he could have anything else he fancied. Marge was approached and told that they had noticed that Trevor was fond of her. That was nice – she thought he was great, too. 'Yeah. We want to tell you that anything he wants, you just let him have it and we'll make it up to you.' There was really only one reply to that and Marge had it: 'How?' she asked. They couldn't understand that Trevor Howard enjoyed Marge's company, usually had dinner with her, but was not about to lay her – ever.

Marge eventually met Helen, in New York. By then she had heard a lot about Helen from Trevor and other mutual friends, and for no good reason had supposed her to be very British and starchy. When Trevor told her that Helen had arrived in New York and that she must meet her at once, Marge was really rather frightened. Trevor and Helen were staying at the Plaza and Trevor knocked on the door and said, 'Henny, I'm coming in with Marge.' Marge had never seen such a beautiful woman and they became the greatest of friends. When Marge was in Los Angeles during an earthquake, Helen called someone she knew in the White House and asked them to find out whether Marge was all right. Marge was not only impressed, she was also very touched.

Through Marge, Trevor also met Robert Mitchum, who was filming *Bandido* in Mexico. They became good friends and were to work and play together in later years.

For Trevor Howard, his friendship with Jane Greer and Marge Gutterman was probably the best part of *Run for the Sun*. It was far from being a good film.

CHAPTER NINE

By 1956, Trevor Howard had appeared in twenty films. Of that number, four were memorable, two of them largely because of his performances, and two became classics. In them all he had received personal notices such as many actors never achieve in an entire career and he had been equally acknowledged for his five appearances in the theatre. Although he had played a number of roles representing integrity and a stiff upper-lip, as the supposedly typical Briton, he had never been type-cast to the point of exclusion of anything else. He had proved his range and versatility as an actor of talent. But there were no great parts for him, nothing which would use his remarkable abilities to the full and stretch him beyond them.

True, he didn't court directors and producers, he never angled for invitations to the right parties in order to corner the right people and sell himself. Nothing in his nature would have made such a ploy possible, it was a talent he lacked and wouldn't wish to acquire. Selling Trevor Howard was his agent's business, for Trevor the right party was among friends and was to be enjoyed, not to be used as a private market-place.

At this point in the game, Trevor Howard might have been forgiven if he had devoted his time to 'hell-raising' and cricket – until the former bowled him out. Instead, he agreed to appear in a film that was well below his usual standard. This was *Interpol*, another Warwick production and another lure from Euan Lloyd: 'It isn't very good, but you're not doing anything else – so come on.' Trevor went; so did Victor Mature. The film was shot in Rome and Genoa and finished in a British studio. Trevor liked Victor Mature, who, according to Euan Lloyd, was a lousy actor by his own definition but great fun to be with.

Euan Lloyd admits that *Interpol* was a film that should be forgotten and that Trevor really shouldn't have done it. Most of the drama that might have gone into a good film went into the promotion of a bad one and the publicity stunt in Frankfurt nearly lost Trevor Howard to screen and stage forever.

There was an early morning press meeting at Police HQ to enable them to watch the machinery at work when a criminal was being pursued. Trevor was the sole passenger in a car with a police driver and they were given a ten-minute start to drive anywhere in the city before the police were alerted to pursue and bring them in. Off they went, leaving the press behind to watch the sport on a large screen. Trevor and his driver were in a red Mercedes and as they roared towards the centre of the city, they came up behind a queue of cars awaiting the pleasure of a policeman on point duty – the traffic lights were out of action and the policeman was slowly controlling the traffic from a high stand. Trevor's driver had been told to take any action necessary to escape, so he pulled out of the queue and drove around the traffic policeman at great speed. Unfortunately, the policeman had not been informed of this little caper; but he did know that the previous day there had been a major bank robbery from which the villains had escaped in an identical red Mercedes.

Seeing a police car apparently chasing the bank robbers, the traffic controller pulled out his gun and fired two bullets into the red car. He would have continued to shoot, but the pursuit car had also rounded the queue, come abreast of him and told him to cool it. As the pursuit car was driven by a police inspector, he did.

Meanwhile, Trevor's driver thought this was all part of the plan: shots maybe, but blanks certainly. Trevor was not so sanguine. He was right since, during this entire balls-up, nobody had thought to make use of radio communication to prevent possible tragedy. Finally it became obvious to one and all that this had become a very dangerous game, so the radio was used, but only to say, 'All points – emergency – stop them.' All police cars converged on the red Mercedes beside an unfenced electrified railway which ran from the airport into the city. Trevor had been told that the press would be waiting at the point of capture so, 'When the car stops, get out and run.' As everything screeched to a halt, Trevor leapt out of the car but could see nowhere to go except over the railway: so he went over the electrified lines. The police stood open-mouthed – there was no earthly reason why Trevor Howard shouldn't have been burned to a crisp.

Luckily for all concerned, he was scared and shaken but unhurt. Meanwhile the hunger for publicity had been appeased, the coverage in all the media was enormous, destined to plug a movie that was at very best mediocre. Well, it needed help.

'But that night, back at the hotel, feet up and a jar in hand, it was all forgotten. Not many artistes would go through that.' Not many people would have expected them to, and not many police forces would have taken such mindless chances. For the London opening of *Interpol*, Euan Lloyd himself devised a less lethal approach to publicity: on the backs of buses, on hoardings, on tree trunks, anywhere that a police-type poster could be stuck was a mug shot of Trevor Howard. 'This man is wanted by Interpol.' It might have been embarrassing, but it was better than being shot in the back.

In July 1956, Euan Lloyd went into the witness box on Trevor Howard's behalf. For the second time Trevor was up for a driving offence, but this time there was some doubt about his condition: he was sober enough to have been frightened into behaving reasonably when picked up. Trevor's defence counsel had heard Euan talking about the actor's odd behaviour in various parts of the world when completely sober, and thought some examples might help his client's cause in court.

Euan had a beauty: 'Last summer, Mr Howard and I were driving along Piccadilly with the car radio on. We were about to win the Ashes and it all depended on two final runs. We were stuck in a traffic jam when finally somebody hit a four which won the game. Mr Howard jumped out of the car in front of Fortnum & Mason's, danced on the pavement, let out a roar, then jumped onto the bonnet of the car, peered at me through the windshield and yelled, "We've done it! We've done it!"'

That well-known titter ran through the court and Trevor Howard was acquitted. It was a story which had to be true since nobody could have possibly made it up.

At last it was Guardian Angel time again and Trevor had a film which was hailed by some critics as his best since *The Third Man*, and a headline called it 'A Winner for the World'. *Manuela* was British made, directed by Guy Hamilton, formerly Carol Reed's right-hand man, and produced by Ivan Foxwell.

The film was shot mainly on location in Spain in Cartagena, Alicante, and on an island just offshore on which no motor cars were allowed.

Trevor celebrated his arrival on location by having a drink, as he usually did. He was far from being alone among actors in this; a bar is a natural place for the cast and members of the unit to meet, relax and become acquainted. Working with a film unit, particularly on location, is like a little life. Everyone has to live together as amicably as possible while it lasts and when it's over, as cast and unit go their separate ways, there is often a hint of sadness, a sense of loss.

At the bar with Trevor on this occasion was the excellent actor Jack McGowran whom Trevor greatly admired. Seeing and hearing McGowran's jollity the producer decided he was a bad risk and wanted to send him home and recast. Just like that. Trevor was outraged on McGowran's behalf, but he rarely operates through anger. He had a quiet word with the producer, pointing out that they were all drinking because work had not yet commenced; he reasoned with persuasive charm and McGowran stayed on the picture. Trevor heartily dislikes this kind of snap judgement: 'You might ruin an actor's career and you might spoil the film. You cannot be sacked for having a drink at the bar before you've started shooting.'

Manuela was shown at the Berlin Festival before opening in London, and there Dilys Powell met Trevor Howard for the first time. She had just arrived from Greece and, due to the usual accidents of travel, was late for the evening showing. She was standing outside the theatre cursing, 'in my terrible Greek. I had it in my head and I was cursing terribly and very loudly in Greek thinking what the hell shall I do. I can't get in. Then Trevor appeared. He was just going in and he took me. We didn't know each other at all and here was this nice man who took pity on some wretched critic who stood cursing in an unknown language outside the theatre.' Hers is a delightfully modest view; most actors would have prayed for a puddle over which to lay their dinner jacket so she could step on it.

Luckily, Dilys Powell liked the picture. Covering the Berlin Festival for *The Sunday Times* she wrote of her delight in seeing a British film which was so superior in craftsmanship that it stood 'head and shoulders above everything else, with a superb performance by Trevor Howard.' When the film opened in London she reviewed the film again, devoting space to an appreciation of the depth and subtlety of a beautiful player: 'I can think of no actor like Trevor Howard for suggesting the heartbreak behind the bleak, the unwavering look.'

Dilys Powell was far from alone in her enthusiasm, both for the film and Trevor Howard. Critics had been starved of British films of which they could be proud and, contrary to the belief held by makers of dull films, do prefer to praise than to punish. In a generally warm review, Philip Oakes noted: 'Trevor Howard gives the film an extra dimension with his painfully precise portrait of the anguished old man of the sea. This is a great performance.'

Nearly thirty years later, Trevor said of *Manuela*: 'Every part was a little jewel – especially Jack McGowran, who went on to play all the Becketts.' He seemed not to remember his own little jewel of a part, possibly because he shies away from talking about his work, or himself, at all. He never gives himself credit for a particularly good performance; it comes from inside and he can feel when it's truly good, like a visceral reaction. Neither does he base his characterizations on observation, remembering a walk or a trick of the head. 'No. It wouldn't be me – and it wouldn't be the character, either.' He finds that approach to be superficial. Once he has accepted a part, he reads the script or play many times: all of it, not just his own role. Once he has studied the script, he needs what he calls 'ping-pong'; someone to hear his lines and give him his cues. Luckily, he married a lady who is a good actress in her own right; Helen plays ping-pong with him. Allowing he is a slow study, he prefers the real to the rehearsal – but likes to wind up during the latter. He also has tremendous faith in his instinct, that whatever goes on inside him will make it all right on the night.

Trevor never gets up to tricks with false noses or any facial props because for him it all comes from inside: 'They wouldn't help. They would get in the way.' He has always used what he has got, preferring to grow his own hair when time allows. His make-up is basically minimal, such as darker eyebrows, but although he claims not to be mad about his face he is also sure that 'if you play tricks you don't get anything. It immediately looks false.'

Neither does he go for the 'method school', or anything remotely related to it. He has never felt the need to act like a bowl of soup or to go up a mountain and shout God Save the Queen for the benefit of his voice.

Trevor remembers dining with Shelley Winters in New York when she was playing in *A Hat Full of Rain*. She was anxious for any pointers he might be able to give her for playing Shakespeare as she was studying with Lee Strasberg and doing exercises from *The Taming of the Shrew*. Since she was already a respected and established actress, Trevor was surprised and delighted by her desire to learn. However, he felt, but did not say, that he doubted she would learn much to her betterment by Lee Strasberg's system.

As a member of the older generation, Trevor is bemused by young actors whose dissertations appear to reveal the nuts and bolts of their craft, like a cooking recipe or a 'how to' manual. He regards them as apprentices, and marvels that they can explain themselves so deftly unless they are thinking it out while they are working – to the possible detriment of their performance. For him an actor is always learning, and there are no absolutes. Certainly few great actors have been able to analyse their work in depth, any more than any other creative artist; the odds are that Fred Astaire would find it hard to 'explain' his dancing.

Insight is a possible keyword to Trevor's best performances. He has searched the character he is playing until he knows and understands his actions and motives. He can share his hate, fear, love or anger; he is at one with him, not just playing at being him. That's his gut-feeling – allied to a huge talent, experience and invisible technique.

Dame Edith Evans might have been speaking for Trevor Howard when she said: '. . . I speak the truth on stage. I don't speak what I've heard other people say, or the way they say it. I say it the way it seems to come to me. And that's all I can say. Speak the truth.'

For lack of a better term of reference, Trevor Howard is called a film star, but he is not just a film star in the common acceptance of the term. He is first and foremost a great actor, which many film stars will never be — and some even acknowledge the fact.

Ability to act well has often had little to do with becoming a 'star', it was a matter of long eyelashes or charisma, an indefinable quality to which the audience responded. In Hollywood they worked hard to create stars, leaving no tooth uncapped, and for years the harvests were great. Stars were not people, they were properties and some were 'hotter' than others; they were mainly under long-term contract to major companies and, give or take a drama or two, everyone was well pleased.

Eventually the trend changed. The audiences became capricious, they had television and stayed at home — *unless* there was a movie that caught fire, that everyone had to see. While such movies were not rare, there were few enough of them for a new word to be coined to go with 'film star'. The word was 'bankability', meaning a blind belief that certain stars ensured that the film would show profit, or even become a blockbuster. Stars were no longer under contract, they were independent and they had the industry by the short and curlies; financial rewards for their services rose astronomically, often taking the budget way beyond any hope of recuperation. Such stars became dictators, they not only demanded script approval, they wanted all the best lines, they wanted tailor-made scenes giving them the edge every time, and they nursed their image on screen to please their fans — or so they believed. Then, when they had played variations on the same theme too often, their bankability slipped. They could no longer hold up production at a whim, disappear from the set in a sulk and make ever-increasing demands for yet more attention: because another name had become bankable and that name was now in the top slot. Some had quite short careers, but they were 'film stars'.

Hence Trevor Howard would prefer to be regarded as a good actor rather than as a film star, both before and after the star war started by the independent names who held the whip hand. If Trevor had been an image-nursing film star he might have turned down his next picture, because the script required that he died half-way through it. Film stars don't do that, any more than they play losers, weaklings, flawed characters or any other role that the audience cannot admire. David Lean asks, 'Why do actors want to be loved?' They don't, they'll settle for being appreciated. But stars have to be loved to maintain their self-esteem.

Although Trevor was due for an early demise in the film, *The Key* was directed by Carol Reed, with Sophia Loren and William Holden, and was made for Columbia Pictures in Britain. For its time (1958) it was an unusually adult film, depicting the ever-present danger of wartime death shadowing a girl whose apartment key became an inheritance for the living from the dead. Her chain of lovers were the captains of battered and vulnerable tug-boats which ploughed into the Atlantic to rescue merchant ships maimed by enemy submarines. Each holder of the key knew that he might have no use for it on the morrow, so he appointed his successor.

Trevor Howard inherits the key and gives a duplicate of it to his chosen heir, William Holden. There is a strong implication that the key leads not only to Sophia Loren, but to death; and so it did – but not for William Holden, because he was a star. When the character played by Trevor Howard died, for many critics so did the film. If he had received good reviews before, as indeed he had, for a performance that lasted the whole film through, by being killed off he won a real bonanza. The critics missed him, and said so. For his untimely death they paid him with eulogies: 'The Howard memory lingers on.' Not too surprisingly, only America's *Time* Magazine put him down by referring to William Holden as 'the hero', and giving Trevor Howard a patronizing pat on the back.

Notwithstanding *Time*, Trevor Howard won the British Film Academy Award for the best actor of the year. The best foreign actor award went to Sidney Poitier.

It is amusing to note that, while they were working together, William Holden's handlers refused to let him travel in the same company car as Trevor – it wasn't grand enough, they said. Of course, they might have been afraid that their runner might catch something – like acting.

By virtue of appearing in several films made by Americans for the American market Trevor Howard became popular there. Admittedly he had played in harness with American 'names', but he had become a desirable British actor. Also his British films had done well, even when they found distribution only in the small art houses. He was known and admired.

When Trevor read Romain Gary's book, *The Roots of Heaven*, he wanted to play Morel as he had rarely wanted to play any role. He had been deeply moved by the book; he feels strongly about the conservation of all species and most particularly he cares about elephants.

It was known that Darryl F. Zanuck had bought the rights to the book and Trevor urged his current agent, the colourful Al Parker, to do his damnedest to get the part for him. Al Parker went to it but he had to report that an American star was first choice, although he wasn't signed because of other commitments. Since such knots are never unravelled overnight, Trevor had to wait, and wait; he agonized over it. Then he learnt that the unit and such members of the cast as were set, were forgathering in Paris – still without Morel. He decided to go to Paris with Helen; maybe if they saw him . . . It was the only time in his life that Trevor Howard chose to be in the right place at the right time to further his career.

It worked. He got the part and joined the considerable cast in *The Roots of Heaven*, to be directed by John Huston, a director to be reckoned with after such classics as *The African Queen* and *The Treasure of the Sierra Madre*. In casting, Darryl Zanuck had made his very close friend, Juliette Greco, the female lead and Errol Flynn the drunken British major who supports Morel in his drive to stop the massacre of elephants by ivory traders, poachers and safari hunters in French Equatorial Africa. Orson Welles and Paul Lukas were also in the cast and, all in all, the production had the hallmarks of an epic.

Trevor Howard and Errol Flynn were born to be soul-mates, sharing as they did a reputation for being hell-raising, hard-drinking, outsize personalities. Neither of them gave a damn for the opinion of less ebullient introverts: Trevor knew he gave of his very best when working and Errol Flynn had been doing very nicely, thank you, for years. Helen remembers Errol Flynn with affection, and her first meeting with him still enchants her. It took place in the bathroom of his hotel suite in Paris and Flynn was in the bath. He looked up at her from the suds, and greeted her warmly saying, 'Forgive me if I don't stand up.'

Helen found him a man of great spontaneity. They were once passing through Paris airport together and Helen casually admired a huge show of roses. The next moment they were in her arms, Errol Flynn had bought the lot for her. She also discovered that he was very knowledgeable about unexpected things, such as geology. Helen's liking for Errol Flynn was very natural, he had much in common with Trevor. Both men had much more depth of character than their reputations suggested but neither of them bothered to make a public display of it.

When John Huston was making *The African Queen*, it was said that he spent almost as much time on safari shooting animals as he did shooting the picture, which made him an unlikely director for a subject dealing exclusively with the conservation of wild life. While elephants were close to Trevor Howard's heart they were nowhere near John Huston's. For some British critics this was reflected in the film, but by no means for all. The theme of the film was big, even noble, and this was noted and appreciated.

Trevor received rave reviews from everywhere, from the prestigious Sundays to the tabloids. 'No other living actor would have been so right for this part as Trevor Howard.' (Fred Majdalany, *Daily Mail*); 'Trevor Howard plays Morel, to my mind without a fault. It's a beautiful piece of acting.' (C. A. Lejeune, *The Observer*); 'For my money there is no major film actor in the world today who can touch the raucous glory of Trevor Howard.' (Derek Monsey, *Sunday Express*).

Dilys Powell detected the flaws in the film, and found them to be mainly in the script, 'The lack of continuing drive affects the acting; even the acting of Trevor Howard as Morel. I regard Trevor Howard as one of the best actors in the world. But he is not sustained here by the pressure of the film itself.' Disaffection wih the script was also expressed in America where Stanley Kauffmann put it on the line, 'The Huston who did *Sierra Madre* would have lighted his cigar with this script.'

Trevor Howard was sadly disappointed by the finished film but, as with most disappointments, took it in his stride, 'It didn't have much chance, I suppose ... making a film about saving elephants with a man who goes out shooting them.'

*

At the end of 1958 *The Roots of Heaven* opened in New York, and Trevor was there, as well as elsewhere in America, helping to promote the picture. He was very much at home in New York; it was a stimulating city and held much to enable him to indulge his private pastimes to the full. Admittedly, it lacked cricket, but it did have jazz joints galore and unoppressive friendliness from strangers. After the relatively small parish of London, where so many people seemed to be waiting for Trevor Howard to do something outrageous and newsworthy, New York offered space and a degree of anonymity, should it be desired. Even when recognized, nobody bothered him in any way. The following letter was received by Doris Lilly, of the *New York Post*, who gave it to Trevor:

Dear Miss Lilly,

I noted your recent remarks about Trevor Howard. The morning after the premiere of 'Roots of Heaven', I was walking on Madison Avenue near the Morgan Library when I saw Howard coming along. When he was abreast of me, a man walking in the opposite direction, young-looking but with gray hair, touched his sleeve and said, 'I have had great pleasure of you, sir.' Howard turned, and simply beamed, and said, 'How very kind you are! I do thank you!' The other man said, 'Not at all, it is I who thank you,' and made an odd little bow. Whereupon Howard bowed to *him*.

It was a charming little scene, I must say . . . very much an eighteenth-century kind of thing.

Sincerely,

Unfortunately, this note carried no address for the sender and an indecipherable signature.

On New York's Third Avenue, there is a shebeen called P. J. Clarke's. For years it had taken its place among many nearly identical ports of call for the famous, the infamous and newspaper stars. In early days the El train ran roof high down the middle of the Avenue. That is long gone, as are most of the predominantly Irish bars. They have given way to bright and shining high-rise office blocks, banks, stores and apartment buildings.

But P. J. Clarke's has survived the developers, thanks being due — it must be supposed — to its owner, Danny Lavezzo. Viewed from across the street today, Danny's premises resemble nothing so much as an unspeakably dirty doll's house with which the child refused to part when the rest of the family moved into a huge new glittering palace.

During the usual, and unusual, hours when a glass in the hand feels like the only way to face another minute, P.J.'s looks and sounds like an old East End of London pub just before closing time on Saturday night. This is Trevor Howard's favourite watering hole in New York, and has been ever since he first worked there in 1953, when the El was still running. Danny Lavezzo is a friend, Trevor is safe there — and the moment he enters the bar, even after an absence of years, somebody behind it says, 'Oh, it's a Ballantyne's Ale with the green label.' Trevor loves that; to him it's a gold medal.

No matter what their religious beliefs may be, talking to Trevor Howard's friends in America about Trevor invariably leads off in a highly charged atmosphere, as though they fear they are going to be driven into negating the life of a much-revered saint. He is accorded the kind of automatic protection that a real Mafia godfather might envy. This is not the routine bromide about being a very, very nice guy, either. They don't bother to call him nice, they say, quite simply, that he's a gentleman — and they love him.

If you run a good, popular saloon to which well-known clients flock, they don't patronize your establishment in order to drink milk — and you wouldn't have much of a business if they did. There are milk bars for such as they. On the other hand, the patron of such an establishment who tells tales out of saloon just might lose hard-won popularity . . . and well loved friends. Danny Lavezzo approached a chat about Trevor Howard as though he had been invited to hand up the nails for a second crucifixion — a very un-British reaction. With few exceptions Trevor's fellow countrymen and women dredge for the light scurrilous. And very dull it is, for the most part.

Danny Lavezzo is far from dull and has no need of kitchen gossip. He enjoys remembering that Trevor used to begin at the end of the bar, on entering, and be served with his Ballantyne's

India Pale Ale. He always started 'clean', sober and straight from work. Danny Lavezzo thinks Trevor liked P.J.'s because 'nobody tried to get into him', he could be almost anonymous – and he was a real bar man. He loved old bars and the casual camaraderie; there was never any sense of 'I am an actor'. By the middle of the evening, Trevor would be snapping his fingers in front of the juke box and having a lovely time with the music. Sometimes he would get a little buzz on, when he always wanted to swop P.J. banners with banners from Paddy Kennedy's Star Tavern in Belgravia – another favourite old bar.

In P.J.'s grill room, which lies beyond the bar, Danny Lavezzo has his own table which is tucked into a private corner. He recalls one evening when Trevor was seated at it with Dorothy Kilgallen and other luminaries. Suddenly a voice rose above the customary din. 'Trevor!' it yelled. Trevor winced and curled over the table, attempting invisibility. The call went out and over again, 'Trevor, old fucko – it's Larry!' This caught quite a lot of attention. Larry? Olivier? Trevor turned slowly. From a table far across the room Laurence Harvey was waving excitedly.

Trevor rose, Larry rose – and they met in what little space was available between tables. 'Larry!' Trevor boomed. 'Trevor, dear heart, lovely to see you!' Backs were slapped with enthusiasm and almost tender enquiries made as to health and professional well-being. They all but waltzed together in the joy of the meeting.

Even the crowd fell nearly silent as they watched the touchingly warm reunion of two British actors on American soil. Final cries of joy were exchanged and Trevor and Larry returned to their respective tables.

Trevor sat down and glanced wonderingly around at his companions.

'In London,' he said quietly, 'we would just have nodded.'

Danny loved it. 'Trevor? He's a very special man. A truly lovely guy.'

Within days of showing the flag in New York for the opening of *The Roots of Heaven*, Trevor accepted an invitation to visit Australia to promote *The Key*. Accepted is perhaps a pale word:

he had never been to Australia and the opening of the film coincided with its Test cricket. He would have hitch-hiked to get there had it been feasible, but as he was on business, he travelled in the style to which he had easily become accustomed.

This was the beginning of a long and faithful love affair – Trevor adored Australia and the passion was mutual. 1959 wasn't a vintage year for the English team but Trevor watched the game avidly and reluctantly hoped for a draw. When he was obliged to leave Australia to fulfil working commitments, he vowed to return, which he did many times; and it came as no surprise that he always succeeded in timing his recurrent visits to coincide with the cricket calendar.

One of the films that Trevor Howard hastened away from Australia to make was *Moment of Danger* with Dorothy Dandridge and Edmund Purdom – and he shouldn't have been in such a hurry. Even his most faithful critics were driven to ask why such a great actor was in such a film. Trevor even replied: 'If I hadn't done it I might have been out of work for two years ... What does one do? You can't do anything better if there's nothing better to do ...' It was a spurious argument and one which was to dog his career, intermittently, from then on. As a successful, distinguished and highly praised actor, he knew he should choose only the best. He was under no financial strain and it was certainly not altruism that sent him racing to the rescue of dross, which he has done time after time. He just couldn't bear to wait it out. His passion for work too frequently blinded his judgement.

Even Trevor's Guardian Angel must suffer impatience with him now and then, but this time he spun the wheel and up came *Sons and Lovers*. Lawrence's autobiographical novel was quite a surprising choice for an American producer, particularly as Jerry Wald did not plan to be in England during the making of the film, which was backed by Twentieth Century Fox. Robert Goldstein, the London chief of Fox, was therefore to hold a watching brief over the production, while the final arbiter was Buddy Adler, the reigning king of Fox. It was a tortuous chain of command which primarily affected the director, Jack Cardiff, and then, indirectly, the cast. Backstage battles on a picture are not, and should not be, the concern of any but the captains and the kings so engaged. Long before the shooting started, Jack Cardiff was battle-scarred, but that's his story, he's writing it, and the final cast was unaware of it. They were to have troubles of their own.

When the leading players were finalized, Trevor Howard was playing Morel, with Wendy Hiller as his wife and Dean Stockwell, their son, Paul. If a young American playing a British miner's son seemed somewhat *outré* it had to be remembered that an American name was essential for an American film. At that time, the most Trevor Howard knew was that he wanted to play Morel. He was not obsessive about it, he just knew that this had to be the best role available at the time. He also knew that Cardiff was struggling for him, because they had conspired together – as one cricketer with another – but he was aware that some outside forces were militating against him getting the part.

. Wendy Hiller was not the first choice, either, but she remembers she was in America, 'doing a terrible something' when she received the script. She then went with her agent to see the producer – a meeting at which she spoke up, loud and clear. She pointed out that, whoever the writer was, he or she had failed to grasp the essentials of Lawrence's story and, in effect, they had better get their act together. She watched her agent getting smaller in his chair, 'all scrunched up', and on leaving the producer's office wondered aloud what his trouble might have been. Well, he thought she wanted to do the film. She did – and she still did. The poor man was obliged to explain that, if you want a part, you never, ever criticize anything in Hollywood. Wendy Hiller was amazed, she couldn't believe that inaccuracies of the most glaring kind should pass without protest. His reply was, 'No. You just don't say those things.'

But she had, and she got the part.

And Jack Cardiff had got the two major stars he had always wanted, schemed for and lied to get. Since there was no definite producer on the spot, make-up and costume stills were sent off for approbation. Now it was Trevor Howard's turn to join the battle. He had chosen to wear a moustache to play Morel; in the book Morel is also bearded. Back across the electric wires the message came: 'Categorically insist no moustache.' Trevor's reply was equally terse: 'Categorically insist on moustache.' Battle was joined. Trevor felt so deeply about not playing Morel as a juvenile lead, which he suspected was in the mind of the producer, that he was prepared to leave the cast. He knew he was playing a character part, the miner father of a grown-up son, in a period piece. The moustache was right, and although Trevor was too harassed at the time to realize it, Jack Cardiff was on his side.

It was the only real argument Trevor ever had with a producer. Usually, if he didn't like a script he turned it down. He felt, and feels, strongly that if you start, you must continue. 'It's a dreadful thing to use blackmail, as it were.'

On that picture he had only just started, but he won his moustache.

Shooting commenced – a certain amount, of necessity, on location, and the main interiors at Pinewood. The rushes were not only seen by the unit on the spot, making the film, they were also flown to Hollywood. Then the real sport began. From Hollywood, Jerry Wald was trying to control what went into the picture by cable. In London, Bob Goldstein was solely concerned with bringing it in under budget and under schedule, so he cut scenes – especially the key scenes, the best ones.

This wide pincer movement could only affect the cast. Wendy Hiller thought she understood what had happened *vis-à-vis* the content of the film: 'The front office in Hollywood was in a frenzy because in *Sons and Lovers* they'd got a story of mother love that had gone wrong. Well, we know that most mothers' love has gone wrong, but they wanted the nice American dream of apple pie and lovely mothers. But that wasn't exactly what they'd got and so the postcards used to come.'

Her use of the word postcards for the miles of cable that issued forth from Jerry Wald is nothing short of superb; it does put the hysteria into perspective.

As the filming and the problems progressed, Wendy Hiller and Trevor Howard formed a cabal of two, fighting together to preserve the key scenes that were being ripped out of the script. She would nip into Trevor's dressing room: 'Shut the door. I only want two minutes. What are we going to do? I'm not going to cut this, will you stand by me?' 'Yes, of course I'll stand by you. What don't you want to do, darling?' Or Wendy Hiller would report the arrival of another 'postcard' and they would work out a way of circumventing another idiotic demand.

Finally, there was total rebellion. Jack Cardiff grew angry at being asked to cut the best scenes in order to accommodate schedule and budget but he knew that no one was more replaceable on a film than the director. They were running two days over schedule, which is far from unusual, but Bob Goldstein had become obsessive. He saw himself as a producer for the first time, and ordered dire cuts. At Cardiff's instigation, the cast sent cables to Buddy Adler threatening a wholesale walk-out. Wendy Hiller and Trevor Howard held the winning hand, and they knew it. If they held fast, the picture would have to be recast and reshot. Bob Goldstein was ordered to restore the cuts.

Infighting while making a picture was completely against Trevor's nature: 'I've never had trouble with people I've made films with — certain disagreements, of course, which were easily resolved, but nothing as big as *Sons and Lovers*.'

Wendy Hiller loved working with Trevor: 'It's such a gift if you have confidence in the other chap and I always had terrific confidence in Trevor. He's much more than a first-rate actor because he's so good at it, you see. I used to make him laugh because I'd say, "You know, you've got the knack. You've got the knack with that camera." I *do* wish I'd done more with him. He's so, so good. And he's always been such a favourite — much loved. I'm sure he's never done anything small. Also he's really reserved. Many people don't know him at all. At the studio there was never any of that boring larking about with stage-hands. Trevor can do with friendliness and politeness and get on with the job. He's not going to give parties, slapping people on the back and pinching their bottoms. And he's never arrogant or rude — the way some are because they don't know what they're doing and are insecure. Trevor is very shy, really.'

In spite of the battles royal, Wendy Hiller wasn't too disappointed in *Sons and Lovers*. 'It should have been forty per cent better but as it was, it was jolly good because it's a miraculous story. One for all time. Mind you, it should be made again now, and made properly.'

Maybe so, but the film didn't do too badly. Jack Cardiff won two awards in New York, the Critics' Award and the Director's

Guild Award. The cameraman, Freddy Francis, won an Oscar. There were Academy Award Nominations for best director, best script, best supporting actress – and Trevor Howard for Best Leading Actor, which ensured that he didn't get it: he was not playing the leading man, he was playing a supporting character role. Had his nomination been for Supporting Actor, he might have won. As it was, he won the best reviews.

With such a success, the last battle on *Sons and Lovers* was for producer credit – Bod Goldstein thought he had produced the picture, but Jerry Wald *knew* he had. Neither contestant had been near the studio while the film was being made.

Sons and Lovers was shown in competition at Cannes Film Festival and again Trevor Howard was up for the male award. That year both the male and female prizes were awarded to ladies, Melina Mercouri and Jeanne Moreau. No male award was made. In jolly mood, Trevor suggested to the organizers that perhaps, if he returned the following year, he might win a girl's prize. He didn't get as much as a smile for that one. Fortunately, Trevor Howard is not a pot-hunter.

If Trevor found the battles on *Sons and Lovers* disagreeable he had no inkling of what was possible; he was joyous when Carol Reed rang him from California and asked him to play Captain Bligh in a remake of *Mutiny on the Bounty*.

CHAPTER TEN

Mutiny on the Bounty was a star's film, made at the height of studio madness when the star's demands not only rose to a point above credence, but were met unconditionally by the backers in the belief that one magic name would guarantee box office returns well above the cost of the picture. In this case the magic name was Marlon Brando, the film was in preparation for thirteen months, cost twenty-seven million dollars – and brought Metro-Goldwyn-Mayer to its financial knees.

It marked the beginning of the end of such nonsense, but that was little solace to the cast and crew who suffered through the making of this epic. Much of the shooting was to be at sea, on location based in Tahiti, and the scheduled starting date was mid-October 1960. Three major British actors arrived in Los Angeles to meet their contracted date: Trevor Howard, Hugh Griffith and Richard Harris. They were on time but the specially built ship, the *Bounty*, was delayed and so was the script. Everyone concerned had been told that December, January and February were the months of rain in Tahiti and shooting finally began in late November.

Helen was with Trevor in Tahiti, which was as well. If ever he needed her comforting and balancing presence it was on the *Bounty* location. Hugh Griffith had only his fellow actors to witness the humiliations he suffered. Fresh from winning an Oscar for his role in *Ben Hur*, Griffith was cast as John Adams, the only survivor of the mutiny. On his arrival, the studio neglected to send a car to meet him, neither was he adequately housed. The script was in disorder – as it was to remain – and suddenly Brando decided that he no longer wished to play Fletcher Christian, he wanted to play John Adams. Just this once the studio was firm and the status quo was restored, but Brando had another card up his frilled sleeve. When called upon to play his scenes with John Adams, he played them without Hugh Griffith, detailing someone else to read Griffith's lines off-camera. This

Griffith regarded as a calculated insult and, since he was treated badly, he rebelled by behaving badly and finally left the picture. In the final film he is buried at sea, slightly ahead of schedule and counter to the history of the mutiny.

Keith McConnell, a very elegant Irish actor who had been working in Los Angeles since he was 'just past being a teenager', was playing James Morrison. He watched Hugh Griffith's humiliation with distress, and noted that his friend Trevor Howard did not fare much better, but 'Trevor behaved with enormous discipline. While Hugh went to pieces, Trevor behaved so well.'

It is possible that Trevor Howard signed on for *Bounty* expecting a certain amount of trouble – he knew that Brando had run every film he'd been in prior to the production. But Carol Reed was directing, and for his favourite director Trevor would have faced short-range gunfire. The first scene between Trevor and Brando marked the shape of things to come.

It was Trevor's scene, with five pages of dialogue for him and a few words for Brando. Every time Trevor hit his lines, Brando fluffed. They went on for eight takes, an unheard-of number for Trevor. Then, when Brando felt that Trevor might be off-key, he threw his line back. It was one of the oldest, and dirtiest tricks in the actor's manual and Brando had perfected it. The crew and members of the cast who witnessed this insolence, couldn't believe that Trevor Howard would go on taking it.

Side bets as to when Mr Christian would get a poke in the eye from Captain Bligh were never called. Trevor maintained his calm and cool throughout. Keith McConnell was amazed at Trevor's dignity and total professionalism. Whatever ploys Brando used, Trevor just got on with his own work without fuss. He even stood firm when Brando took to wearing earplugs to avoid hearing his co-actor's lines. Trevor never lost his temper or showed any distress.

The usual foundation, the guideline, for a film is the script. In this case no final shooting script existed. The producer, Aaron Rosenberg, had started his remake of *Bounty* with a script by Eric Ambler and the belief that Brando had turned the project down. Then Brando expressed interest, but wanted more emphasis on the post-mutiny period dealing with the settlers on Pitcairn Island. He thought that part of the history had a message for mankind.

Aaron Rosenberg not only agreed to alter the script to embrace the fatal settlement on Pitcairn, he also gave Brando jurisdiction on that sequence of the film. This gave rise to Brando's sudden decision to play John Adams, a role which would undoubtedly have become bigger than those of Captain Bligh and Fletcher Christian put together. More writers were put to work on the script and by the time shooting started, the title was held by Charles Lederer. He was not only trying to catch up with the shooting, he was bedevilled by Brando.

Scenes were shot — the actors being given their lines by word of mouth — and maybe the script would arrive later. Or else the script had been received by telex from Hollywood and torn up by Brando. Keith McConnell thinks of the picture as having had hundreds of writers, but no script. He also believes that there are no other roles in a Brando picture, just supporting extras.

McConnell is not only Irish, he is also independently minded, which might amount to the same thing. He grew weary of seeing his friends, Trevor and Hugh, being subjected to daily indignities at the whim of Marlon Brando, and weariness became articulate concern. He decided to approach Carol Reed supposing, not unreasonably, that if anybody could put a stop to the shenanigans, it was the director. He pointed out that Trevor Howard was one of the great actors and that Hugh Griffith was hardly a nothing. Carol Reed agreed absolutely. He knew what was going on, indeed, he could hardly have failed to notice, and it was very bad and very difficult. He could not have been more sympathetic or understanding, 'But, you know, there's nobody like Marlon.' Carol Reed had been professionally seduced. Later he was to be raped.

While the film-makers were going through their particular hell, which included sea-sickness, and Brando was enjoying Tarita, the local feminine lead, Helen was looking after Trevor and exploring Tahiti. Naturally she was interested in Gauguin memorabilia. With Trevor, she had met Gauguin's son who wove baskets, lived on his father's name, was big, fat and white and very unattractive. Helen wanted to go further than that. She was already amazed to find that there was not a street or even an alley named after the great painter. 'Where,' she asked, 'is the shed in which he painted?' She got an answer: 'Oh, they're building it now.' Somehow it was all of a piece with *Mutiny on the Bounty*.

Finally, the rainy season in Tahiti caused Aaron Rosenberg to postpone further work on location. He summoned the entire crew back to Hollywood to shoot interiors. They reassembled in the studio for work, and in the front office for recriminations. Naturally, Marlon Brando had further demands — and Sir Carol Reed was off the picture. It was a quick rape and Lewis Milestone took over as director.

The British members of the cast, and there were many of them, were outraged. They demanded a meeting with Sol Siegal, then head of the studio. With Trevor Howard in the lead they marched into his office. He rose from his desk and greeted them: 'Gentlemen, before you say anything I want you to understand one thing. The only expendable commodity in a great movie is a good director.'

Sol Siegal must have been as aware as the deputation that he had just delivered as meretricious a statement as any yet made in Hollywood, and the standards for such were high. But he had also succeeded in whipping the rug out from under their feet; the wind had left their sails and there was little more to say. They were just broken-hearted at losing Carol Reed.

Of all the miseries Trevor Howard endured on the *Bounty*, the seduction and rape of Carol Reed was the worst.

Even then *Bounty* might have been saved. Carol Reed had shot some magnificent footage around Tahiti. His only crime had been to try to work as he was accustomed to working and bring in a good film; the star-dominated epic was foreign to his talent. Milestone was a highly respected veteran who had directed great films. He was used to working quickly and efficiently. He was also used to *directing*, which meant having the last word. When he realized the film was being made by a committee of three: Brando, Rosenberg and Lederer, he let it ride. There was nothing else to do. His long experience had never encompassed such a situation; he was a professional in an amateur game and *laisser faire* was the only rule.

During the studio shooting, the 'committee' gathered on the floor for every take and hours were spent arguing every line.

From Milestone's point of view, the film was being made beside him rather than by him.

Out of hours the period of studio shooting on the *Bounty* was like Rest and Recreation after what had gone before. Trevor never cared for the Hollywood 'life-style pattern'; he had friends, like Keith McConnell, and other British members of the cast. Trevor has never found the warmth of friendship among American actors, with a few notable exceptions. 'They don't like us, you know,' he says. He also asks, 'What are they frightened of?' There are several answers to that. Trevor has never conformed beyond his own rules for civilized behaviour — and his own rules might frighten a lot of people. He quickly noted an aspect of working in the studio with which he was not about to conform. To have lunch outside the lot was unthought of: it was taken in the commissary — with milk.

This was not for the British contingent. They left the lot to go to The Retake Room, a restaurant close by, where they had their apéritif and lunch like ordinary people. There were two exists which led to the restaurant and they enjoyed darting between the two, further needling the security guards whose disapproval of them was evident. Trevor was puzzled: 'There was never an American actor in The Retake Room — just the Brits. *And* they gave the best performances — which must have hurt even more. A drink before lunch never hurt a true pro, they know what they're doing. Think of those martini lunches on the East Coast. Those chaps are probably none too capable at stockbroking or whatever in the afternoon.' But they don't have rushes, or dailies as they call them in America. And if present reports are to be believed, they don't have the martini lunches any longer either.

The studio work on *Bounty* coincided with the Academy Awards presentations and Trevor had his nomination for *Sons and Lovers*. However, he didn't have the evening suit which was mandatory for the occasion.

Keith McConnell dropped in to see his friend Robert Newton on the evening of the presentations and was astonished to find Trevor there, being dressed for the occasion by Newton, who was 'a madman when drunk, when sober extremely conventional.' McConnell, who is a self-acknowledged dandy, cast a critical eye

CHILDHOOD IN CEYLON: *(above left)* A sailor-suited Trevor Howard

(above right) Trevor Howard with his miniature set of golf clubs

(below) Merla, Mother, Trevor and Father

GROWING UP:
(above) Merla, Mother
and Trevor

(right) Suave and elegant.
Trevor at RADA

French Without Tears Rex Harrison, Trevor Howard, Guy Middleton and Percy Walsh

Declaration of War, Sunday 3 September 1939. On the terrace of the Dirty Duck. Trevor, seated on the wall, with other members of the Stratford Festival Company

The beginning ... Trevor Howard and Helen Cherry in *The Recruiting Officer*

1945: Trevor's first accredited film, *The Way to the Stars*.
Michael Redgrave, Trevor Howard and John Mills

The evergreen classic: Celia Johnson and Trevor Howard in
Brief Encounter

(above) *Brief Encounter* Trevor Howard and Celia Johnson

(right) The Old Vic Company. Trevor triumphed as Petruchio in
The Taming of the Shrew

Cayet

THE THIRD MAN: *(above)* Alida Valli, Joseph Cotten and Trevor Howard
(below) Trevor Howard and Bernard Lee

evor Howard's Film Star XI played Kenneth Cranston's XI at Oxley and
evor as winning Captain signs a bat for the Mayor of Birkenhead.
nmy Hanley is in the background and Kenneth Cranston on the left.

As Scobie in Graham Greene's *The Heart of the Matter*

ons and Lovers Wendy Hiller and Trevor

utiny on the Bounty with Marlon Brando

Trevor and Ingrid Bergman in the BBC–CBS production of *Hedda Gabler*

Fame at last: starring in *Flook*

Ryan's Daughter Sarah Miles, Trevor Howard and Robert Mitchum

Catholics Trevor Howard as the Abbot

The highly successful reunion of Trevor with Celia Johnson in Granada's
Staying On

In the anarchical British film *Sir Henry at Rawlinson End*, Trevor as Sir Henry

No Country for Old Men Trevor Howard as Jonathan Swift, with Cyril Cusack

Dust Trevor with Jane Birkin

(above) Appearing together in *Conduct Unbecoming*

(left) a hilarious welcome home

(below) On holiday in the Bahamas

over Trevor in Newton's beautifully made evening suit and found it too big: 'Trevor comes over as bigger than he is because of such great presence.' Why had Trevor not chosen something from the studio wardrobe? Because the suits were not practical, they didn't have pockets and Trevor was still a smoker. As far as Trevor was concerned, the suit was fine, the jewelled cuff links were exquisite and the patent leather bedroom slippers were comfortable. A final tweak at the bow tie, then Newton clapped a straw hat on Trevor's head and he was off. It is generally believed that the straw hat was discarded before Trevor took his place at Hollywood's night of the year.

Trevor Howard did not receive an award, but he did get to dance at the reception later in the evening. He was a little nonplussed when one charming partner gave him the once-over and said, 'That's not your suit, is it?' The lady ultimately became Mrs Greg Bautzer.

Keith McConnell has a friendly lawyer and one evening they were both having a drink with Trevor when the lawyer thought to ask if Trevor had made a will. Trevor hadn't even considered such a thing, but he was urged to do so. After all, he was going back on location and God only knew what might happen the second time around. There was all that work at sea and so on. Finally Trevor was persuaded to make an appointment with the lawyer's office; it wouldn't take long and it really should be done.

Trevor arrived at the appointed time. The lawyer was waiting with his secretary who, notebook in hand, was poised to take down the Last Will and Testament of Trevor Wallace Howard. Trevor looked thoughtfully from one to the other and said, 'Yes.' He paused and then went on, 'I think you should put down that I leave all my assets to the elephants – and five thousand pounds to Helen.' The room became very still indeed. Then the lawyer hedged. Perhaps, after all, this wasn't the best day for such a serious task, maybe it would be better all round if another appointment could be fixed. Trevor was quite agreeable so another day and time was arranged.

Punctual as ever, Trevor arrived for the second appointment and they started again. Trevor leant back in his chair, stared at the ceiling for a while and then gave voice, 'I suggest we leave all my assets to the elephants and . . . and two thousand pounds to Helen.'

The lawyer decided to leave the whole business alone, which was most likely what Trevor had in mind. Reminded of this little game in later years, Trevor smiled his best smile and said very softly, 'It wouldn't be very fair to Henny, would it?'

Keith McConnell has a dictum, 'At the beginning, acting was a form of revolution and most actors are not gentlemen – but Trevor Howard is. He has the talent and the background of a great actor while being very un-actory. He puts his talent into his work and his genius into his life – so when you know Trevor as a friend, you don't know an actor, you know a friend.' It's a remarkably good assessment.

The relative delights of R and R were over, and by the end of March 1961, everyone was back in Tahiti and on the *Bounty*. Things were not any better. They weren't even the same – they were worse. Brando's disdain for Milestone's direction was now overt. While the rest of the cast accepted direction like professionals, Brando made his own arrangements in every way. While everyone else rose early in the morning to board the *Bounty* for the day's work, Brando had acquired his own motor launch and might join the company at about eleven, if he was on morning call. Meanwhile, cast and crew waited in the heat. Sunday must have been a particularly arduous day on Tahiti because the star became known as Never-on-Monday Brando. When he did appear for work he lost his lines and would mumble his way through an unheard-of number of takes. He even resorted to having his lines written on pieces of paper which were attached to the costumes of the actors with whom he was playing a reverse shot.

As the major part of the *Bounty* was shot at sea, Trevor Howard was allocated a cabin on board – in which the director spent a fair amount of time asleep, when he didn't nod off on deck. Nobody blamed him: he was no longer a young man, ten hours in the gruelling heat was a lot to take, and he wasn't left with much to direct. On occasion, Aaron Rosenberg took over and Keith McConnell recalls being directed by him, 'Keith, we've got to give this scene balls.' It was a flogging scene. When the next set-up was ready, Milestone was seen to have his eyes open. 'Milly, we're ready, would you . . .?' 'Oh, I don't think so. After all, Aaron Rosenberg directed the last one. I don't suppose there's any reason for me to do anything more about it.' McConnell had great sympathy for him, 'He'd heard it all. He'd made the great pictures, he knew *Bounty* was going to be a terribly expensive fiasco. So he just took the money.'

In spite of his rigid professional dignity, Trevor Howard suffered deeply on Tahiti. Helen had returned to England and he missed her. He even declined a drink on the grounds that, 'I don't enjoy it any more. I don't enjoy anything very much any more.'

Trevor has a reputation which is nonpareil for never bad-mouthing another actor, but Brando's antics had to grind something out of him, even years later and in private. He recalled having seen Brando trying a ju-jitsu trick on a young Tahitian: 'He looked big and tough and the Tahitian beat him. So he called for his boat and sulked for the rest of the day. We couldn't work. Really he should be pitied, because he only liked to associate with people smaller and weaker than himself.'

There was one long scene between Trevor and Brando which Keith McConnell remembers very clearly. The dialogue was evenly distributed and after many takes Milestone took Trevor aside. 'Trevor, you're doing wonderful work,' he said. 'We all admire you and you're a great actor. But you seem to be sticking on your lines . . . you know? You're coming in a bit slow all the time. Is there any kind of problem?'

Trevor shook his head. 'Oh, no. There's no *problem*. I admire Mr Brando's work very much, as do we all. And the dialogue he is creating as we go along is, I am sure, very good. The only *difficulty* is that I never know when he has finished.'

That was grace under pressure.

During the four-month torment, Trevor remembered Graham Greene speaking of the opium pipe, and how wonderful it was when prepared by beautiful oriental girls. Trevor was prepared to try anything once and Keith McConnell elected to set it up: by now he had many connections on the island. Keith fell to his work and the arrangements were made.

On the night they went to the appointed place and were faced, not with beautiful oriental girls, but with an elderly, asthmatic Chinese gentleman. They took their places on the palliasses provided and smoked their pipes.

The effect on Trevor was startling. He took off, having seized a car, and drove round the island a number of times like a maniacal Jehu. He followed that act by dancing all night.

Keith McConnell remained on his palliasse, becoming greener and greener as he developed a crashing headache. He finally made his difficult way back to the hotel where he went out for the count for several hours. The following day, notes were exchanged. Keith allowed that he had found the experiment simply painful. Trevor admitted to having felt wonderful, 'But we lost a lot, didn't we? Going from beautiful oriental girls to an elderly asthmatic man. I mean, we didn't get the half of it, did we?'

Nearly two and a half decades on, Graham Greene agrees that he might have described the pleasures of opium-smoking to Trevor, 'It's a calming thing. You become a bit talkative, but it's very restful and calming.' He regretted that their first experience should have been on Tahiti. He had smoked there himself, but with difficulty: 'Very *sub rosa*, crawling on hands and knees in order not to be seen.'

The time finally came when, if not crawling on hands and knees – to which he might well have been brought – Trevor Howard finished being Captain Bligh on His Majesty's Ship *Bounty*. It left him with a distaste for star-controlled epics that amounted to nausea. When he was offered the role of Caesar in *Cleopatra*, he turned it down without a second's pause.

While the film was being finalized, and giving financial headaches to the MGM hierarchy, Trevor went on to do other and more agreeable work. But he was far from seeing the end of Captain Bligh. When *Bounty* had its worldwide release at the end of 1962, Trevor was co-opted to help with the promotion. With Helen, he went to Japan where they were rewarded for the months of purgatory with the most thoughtful hospitality imaginable; occasionally it appeared to be a touch too thoughtful.

In Kyoto, Helen and Trevor made friends with 'a lovely man who was an artist and looked exactly like Picasso.' They were invited to his home and met his wife, who served Helen with saki, but took none herself. They were to go out to dine with their host, but without his wife — evidently it was not customary to include wives, other than barbarians — in a dinner party held outside the home.

Somewhat to Helen's dismay, their host said it would please him very much if she would dress in a kimono for the occasion. Dismay was truly not the *mot juste* — Helen was appalled. Kimonos, she felt, were really not her style. However, her manners are impeccable, so she was game. She was taken off by her hostess into a room filled with shelves, piled with kimonos in every possible colour, and she was invited to choose. 'I chose a black number with an orange obi. Although I was much taller, it fell to the ground on me because Japanese ladies hoist them up at the waist to make that square shape. I just let it hang and added the obi. In fact, it looked lovely.'

They went off to dine and then on to a night club, where they were joined by a Japanese hostess — which was par for the course in their previous experience in Japan. Suddenly their host announced that he had to play Cinderella: if he were not home by midnight, his wife would lock him out. Fine. They had enjoyed a splendid evening, Trevor and Helen would take their host home and then see the young lady safely back to wherever she lived. The first part of the plan went beautifully. They left their host and then Trevor asked the young lady where she would like to be taken. To Trevor's dismay she replied that she would return to their hotel with them.

Helen muttered to her husband that the girl was a present to him from their host, it was a Japanese custom. Trevor was horrified. Where was she going to sleep? Helen told him not to worry, she would move into the spare room in their suite so that Trevor could enjoy his gift. That really set Trevor a-murmuring. 'Don't be so ridiculous. Of course she's not really coming to the hotel.' Helen shrugged. 'You'll see. When we get to the hotel, you'll see.'

Trevor did see. When they arrived at the hotel, he bade the girl a firm 'Goodnight' only to receive the assurance, 'No, no. I come. I come.' In the hotel lobby, Trevor begged Helen, 'For God's sake, get rid of her.' Helen shook her head. 'We can't. It would be so rude. You must be grateful for a very nice present.'

So they all went up to the suite. By this time Trevor was shaking. He didn't know what to do, or how to escape.

Only Helen knew that the girl was not a night-club hostess because only Helen knew that the girl was there to collect the kimono and take it back to its owner. It was a royal 'Trout'!

Not all the evening engagements ended so well. In Tokyo, Helen and Trevor had made friends with Paco Rodriguez, MGM's man in Japan. Inevitably, the promotional paths of Trevor Howard and Marlon Brando crossed right there: in Tokyo and in the same hotel. Since Trevor doesn't talk about himself, his work or his fellow actors, outside a very small circle, Rodriguez had no reason to suppose that the two stars were other than the best of friends. So he arranged to take them out on the town for a 'men only' evening.

They went to a very nice, cosy club with a small dance floor. As was usual, three ladies joined them, they all had one routine dance and the girls stayed to have a drink. Suddenly Brando pulled a huge roll of money from his pocket, leant across the table to a candle and set fire to the lot.

'Not only did it ensure that he wouldn't pick up the tab, but those girls could have used the money. It would probably have kept all three of them for God knows how long.'

Trevor Howard rightfully claims that Marlon Brando is the only actor he has ever publicly savaged, yet the most he has been quoted as saying is, 'The man is unprofessional and absolutely ridiculous.' Without trying, citizens have been known to be more savage than that in a bus queue on a rainy night.

Privately, Trevor admits that working with Brando on *Bounty* was absolute hell. But he rationalizes it, 'They say people won't go to the cinema unless they can see stars. Film companies can't make stars overnight, so they can be held to ransom by people like Brando who get paid far too much for far too little.' That's not savaging, that's pretty well factual.

In October 1962 Trevor was amazed to receive a long, long letter from Brando. In it, the hunter had become the hunted. His sufferings on *Bounty* had been immense, the frustrations unbearable and, this above all, he had been hurt and shocked by Trevor's quoted remark that he was unprofessional. He was torn between being sure that Trevor hadn't really said it, and won-

126

dering why Trevor had failed to confront him with the accusation. As far as he knew, he had never before been criticized in any way by other actors with whom he had worked.

Well, that was as far as he knew.

The quoted remark made by Trevor that had so affected Brando's tender susceptibility appeared in an article by Bill Davidson for *The Saturday Evening Post*. It was a well documented, hard-hitting piece which held Brando very largely responsible for the *Bounty* fiasco. Brando lodged a lawsuit against the publishers. Two years later, thanks largely to Trevor Howard, Keith McConnell and Aaron Rosenberg, he won it.

So far as the roles of Captain Bligh and Mr Christian were concerned, Bosley Crowther of the *New York Times* probably had the last word: 'Where Trevor Howard puts wire and scrap-iron into the bulky, brutal character of Captain Bligh, making him really quite a fearful and unassailable martinet, Mr Brando puts tinsel and cold cream into Christian's oddly foppish frame . . .'

Mutiny on the Bounty was said to have recouped just ten million dollars from the twenty-seven million it had cost.

When their promotional tour of Japan was over, Helen and Trevor flew to Hong Kong. As they flew in over the islands, Trevor was up front with the captain listening to the Australian Test scores. Helen hoped somebody was minding the store. Trevor enjoyed Hong Kong and he liked having suits and shirts made there. Between, and during, fittings he listened to the Test and learnt that England was playing a winning game. In a burst of euphoria he announced to Helen that he was going on to Australia, apparently alone. By then he had borrowed all Helen's money to pay for his purchases, leaving her with seven pounds ten. 'To be fair,' Helen says, 'I did have my ticket home.' Luckily Helen Cherry is unflappable and resourceful − Trevor Howard's wife would need both those attributes. She rang Paco Rodriguez, rebooked the suite they had just left and flew back to Tokyo. On arrival she rang the friends they had made there who were delighted by her return. When she was not being entertained at lunch or dinner there was always room service. She was back on MGM's expense account. When she returned to England her seven pounds ten was still intact.

Safely in Australia, Trevor informed enquiring journalists that his wife had decided to remain in Hong Kong to do some shopping. He invited them to imagine leaving a wife among all those shops, with a free hand and nothing to do but spend money!

Trevor arrived in Australia in January 1963 and, whether he knew it or not – and he can no longer remember – *Bounty* was about to open in Melbourne and Sydney. He was swiftly gathered up by Bill Band, chief of publicity for MGM in Australia and New Zealand; they were to remain close friends until the end of Band's life. Trevor's name for him was Handholder, because he was always there to guide him through personal appearances, premières, interviews and television appearances. Band took over as Nanny-Extraordinary when Helen was not around. Another comforter was Ossie Bates, a great friend of Band's and, having spent fifty-five years in show business, he was well equipped to take over from Band if necessary.

Ossie remembers that although Trevor's primary interest was the cricket, he did a remarkably good job of promoting *Bounty*. He tempered his interviews with a shrewd eye on the requirements of the various publications. They ranged from amusing and audacious to serious and thoughtful, skilfully avoiding any comments on problems which arose during the making of the film.

He attended the première in Melbourne, a Hollywood-style event graced by *le gratin* of Society. He then returned to Sydney for another high-gloss opening to which, at his request, both cricket captains had been invited: Ritchie Benaud for Australia and Ted Dexter for the MCC. The latter had already been victorious in Melbourne, and the Sydney première of the *Bounty* enabled Trevor to watch the third Test, which began in Sydney on January 11.

CHAPTER ELEVEN

There are no longer actor-managers, in the former sense, but a number of actors have become directors for stage or screen, or both; outstanding British examples being Sir Richard Attenborough, Sir John Gielgud and Lord Olivier. In America both to direct a film and star in it is now commonplace. In spite of his passion for work, Trevor Howard has never contemplated turning director. The furthest he will go in discussion is to allow that he might have been interested in directing children on stage, but the interest was tenuous, to say the least.

He is certain that he would never attempt to direct a film because he is not a technician and he feels that a film director must understand all the technicalities that go into the making of a film, from camera to cutting. A film unit is comprised of a large number of specialists and Trevor cannot see how anyone can direct unless he knows how they work: 'A truly good director must know enough about all the facets of film-making, which doesn't mean a passing actor who puts himself in the hands of specialists and then *calls* himself a director.'

His is a very idealistic view since there are many reputable directors who are content to work with the knowledgeable men and women whose function it is to help them towards their goal, their vision of the finished film, and they choose their units accordingly if they have a choice.

Trevor's strictures are born of being first and for all time an actor. He is prepared to examine a lack of desire to direct but has a basic reluctance to know more than he needs to know when he walks onto the set and meets the cast. That's when he gets his feeling about playing his own role: 'It's no good setting a character until we start to know how it's to be played. It depends on positioning and the people you're working with. Otherwise you'd just say the lines the way you learnt them at home. And the most important thing about acting is to re-act – and to listen.'

Awareness of the mechanics involved might get in his way – he doesn't want to know whether the light goes out when the refrigerator door is closed. Neither did he have time to find out in 1962. Between playing in *Bounty* and promoting it, he made another film, returned to the theatre and did a play for television.

The film was *The Lion*, with William Holden and Capucine. It was an American production to be directed by Jack Cardiff and shot in Kenya and Britain. Helen was able to go with Trevor on location, based at William Holden's Safari Club in Nanyuki, some miles north of Nairobi. It was a no-hardship location which even included cricket. Jack Cardiff is another enthusiast, although he admits to being a lousy player; he and Trevor played in several matches in the area. Jack remembers that for some reason Trevor was unable to play in their first match, so he umpired and was behind Jack when he was batting.

Jack was playing a saving game, very defensive and not at all bold. As time passed without much action, Trevor murmured, 'Yes, Jack. You're doing all right. Keep it at that and you'll be here all day.' Jack still admires the exact note of sarcasm in Trevor's voice.

He also has great admiration for Trevor as an actor: 'Holden acted his part to the letter of the script and did it perfectly. You never knew how Trevor would play, but it was always exciting and not necessarily following the script directions. There was a scene, in close-up, when he had to scream at his wife, in rehearsal he whispered the line. It was marvellous. Nobody had thought how much depth and venom could be better expressed in a whisper. The script said shout, but we shot it his way. Some actors have made up their minds about playing a part and are therefore in-directable, but not Trevor. He never argues about direction, never does a star turn, but he can surprise and delight you with his interpretation. He's not a line-changer, either. He just works out a way to use them.'

During the location Trevor had news from America telling him of cuts affecting his performance as Captain Bligh, which depressed him acutely. Jack Cardiff was having dinner with Helen and Trevor when Trevor said, 'Look at me. I'm an actor.' It was said in the pejorative sense and out of real despair. Helen was quick, 'Of course you are, darling, and you're a bloody marvellous one.' But the mood persisted for a few days before lifting.

On the whole it was a happy location, but few pass without incident. Helen and Trevor had met a young British officer serving with the King's African Rifles and one day he offered to drive them to Murchison Falls in his little Volkswagen. They all had lunch at the Safari Club and then set off. They had gone about half a mile when Helen, seated behind the driver, saw an army truck about to make a right turn in front of them. The African driver gave all the right signals and Helen naturally expected their driver to notice and heed them. He didn't, because he was talking to Trevor. Then Helen knew the crash was coming – and it did.

Trevor's face was cut and covered in blood and Helen's hand was hanging the wrong way round: her arm was broken. The young subaltern was unhurt. Helen and Trevor were taken to hospital where Trevor had three stitches in a cut lip and Helen had her arm set. While she was in hospital the subaltern went to apologize, taking her a bunch of flowers. 'He must have picked them in the veldt because they still had roots and the earth fell all over the bed.' Trevor was unphotographable for a few days during which time Helen was restored to the Safari Club. Then they were asked to go into court to speak in defence of the young subaltern. Helen would have none of it. If she went into court, she would tell the truth. It had not been the African driver's fault, he had given clear signals and she was not about to help the Army to make him a scapegoat. She was not called to court and neither was Trevor. The case was heard and summed up as 'An error of judgement'. The subaltern got away unscathed. 'He's probably a general now,' Helen smiles.

When *The Lion* was shown later that year, it set no critical hearts a-beating, nobody cheered.

When Trevor Howard finished on the picture he hardly had time to unpack before starting rehearsals for John Mortimer's *Two Stars for Comfort*. This was Trevor's first appearance in the theatre since *The Cherry Orchard*, eight years previously. It is an act of courage for any actor to return to the boards after a long spate of filming and many fumble it through nervousness born of true fear. A theatrical performance must be sustained, it must flow, the lines must be remembered; a dropped stitch can be picked up when filming but not in theatre at its best.

For the theatre, as for films, Trevor believes firmly that there has to be someone who has the last word. Even if it's the wrong one, it has to be the director's decision. 'They might be able to drag from you more than you think you've got or they might leave you to do your own thing. The rare ones have a vision, and if you can catch up with it, that's marvellous.' He feels that theatre directors often use their position to be unkind, even brutal, to be self-important. These are the ones who don't like actors and who often bully the small fry in the cast, which Trevor finds detestable: 'They are the "unkind-to-waiters" people.'

Trevor remembers a director who approached him during the run of a play when his break date, or contractual option, was drawing near. 'I understand you might be leaving us to make a film,' he said. Trevor considered it. 'Maybe I am, maybe I'm not.' The director was far from pleased: 'It would be very unfair to the rest of the cast if you did.' The director himself was leaving the show to visit Russia.

There were no such problems during *Two Stars for Comfort*. For Trevor it was a joy, 'a very good choice – about the only good choice I've made.' The director, Michael Elliott, loved the theatre and loved actors. During the run of the play he told Helen, "Trevor is absolutely remarkable. If I'd asked him to stand on his head, he'd have done it.'

Obviously a good and sympathetic director is a boon to actors, but so is good writing. A bad script is very hard to learn, but John Mortimer doesn't write those.

In his autobiography, *Clinging to the Wreckage*, John Mortimer writes: 'An actor who never runs out of his own positive personality and who has no need of a stick of make-up or an inch of false hair is Trevor Howard. I had met him when he was doing a remake of *Mutiny on the Bounty*, in a bar just outside the teetotal desert of the studio where we were both working. I had made an exceedingly pretentious remark about Hollywood being the "suburbia of the soul" which he had somehow appreciated and he agreed to be in a play I had written called *Two Stars for*

Comfort. He gave a performance which combined great strength with vulnerability, influenced a good deal by the brilliant but wayward actor Wilfrid Lawson, whom he greatly admired.' The bar was at The Retake Room in Hollywood.

The play opened in Blackpool during a Student's Rag Week and for Trevor Howard this proved to be dangerous timing. As he was leaving his hotel one afternoon, he was surrounded by jolly students, bundled into a car and driven to a house where he was locked in a broom cupboard. Although Trevor can be quite jape-ish in his own fashion, he is also meticulous about being on hand in good time for a performance. His main fear as he beat upon the door with a broom handle was that the so-called joke might continue beyond the hour for the curtain to rise. In fact, he was released in time but John Mortimer believes that 'he found the kidnapping incident rather humiliating since he really didn't talk about it much.'

The play was a success and the critics welcomed Trevor Howard back to the theatre like a prodigal son. When the play opened at the Garrick Theatre on 4 April 1962, T. C. Worsley wrote in the *Financial Times*: 'I am jealous of the films for having kept Mr Howard out of the theatre so much. He is one of our really superb actors, the best Lopahin in *The Cherry Orchard* and the best Petruchio I remember.'

In many ways the character of Sam Turner in *Two Stars for Comfort* could have been drawn from Trevor Howard himself. There is the charm, the humour, the ability to entertain; he even sings 'Stars Fell on Alabama', and plays the drums. Then there is the rebellious spirit expressed in Howardian lines: 'Why not let him do as he likes?' he shouts in court when defending a minor felon, thus ending his legal career without a moment's regret. As a pub owner by the River Thames, he dispenses comfort and pleasure to all about him. However, a joyous life is only the tip of the iceberg: beneath lies an indefinable torment, a sadness that is recognizable in Trevor Howard. In the *Daily Telegraph*, W. A. Darlington wrote: 'I have never seen Trevor Howard do anything better or more understanding than his Sam . . .' There is no doubt that Trevor understands sadness – Helen has described her husband as 'the saddest man I have ever known.' Many who believe they know Trevor Howard might well argue that this is not only untrue but also unpalatable, but the sadness is there in the fine brushwork if not in the broad strokes of colour.

Two Stars for Comfort ran for six months in the course of which Trevor Howard also played Lovborg in an Anglo-American production of *Hedda Gabler* for television. It had a fine cast with Ingrid Bergman as Hedda, Ralph Richardson as Brack and Michael Redgrave playing Tesman. The production was shared between the BBC and David Susskind and was directed by America's Alex Segal. In his end-of-the-year résumé of television drama, Philip Purser expressed certain dissatisfactions with the overall impact of *Hedda Gabler* but wrote that, 'Trevor Howard's tight-jawed, doomed Lovborg and Michael Redgrave's fussy Tesman were performances to be proud of . . .' (*Sunday Telegraph*).

Any truly professional actor is a remarkable human being because no personal adversity may be permitted to flaw a single performance. This is not to say that all performances are evenly the same, they are not. But domestic problems, overdrafts, the bailiffs waiting at home or an ingrowing toe nail have to be expunged from the conscious mind so that the role of the moment may fill it. The show must not only go on, it must be the best show possible.

Two Stars for Comfort had been running for exactly two months when Trevor Howard was picked up for a driving offence for the third time; he had once lost his licence for a year and once been acquitted. Whatever the results of previous charges have been, three accusations place the offender in a very vulnerable position, and Trevor had to be aware of the fact because many of his friends had been there before him.

After the performance on 5 June, Trevor believes he had a few in the pub before going on to a party given by his agent, Al Parker, to celebrate the final day of recording *Hedda Gabler*. This would bear out his theory about drinking to celebrate a job well done, or memory might have played him false and he was drinking because he was thirsty. Whatever the cause, the effect remained. He thinks he left the party at about one or two in the morning and drove off to Arkley. When in striking distance of home he approached some road-works and failed to skirt them successfully, knocking over a hurricane lamp and a pole. He also failed to stop and pick them up. Within seconds, he was flagged down by the law and taken to Edgware to be examined and subsequently charged. On his own admittance, he gave the police a hard time, taking the view that they were public servants and should be taking care of him instead of subjecting him to such nonsense as walking the white line. At the time he was aware that 'it didn't go down very well.' He was right about that, particularly when his views were later intoned in court.

When Trevor had finished haranguing the police and the police were satisfied that he should be charged, Helen received the middle-of-the-night call telling her she could collect her errant husband and take him home. In such circumstances, many husbands would prefer to spend the remaining few hours in the cells – or in a railway tunnel – but Trevor's faith in his wife's capacity for endurance is not misplaced. She doesn't even let it look like endurance.

So the show went on until the case came up at Middlesex Sessions in September, before a jury of nine men and three women and with Mr Ewen Montagu, QC, as chairman. Trevor Howard had Mr Christmas Humphreys, QC on his side. Mr Humphreys opened the batting by describing his client as 'a man who at the time was at the end of his tether'. This stretching of the rope having been occasioned by working for ten months without a holiday followed by a month during which he worked for sixteen hours a day, filming and also rehearsing a play. He allowed that the accused was drinking more than was good for him, 'to give him energy to carry on a task which was almost more than he could bear'. He also told the court that disqualification would mean that Mr Howard would have to employ a chauffeur and that he was going to take a substantial holiday as soon as his current commitments would allow.

Mr Humphreys gave it the old college try with a 'Not Guilty' plea, but he couldn't have hoped to win. They had Trevor Howard bang to rights and he was up before Mr Ewen Montagu. The latter's summing up lasted forty-five minutes during which he caused the clock to be stopped while Trevor Howard's verbal attack on the police in Edgware was read to the court. The jury appreciated that. He also allowed that the defendant was a man who would not dream of committing a crime, who was admired by thousands and had given a lot of pleasure on stage and screen: 'People who offend in this way believe it can't happen to them. It is not a deliberate offence.'

The jury found Trevor Howard guilty and, before passing sentence, Mr Montagu had rather more to say: 'You are a man who drinks vast quantities every night . . . Yet you have so little care for your fellow citizens that you are willing to drive.' He pointed out that the normal procedure in such a case, when the offender had received a previous warning, would be a prison sentence, but had decided that it would not be either to the public good or to Trevor Howard's own good to send him to prison. However, he felt that an example should be made of the offender in order to discourage like-minded users of the road: 'We feel that the public must be protected and having regard to the consequential financial burden the sentence is going to cause you, our sentence will be *less than normal* for a second offence.'

Trevor Howard was fined fifty pounds, ordered to pay thirty pounds costs – and disqualified from driving *for eight years*. It that was less than normal, what in the name of justice might normal be? Allowing for the fact that drunken drivers are a menace and a danger, that was a punitive disqualification in the circumstances; no damage had been done, no other car was involved and nobody had been hurt.

Following the press reports on the case, Trevor Howard received many letters filled with furious commiseration from all over the country. One such, from a dental surgeon, reflects them all:

> *Dear Mr Howard,*
> You have been most unjustly treated and you should appeal against your savage sentence. You are being made to suffer because of your position and as an example to others and that is grossly unjust. No doubt you feel like quitting the country and no one could blame you if you did, but couldn't you try to right this wrong first?
> Such a sentence is vindictive madness and all reasonable people are appalled by it – this note is just to let you know so.
>
> *Yours sincerely,*
> (Signed) G. D. Jameson.

On 18 February, 1967, the *Daily Mail* reported that three Appeal Court judges had quashed a dangerous driving conviction because they found that Mr Ewen Montagu, QC, chairman of Middlesex Sessions, had harassed defence witnesses and impeded their evidence. His behaviour had been so prejudicial that nobody in court could have believed that the offender had a fair trial. Four other cases were listed citing criticism of Mr Montagu by Appeal Court judges.

Twenty-three years after Trevor Howard's case, the late Sir Ewen Montagu, QC, was prepared to discuss the sentence providing he was not quoted verbatim. He remembered the case clearly but seemed to be slightly astonished by the eight-year sentence – of course, that would have been partly the responsibility of the two magistrates on the bench with him. In order to protect the public, the usual practice would be to double the previous disqualification. So multiplying it by eight was not normal; neither is it abnormal when the court is certain that, at the time, the offender is an alcoholic. No medical proof is needed to support this assumption, the court is guided by the pattern. Thus one conviction plus one acquittal equals alcoholism.

Sir Ewen denied that he had expressed his intention to make an example of Trevor Howard but admitted that there was no rule laid down by law that included a disqualification of eight years. His judgement was based on a study of character. By watching and listening to the offenders brought before him he could gauge their attitudes: he was not looking for remorse but for the aura that indicated total impenitence and the ready-made decision to continue to drink and drive unless halted by disqualification. In effect he thought he detected in Trevor Howard an aura that said, loud and clear, 'Bugger everybody else.'

It is a singular system for jurisdiction considering the natural nervousness of any individual who appears in court on the wrong side of the bench, but perhaps Sir Ewen acquired his parapsychology during his six years in Naval Intelligence during the war. He also acquired the idea for his book, *The Man Who Never Was*, which was made into a film. One of the roles was played by Robert Flemying after it had been turned down by Trevor Howard.

After the run of *Two Stars for Comfort*, Helen and Trevor went on holiday to their favourite little hotel in Villefranche, near Nice. Never one to let sleeping dogs lie, Trevor allowed himself to be photographed at the wheel of Helen's car when it was not only stationary but lodged directly in front of a-large sign on which was painted: Car Park. No one should have been surprised when the photograph found its way into Fleet Street. It was printed over a caption which suggested that Trevor Howard might not be allowed to drive in Britain but took his chance in France. Maybe the picture editor thought car park was French for bus stop.

After flogging *Mutiny on the Bounty* in the Far East and Australia, Helen and Trevor went on a skiing holiday in Switzerland, before Trevor was due to return to America. This time he was to work with George Schaefer, probably America's finest television director, in *The Invincible Mr Disraeli* for the Hallmark Hall of Fame.

Greer Garson played Mrs Disraeli, Kate Reid played Queen Victoria and the outstanding cast also included Hurd Hatfield, Geoffrey Keen and Denholm Elliott. It was a very happy time for Trevor, he loved playing Dizzy, he was delighted with Greer Garson and admired George Schaefer enormously. It was true Guardian Angel time.

When Trevor is cast in an historical role, he does his homework. He reads as much about the man as possible. Before playing Captain Bligh he had read a great deal about him, not that the true nature of Bligh was either in the script or required on the screen. 'Bligh had to be a baddie instead of the great man he really was.' The study of Disraeli was to prove much more worthwhile.

The company was rehearsing in New York when St Patrick's Day rolled around and, although no one involved in the making of *Disraeli* was dedicatedly Irish, the day is inclined to make its presence felt all over town. During the lunch break, several male members of the cast made their way into McSorley's Tavern which was run by ladies for gentlemen only: a nice case of inverted sexism. In the Tavern they found Jason Robards playing the violin dressed in white tie and tails. He was left over from the previous evening when he had attended a boxing match with his wife, Lauren Bacall. Like most of the gentlemen already *in situ* he was also wearing a green hat and an extravagant boutonnière of shamrocks. Trevor Howard is mad for hats in any weather and he wasn't about to be cheated out of a green pixie number. Before anybody could say begorrah, George Schaefer's distinguished cast had clapped on green hats and covered themselves with shamrocks, overdoing it up to the hilt in order to give the best possible impression of a load of drunks on St Patrick's Day. They then returned to rehearsals for the pleasure of seeing George Schaefer's face at the spectacle of his cast arriving pissed.

But George Schaefer didn't win all his awards for nothing, he quickly realized that his crew was entirely sober and good for work: it was off with the hats and on with the show. It was exactly the sort of story that could have spread alarm and despondency had some lucky journalist caught it: 'Poor George Schaefer couldn't work that afternoon.' At least they didn't take Jason Robards with them. He thought it was about time to get out of his tails.

While Trevor was enjoying being Dizzy, Helen was working on a television series in London. Early one morning she was reading the *Daily Mail* while having her coffee in bed and turned to the Flook strip cartoon. Among the characters in it, she saw one who looked exactly like Trevor, but she couldn't believe it. She went to the studios where Maurice Kaufman asked whether she'd seen Trevor in Flook that morning. She still couldn't believe it. At the time Flook was created by the artist and jazz musician, Wally Fawkes, and the writer and jazz singer, George Melly. Helen wrote to George Melly telling him how delighted both she and Trevor would be if the character really was meant to be Trevor. She thought it might be and the people she was working with were sure it was. Then she took a chance and sent a cable to Trevor: FAME AT LAST YOU ARE IN FLOOK. LOVE HELEN.

Melly and Fawkes were equally joyful because their editor had cut the key line. 'What a marvellous part for Trevor Howard', on the grounds that the character was a British Consul with a weakness for drink and he was sure Trevor Howard would sue. Helen's letter was put before them at one. She had also written that Flook was the main reason the Howards took the *Daily Mail*, to the cartoonists' great glee.

In New York the cable made Trevor's day. On his way to work he hunted for a *Daily Mail*. 'Being in Flook was better than a gold medal.' He thought it the greatest compliment he had ever received. Later he was sent the original cartoons in which the Consul's post is called Greeneland. Trevor and Helen believe it was the first time the term had been used.

Although Trevor is a jazz buff he had never heard Wally Fawkes play or George Melly sing. He knows every jazz club in New York but never seeks them out in London. Just once, he had a call from Wild Bill Davidson who told him he was playing at Ronnie Scott's and Trevor dashed into London to hear him. In New York, known faces in a night spot are taken for granted and left alone; the reticent British regard them as personal property and treat them accordingly.

If Trevor Howard thought featuring in Flook was better than a gold medal, he won two awards on that trip to New York. When *The Invincible Mr Disraeli* was shown in April he won the Emmy for the Best Actor. The production was such a success that it has recently been reissued without the commercials, and is now on video cassette. In the *Los Angeles Times*, Cecil Smith wrote: 'Trevor Howard's performance as the immortal "Dizzy" was as lustrous a piece of work as these tired eyes have seen in many a year ... The cast was without blemish, and George Schaefer's color production, as usual, was superb. But, ah, that Mr Howard!'

George Schaefer remembers that working with Trevor Howard was a most exciting experience: 'He not only looked like Dizzy but the play had wit. Dizzy was a very amusing man – everything had a little hook to it which Trevor did effortlessly, those things he can do with his voice. It wasn't an easy script because Dizzy's life was all over the place. I didn't regard it as sure-fire, but Trevor brought so much to it.' In those days they taped in very long sections because tape couldn't be edited as easily as it can today. Fifteen-to-twenty-minute scenes were shot using four cameras, rather as live television is shot. 'Trevor managed the long speeches with ease and all through rehearsals and shooting he was totally sober. But when the last shot was in the can he was entitled to a party.' That's the Howard system: to celebrate when his gut-feeling tells him he has done good work.

The Invincible Mr Disraeli was a joyous production for Trevor Howard and the peak of pleasure was reached when, after his last long speech in the House of Commons scene, the entire crew lined up and applauded him. Such occasions are rare in the life of an actor and therefore much cherished.

Although the crime was not seen to have been perpetrated until the following year, 1963 saw the launching of a new facet of Trevor Howard's talent. It can only be called grand larceny and the first offence was to be followed by many more. Hitherto, whether the films in which he had played were large or small, good or bad, he had earned his name above the title in a major role. The one exception being his 'cameo' appearance in *Around the World in Eighty Days*, but that put him in there with every star in the firmament. Now he was playing as a 'guest star', so for *The Man in the Middle* his name was above the title but he was on-screen for roughly ten minutes during which time he effortlessly stole the picture, nicking it from under the noses of Robert Mitchum and France Nuyen among others. It was his first 'guest-star' appearance and must have caused a deal of finger-flipping in actors' ranks. Felix Barker described Trevor as 'the sort of guest who turns the rest of the house-party into pigmies.'

The story of top brass trying to rig a court martial was not the stuff of which epics are made but it was directed with assurance by Guy Hamilton, and Robert Mitchum was a box-office delight. In the *Sunday Express* Michael Thornton wrote: 'But there is still Trevor Howard. And in ten priceless, unforgettable minutes he elevates the film to greatness and shows Mr Mitchum and Miss Nuyen what acting is all about.'

Mordecai Richler noted, 'another piece of good luck is Trevor Howard, easily the best film actor in this country.' Felix Barker's review in the *Evening News and Star* carried the headline 'Mitchum is the star but ... Howard Takes Command.' It says much for both gentlemen that Trevor Howard and Robert Mitchum became firm friends while working on the picture and have remained so.

*

Trevor Howard made another enduring friendship in the summer of 1963, while watching England play the West Indies at Lord's. By chance he sat next to Michael Meyer, whom he had never met. Not unnaturally, Michael Meyer recognized him, they chatted and became friendly watching all five days of the exciting match together. While Michael Meyer was well aware who his companion was, Trevor had no knowledge at all of his. He didn't know he was watching cricket with one of the best translators of Strindberg and Ibsen – and a topmost authority on the latter. Meyer was a former lecturer at Uppsala University in Sweden, and a distinguished man of letters who had also edited a volume of poetry by their mutual friend, Sidney Keyes. This last bond did not even come to light until they had been friends for several years.

Michael Meyer had seen and admired Trevor in *The Recruiting Officer* and 'I remember seeing a marvellous performance he gave as Lopahin in *The Cherry Orchard*. Wonderful he was – a wonderful stage actor.' As they watched the cricket, Michael Meyer remembered that Casper Wrede wanted very much to stage his translation of Strindberg's *The Father*, a play that needs a special kind of tragic actor: 'He couldn't think who could do it and at one stage of the match, when England was doing badly, I glanced to my right and there was this marvellous tragic mask in profile – Trevor suffering the agonies of the damned – and I thought, *The Father*.'

Without a word to Trevor, Michael Meyer passed the idea on to Casper Wrede with whom it found great favour. He in turn rang Trevor, who knew it was a marvellous part; he had seen and loved Wilfrid Lawson playing it. But Trevor demurred a little on the grounds that, although it was a splendid play, he didn't think there was a good translation around. Casper Wrede pointed out that there was a chap who translated very well from the Swedish – a fellow called Michael Meyer. Trevor appeared never to have heard of him so Casper Wrede said, 'I think you do know him a little because he sat through a whole Lord's Test with you.' Trevor was dumbfounded. 'That fellow? Does he translate from Strindberg? Why didn't he tell me?' Casper Wrede replied, 'I don't suppose he thought it very appropriate, in the middle of an exciting Test match, to say, "By the way, I happen to translate Strindberg."'

So Trevor Howard started rehearsing *The Father* in December 1963, with Joyce Redman playing his wife.

As Helen was filming in the Bahamas, Trevor stayed with friends in Cheyne Walk while he was learning his lines. As he paced to and fro daily, he noticed the regular passage of a barge called *Conformity* sailing by every day at roughly the same time. As such a word doesn't figure much in Trevor's personal dictionary, he was sufficiently amused by it to mention the barge to an interviewer. When *The Father* came into London Trevor received a good luck telegram from the captain and the crew of *Conformity* on opening night.

The Father had an advance date in Brighton and Michael Meyer remembers that Trevor had a little difficulty with his lines for the first few performances but had got them nailed by the end of the first week.

Behind the Theatre Royal in Brighton there is a pub called The Wheatsheaf where Trevor and Michael Meyer soon became friends with the very fat landlord named Laurie. At one matinée, Trevor astounded Michael Meyer with his last line in the first act, replacing 'Harness the sleigh. I'm going out and I shan't be back before midnight', with 'Harness the sleigh. I'm going to the Wheatsheaf and I shan't be back before midnight.' After the performance Michael Meyer was in Trevor's dressing-room before the last curtain call. 'I must be mad or drunk or something,' he said to Trevor. 'I could have sworn you mentioned The Wheatsheaf.' Trevor looked surprised. 'Yes. Didn't I tell you? Laurie bet me a pound – or a fiver or something – that I wouldn't refer to The Wheatsheaf during *The Father* and I took him on.' Michael Meyer told him he was disgraceful, fancy introducing an English pub into a Swedish play! But he went with Trevor to collect the bet.

They bounded into the pub, Trevor calling, 'Laurie, I'm going to collect that bet from you. I've got a witness to the fact that I mentioned The Wheatsheaf.' Laurie looked at him sourly. 'In a matinée? In a fucking matinée with six old ladies drinking tea? You bloody shit! If you'd done it in an evening show I'd have given you twenty quid.'

From Brighton, *The Father* went into London, to the Piccadilly Theatre, where it did very well. From there it transferred to the Queen's where it did less well and came off.

During the run, Michael Meyer saw the play frequently and thought Trevor was wonderful: 'Of course, one might say he varied, but he varied, I should say, between seventy-five and ninety out of a hundred. I would have thought, for that part, nobody would get hundred out of a hundred every night. It's one of those parts, like Othello. You've got to play it on your nerves. Trevor only varied in the sense that sometimes he'd be absolutely astonishing and sometimes he'd just be very, very good.'

The critics and the translator were largely in agreement. Philip Hope-Wallace wrote, in *The Guardian*: 'But of course Trevor Howard's study of pathological dissolution, so strongly and naturally conveyed that it seems inevitable, is what makes the evening memorable. The audience was not in doubt.' And Michael Meyer was complimented by W. A. Darlington on his 'new, smooth translation'.

Trevor Howard's friendship with Michael Meyer continues: 'We've been very good friends for twenty-one years but I can't claim to *know* him. There's a great deal of private in Trevor. I'm very fond of him and I can't imagine anyone not liking him. We meet at Lord's and if Trevor is at a loose end in London he pops in to see me. We get along very well because we talk about, well, mainly cricket.'

In 1972, they played cricket together. Michael Meyer was asked by his old school, Wellington, to put together a motley eleven to play an Irish side called the Pembroke Cricket Club – 'a lovely lot they were, mad Irishmen.' He co-opted Trevor, Tom Courtenay and Tom Stoppard, who was a very good wicket keeper, and 'seven non-famous people to do the bowling and batting'. During play a storm hung over the pitch, but didn't fall. It just hung there, getting darker and darker. By the time Michael Meyer's side went in it was night-dark. Trevor found himself at leg slip and was nearly beheaded by a ferocious hook then, when he went in to bat, it was impossible to see the bowling and he was run out for nought.

A few days later, Trevor and Helen were leaving a theatre when Trevor was hailed by a crowd of none-too-sober Irishmen. It was a moment or two before he recognized the Pembroke Cricket Club. He presented them all to Helen, saying he was afraid he hadn't made any runs during their match. One of the

Irish team turned to Helen, 'Ah, madam, he was the victim of a dastardly run-out.' As Michael Meyer says, 'a lovely phrase'.

Like many an admirer, Michael Meyer is sad that Trevor didn't play more of the great classic roles in the theatre: 'He'd have been perfect for a lot of those Strindberg and Ibsen characters. There wasn't time, I suppose.'

Of course, there had been time. There had been frequent stretches between films when Trevor Howard was crying out for work, and accepting mediocre films in consequence. It is no secret that the financial rewards for acting on-screen are far greater than they are for playing on-stage, but this was the last consideration for Trevor. He never measured his talent against money and, now nearing fifty, he could very easily have afforded regular sorties into the theatre. But theatrical impresarios were not to know that, and he could hardly advertise. Since it is a *sine qua non* that film stars are highly paid, theatre producers tend to feel they are out of reach, particularly for 'special' plays such as those of Strindberg and Ibsen. It was a lucky meeting at Lord's that put Trevor Howard into *The Father*. Although he would have accepted other such roles, he was too shy and too lazy to ferret for himself: that was a matter for his agent, Al Parker.

As an agent, Al Parker was second to none when it came to making deals for his clients. He was an extraordinary and very tough American operating in London, he rode managements and producers hard on behalf of his actors and actresses but, like many other agents, he didn't read scripts – he went for the deal. With a large and flourishing stable, he had neither the time nor the urge to seek out theatrical productions for Trevor Howard which might have stretched his talent and added to his stature, if not to his bank balance.

So Trevor Howard continued to make films and become more and more adept at stealing them from Hollywood's 'big names'. He made *Father Goose* with Cary Grant and Leslie Caron, and *Von Ryan's Express* with Frank Sinatra. Donald Zec wrote: 'Every leading Hollywood actor with whom he has started – they include William Holden, Cary Grant and Bob Mitchum – will candidly admit to having to "work their asses off" (or so they've told me) to stay on level terms with him.'

*

No such stress was registered by Frank Sinatra after working with Trevor on *Von Ryan's Express*. It was a film Trevor enjoyed making and he regarded it as one of the better American offerings. He also liked working with Sinatra but always felt he was rather remote: possibly Sinatra's fairly large retinue of protectors, or handlers, created a barrier against mateyness. The film was made in Rome, Malaga and Cortina, and then the unit returned to Hollywood to shoot interiors.

Helen joined Trevor in Cortina, travelling independently and losing her luggage on the way. She was waiting for Trevor in the hotel bar when she was joined by a slight and bald man who had also lost his luggage. They chatted amiably and her new acquaintance bought her a drink. Finally Trevor arrived. 'Ah,' he said, 'I see you've met Frank.' Helen had been talking to Frank Sinatra and had no idea who he was. To take the sting out of that she claimed she couldn't see very well. She too thought Sinatra was charming.

While working on the set of *Von Ryan's Express* in Hollywood, Trevor Howard was visited by Aaron Rosenberg of *Bounty* fame. The producer was working in the same studios on a film called *The Saboteur, Code Name Morituri*, starring Yul Brynner and Marlon Brando. The burden of Rosenberg's message had been loaded by Brando who wondered whether Trevor Howard might have a few days free after his present film because Brando would very much like Trevor to make a guest appearance in *Morituri* for old friendship's sake. That was a stunner, as was the disproportionate figure suggested for a few days work.

Trevor Howard thought about it and then, having rowed his friends Gil Stewart and Keith McConnell into the same act, he agreed. At the time he didn't know that Brando had a very particular reason for wanting him in the film – any more than Brando knew that Trevor Howard had an excellent reason for accepting such a fee for a modicum of work.

At this time Brando's case against the *Saturday Evening Post* had not yet been resolved, but it was nearing court time. The implication of the article was that Brando's behaviour on *Bounty* was such that no British actor of any stature would ever work with him again, at least this appeared to be the main line upon

146

which the case was based. By having the same producer and working with three of the British actors who had been in *Bounty*, Brando was able to win his case. In Trevor's words, 'Bloody clever of Brando.' Would Trevor have worked with Brando again had he known that he was, in effect, being used in a legal ploy? Probably not.

Helen, however, remembers the situation differently: 'I know very well why you did *Morituri*.' Trevor's selective memory baulks at that. There was obviously some little incident he didn't care to recall. Helpfully, Helen reminded him of a party given by the writer Alec Coppel. Trevor tries a smile, the kind that Keith McConnell calls his crocodile smile although it more resembles an outsize wince than any expression of pleasure or humour. 'That's right. We all got stoned. But that was nothing to do with Brando, he wasn't there.' Helen looks at him, waiting. Finally, 'I know why I did it. Of course I know.' 'Why?' Trevor shifts about. 'To pay for the broken cars.' Helen nods, 'Exactly.' Trevor stares at her. 'Who told you that – Michael Wilding?' Even Helen couldn't believe it, '*I was there!*' 'Oh yes, I had to buy a couple of cars, that was all.'

It was one of those more memorable parties, filled with laughter and drink. When Helen finally persuaded her husband that he'd had enough of both he decided to do her the favour of extricating her car from the mass of others in the driveway. He went forward into one, backed into another and shunted the next two in line fore and aft. Michael Wilding quickly took charge, arranged for the substantial repairs to be made and Trevor paid the bill – from fees earned on *Morituri*. There was a kind of poetic justice lurking in those back axles.

Later, in 1965, Trevor Howard was once more safely in the hands of George Schaefer, playing in *Eagle in a Cage*, a television special about Napoleon's exile until death on St Helena. The original play was by R. C. Sheriff but George Schaefer bought the rights and caused it to be rewritten by Millard Lampell. The latter had suffered during the McCarthy era and this was to be his comeback. Casting about for a Napoleon, George Schaefer wondered what Trevor Howard would be like: 'There was a vast difference between Dizzy and Nappy, but Trevor can do anything so we sent him a script — and he did it.'

Although Trevor Howard was nominated for an Emmy, he didn't win it. George Schaefer thought he should have done so because, 'It was a brilliant performance in a difficult part — using elements of his skill that he doesn't often get a chance to use.' The critics agreed, they were all for Trevor but one or two were vastly unfair to the writer, Millard Lampell. They suggested that the young girl, Betsy, had been invented by Lampell as a convenient character to play touching scenes with Napoleon. Betsy Balcombe was very real, she spent very much time in Napoleon's company while he was living out his last days in the Pavilion on her family's estate. In the role, Pamela Franklin won her just share of acclaim.

After the wrap-up on *Eagle in a Cage*, Trevor Howard went off to have a few and listen to some jazz. He was returning to England by one of Cunard's *Queens*, so had the night ahead of him before sailing in the morning. As he moseyed around the jazz clubs he ran into his old and dear friend, Buster Bailey, the great jazz clarinettist. They drank, listened and chatted, and Trevor thought to ask his friend to see him off on board the following day. Then he remembered that Buster Bailey and the band were playing an all-night session recording a disc, so he would naturally be too tired to see anybody anywhere. Buster Bailey let it float.

The following day Trevor went aboard and went directly to his stateroom. Suddenly the telephone rang and he was told that Lord Louis Mountbatten was on board and would like Trevor to join him and others for a drink. While making his way up to the stated bar, Trevor saw Buster Bailey and his eight grandchildren making their way down the gangway away from the ship. Clearly they had come to see him off and had been turned away. Trevor was furious. He roared into the bar and tackled a Cunard official, demanding to know why he had not been informed that his friend had been to see him and, above all, why he had been turned away. Several red faces later Lord Louis joined in. He requested that Trevor Howard's friends be brought back on board and treated properly. And so they were. Refreshments were provided for the children, champagne was poured for the adults and everybody had a nice time. The liner was late sailing but honour had been satisfied and noblesse had obliged.

A few weeks later Trevor received a copy of the record that had been cut the previous night signed on the cover by every member of the band. It would have been perfect had they sent one to Lord Louis Mountbatten as well, but maybe they didn't have his address.

CHAPTER TWELVE

The Poppy is Also a Flower was an interesting film, not because of any quality in the final production but because of the financial structure upon which it was made — and the reason for it being made at all. The producer, Euan Lloyd, still retains a slight sense of amazement at the original set-up. It seems that in the mid-Sixties, the image of the United Nations was not very glowing. A number of high-powered Americans evolved a plan to make a series of films for television which would demonstrate the work being done by the United Nations while also aiming at being entertainment for the viewers; maybe the sort of semi-documentaries that were once made with expertise in Britain.

Xerox put up three million, six hundred thousand dollars to finance six 'Movies of the Week' to be shown on television in America and distributed through cinemas overseas. Eminent directors and producers were approached by Adlai Stevenson, who was then Ambassador to the United Nations. He was fully behind the project and, very naturally, caught the attention of a lot of directors, such as Alfred Hitchcock, Otto Preminger and Joseph Mankiewicz. The latter made the first 'Movie of the Week', a modest production which failed to move on after being shown on television. At the time a British director, Terence Young, was current and choice, having made a smash hit with the first Bond film, *Dr No*. Somehow, Terence Young got alongside the Xerox funding, taking Euan Lloyd with him as producer. They acquired the six hundred thousand dollars from Xerox and then the director became ambitious. He persuaded himself, then Euan Lloyd and then the market, that if they could get a star-studded cast they could get more money and make a bigger picture — so the budget went up to six or seven million dollars.

Someone at Xerox had heard about escalating budgets and when they had set up the funding they had done so on the basis that beyond their contribution the film-makers would put up something in return. Terence Young had a nimble solution to that: 'We'll all work for a dollar a head. We'll have expense money but that's our salary.' Euan Lloyd bit on that bullet. 'You mean the artistes as well?' 'Yes. That's it. Do you think we can do it?' It was a very tall order indeed, but with Ambassador Stevenson and the White House hierarchy behind the drive, it had tremendous push and it fired the imagination of the film industry.

Euan Lloyd's first task was to get a cast together – there were to be two sustained roles and a number of 'guest' appearances. He did very well with the guests, capturing Omar Sharif, Yul Brynner, Jack Hawkins, Rita Hayworth and Marcello Mastroianni, among others. There remained the two central characters, a CIA man and his opposite number from Scotland Yard. E. G. Marshall committed himself to fourteen weeks' shooting for one dollar and then Euan Lloyd decided to go for his friend Trevor Howard. Terence Young was becoming choosy: he thought Trevor was rather older than the character he had in mind. The producer stared at him: 'Well, you find a younger fellow for a dollar.' Then he set off to Arkley to have a lovely Sunday lunch and chat up his friend.

He gave him the locations first: Naples, Rome, Teheran, and the South of France. Trevor found all that very interesting, 'France? Jolly good. Victorine Studios? The food is good there.' 'Yes, very. Now comes the bad news . . .' Trevor looked at him curiously, 'One dollar?' 'That's all. But you'll have generous expenses and you'll be travelling.' Trevor smiled, and agreed. 'So he did it – and they all finished up with one dollar each. The contracts still exist. The Tellson Foundation took over the film in the States and it is still being run on television. It raised one million dollars which was given to UNICEF – who promptly furnished a building in Paris with it.'

A view of the contracts might be of passing interest but a study of the fiddle sheets should be mind-blowing.

Trevor Howard's last scene for the film was filmed at Monte Carlo harbour, where he was to be bumped off by Gilbert Roland and fall into the water. For the fall a double was standing by. Then Terence Young had a better idea and approached Euan Lloyd with it: 'Euan you know Trevor very well – and it would give him a good send-off. D'you think he'll go in?' Euan Lloyd was appalled, 'Are you serious? Have you seen the filth in the harbour? Forget it.' But the director didn't want to forget it. He continued to press the producer to put it to the actor. Finally, Euan Lloyd gave in. 'Trevor, I've got one for you. Mr Young would like you to play the scene right through to the end, into the drink.' Trevor smiled, 'Oh, Mr Young would like that, would he? Well, I doubt it will happen, but I'll do it if he'll do it.' Euan Lloyd returned to the director: 'Terence, I've got the solution. Trevor will do it, but he wants you to do it first.' Terence Young laughed that off and the stunt man finished the shot, which nearly finished him. He hit his head very badly on some floating wood and had to be rushed into hospital.

Whether it was conscience or natural generosity that prompted Terence Young's end-of-film present to Trevor Howard, it was impressive: a gold Cartier wristwatch. It was a very nice watch and Trevor was touched and pleased, but he is not a man who dotes on possessions. In Helen's view, if he was robbed of everything, even his collection of jazz, his sense of loss would not be great. Some time later, Helen and Trevor were enjoying a yachting holiday in Greece with Rex Harrison and his wife. They had all been ashore for lunch and a swim. Back on board, Trevor realized he had left his watch in the restaurant. Helen urged him to go back for it, but Trevor wasn't bothered. 'It didn't go, anyway,' he said. Helen shook her head, remembering the loss, 'Of course it didn't go. It didn't go because he never wound it.'

By some legerdemain of film finance, the end money for *The Poppy is Also a Flower* was put up by the City of Vienna, so the world première took place there with as many of the stars as possible in attendance. The producer was delighted: 'It was a formidable turnout, a wonderful success. The film became a collector's item in Vienna, it's still showing in art theatres and, believe me, it's not an artistic achievement.'

A year or two after the première of *The Poppy is Also a Flower*, Euan Lloyd had a call from a Viennese journalist who was organizing a big charity evening. The film was to be shown again, the evening before the charity function, and could Euan Lloyd provide some stars from it? Not surprisingly, Trevor headed the list and they went to Vienna. Euan Lloyd, possibly recalling the drama with *Interpol* in Frankfurt, made haste to enquire as to what was expected of his team and, most particularly, what did they want Trevor Howard to do. The reply was not altogether reassuring. They begged him not to be frightened but they had a real, live circus and wanted as many artistes as possible to participate. Trevor thought it sounded fun and being mad about elephants, was more than prepared to play with them. However, Marianne Koch − an actress who was also in love with elephants − had pre-empted that act. She was to be lifted onto the elephant's back by his trunk, and also to lie prone with his foot placed just above her breast. Even Trevor was relieved not to be part of that one: 'I'm glad she's doing that. It's not for me.'

The organizer of the show then said he had something very spectacular for Trevor, but it was entirely safe. So what was it? They just wanted him to go into the lion's cage − 'Who, me?' − yes, but don't worry, 'Just the fact that you're inside and we can get pictures, that's all we require.' So Trevor went into the lion's cage and his escape from it was through a tunnel like a circular tube. He was in the cage for the pictures and then the lion showed signs of becoming rather too lively, so he made for the tunnel at speed. But once inside it, he found himself face to face with polar bears, who were on their way into the ring. It was a heart-stopper. When those responsible realized that Trevor was in danger, keepers joined him and the bears, prodding the latter with forks to keep them off. Apart from being scared witless, Trevor remembers that he was also conscious of fearing that the forks might 'fail to penetrate the bears', well, feelings,' Wherever the forks were aimed, they finally did their work and a very shaken Trevor Howard emerged from the end of the tunnel. Euan Lloyd was proud of him: 'He was very brave. He did most of the things we asked him to do at any juncture around the world.' After Frankfurt and Vienna, Trevor might have asked himself whether Euan Lloyd might not prove to be a touch too dangerous as a playmate.

The Poppy is Also a Flower was shown on television in America in April 1966 and some time later went on release. The *New York Times* regarded the illicit traffic in opium as being 'altogether incidental to a heavy-handed and old-fashioned melodrama.'

Trevor Howard has been quoted as saying that he has been

offered more rubbish than the dustman and even acknowledged that he has accepted some of it. In 1966 *The Liquidator* was released after a two-year legal wrangle over assignment of rights. The film was conceived as a spoof of the Bond series, but by the time it reached the screen the genre was already familiar and *The Liquidator* was not good enough. *The Observer*'s Penelope Gilliatt vouchsafed no praise for the film but devoted space to an appreciation of Trevor Howard's talent: 'Trevor Howard is worth going a very long way to see, even in an hour and forty minutes of punk. His shot-riddled face is one of the most moving proofs in the cinema of the simple rule that a great film actor can always be seen to be thinking the thought that produces his next action . . . the opinions and decisions that chase across Trevor Howard's face are as absorbing as the levels of his voice.' His next film *The Long Duel*, with Yul Brynner, also misfired but Trevor emerged unscathed. Although he has sternly refused to become involved in soft or hard pornography masquerading as *avant-garde* art, he has done time in some dim productions that, according to many critics, had nothing to recommend them except his performances. It's Sod's Law that if an actor wants to act and is offered nothing of true value, he accepts the dross and makes of it what he can. As Dilys Powell says, 'He's done the most extraordinary things and when I say he's ready to do anything, I mean anything that exercises him. And, of course, he's saved a number of films. One is always so thankful to see him because when he's there it's going to be all right – and when he's gone it's going to be all wrong. If he had rejected some of the films he's saved, his reputation would have been grander. I don't think he has the reputation he deserves because he's really a great actor.'

One film that even Trevor Howard couldn't save was *Pretty Polly*, released in 1967 and re-titled *A Matter of Innocence*, in America. Based on a short story by Noël Coward, it was made in Singapore with, among others, Hayley Mills and Shashi Kapoor. As far as Trevor was concerned, the highlight of the location was his meeting with Lorne Polanski, an American then working with IBM. They met in a hotel lift and their friendship was instant and enduring. Lorne Polanski is the perfect companion for Trevor: he is an admitted actor *manqué*, has great charm and wit, but is also a sensitive observer, recognizing highs and lows. With Trevor's help, Lorne did a little moonlighting on the film as an extra, playing a drunken sailor – which delighted him. Off duty, they wandered the now defunct Bugis Street together and generally enjoyed a high old time. Lorne marvels that no matter how hard they played at night, 'Trevor was always on time on the set, always knew his lines. He was entirely professional and greatly respected for it. There aren't many of his kind left.'

Lorne Polanski is the first friend Trevor contacts on arrival in New York, often arriving in his office unexpectedly and shouting with glee. After his stint with IBM in Singapore, Lorne worked for a while with the company in France and then wished machinery a fond farewell and returned to New York. He has created an answering machine service for young actors and actresses who also man the switchboard when becalmed. It is work very close to Lorne's heart, and to Trevor's, who loves him for dreaming up the idea and making it a success.

As for the film, *Pretty Polly*, Noël Coward noted in his 1967 diary that 'the first script was common, unsubtle and vulgar. Nobody was good in it and Trevor Howard was horrid. When I think of his charm and subtlety in *Brief Encounter*.' Wilfrid Sheed lowered the tombstone into place, 'It came and went this winter, leaving a slight trace of camphor and old knitting needles.'

By now Trevor Howard might have wondered whether his Guardian Angel had retired or was taking a quiet holiday guarding somebody else. Then came an epic with a beauty for Trevor: the role of Lord Cardigan in Tony Richardson's *The Charge of the Light Brigade*. The film had been in preparation for nearly four years. While Richardson was directing other pictures, his military historian, costume researchers, script-writers and location reconnaissance teams had been spending a large part of the budget on getting everything right and ready to go. By then the allocation for the cast had shrunk and cuts in salaries were suggested, and accepted: it was to be a prestige picture, and to appear in such a rarity was almost worth money. Apart from Trevor Howard, Sir John Gielgud and Harry Andrews were signed for Lord Raglan and Lord Lucan and the cast included some very fine players, such as Jill Bennett, Norman Rossington, David Hemmings and Vanessa Redgrave.

The Valley of Death was finally found in Turkey not far from Ankara, where lay two villages, Pacenek and Saraycik. Also the Turkish government were pleased to supply a force of cavalry. No part of these preparations had been easy, indeed they had been fraught with difficulties of every kind, but all was done, and cast and crew left for Turkey in May 1967 to shoot the film.

At thirty-eight, Tony Richardson was probably the youngest director Trevor had worked with for some years. He was also of the school that believed in a certain amount of *laissez faire*, encouraging the artistes to improvise within the framework of the character. Trevor was used to the old-guard directors who rehearsed meticulously, wanting to know what they were going to get before the camera turned. Trevor found that both systems suited him and he enjoyed working with Richardson: 'He gave one a free hand and had ideas of gutsy things, strange things. He was very easy to work with – gave me confidence.' The pleasure was mutual. Tony Richardson speaks of Trevor as, 'a lovely actor – but a most un-actory actor.' It was always a fine compliment.

For some reason Tony Richardson decided to forgo the customary press show in London. It was an odd decision and not one calculated to endear the film-makers to the press. On the other hand, it engendered more pre-publicity for the film than was usual, and most publications were prepared to stake their critics the price of a ticket to review the film independently. Sadly, in spite of the time, money and care spent on the production, it was not hailed as a masterpiece. Criticism was levelled at the social satire that had been injected into the script, the disparities between upper and lower classes and between officers and men. This was a view shared by Trevor Howard who felt that such underlining had little to do with the story being told. The story was another point at issue since many found it to have become muddled in the telling: 'Notions for at least three interesting films are on view ... what seems signally lacking is a guiding hand, an overriding purpose.' These were John Coleman's findings.

The actors fared better than the director. Trevor Howard received his accolades, as did Sir John Gielgud. But disappointing reviews for an epic blur individual successes and work against even the best actors rather than for them. Rave reviews for a performance in a popular film form the alchemy that keeps the offers coming.

The film had a better reception in America, where Trevor Howard went to promote it. Since Americans have always known that the British are snobs, they were all content to accept manifestations of the national disease on the screen and applaud them.

Keith McConnell was in New York when Trevor was engaged on publicity prior to the opening of the film, and he recalls with delight one of Trevor's appearances on a television chat show. The interviewer led off: 'You know Mr Howard, it's a great pleasure to have you here. You're such a wonderful actor and your performance in *Charge of the Light Brigade* is just so great.' Trevor stared at him. 'Oh, really, did you see it?' The interviewer fumbles: 'Well, now – I – I – er . . .' 'Did you *see* it?' Mumble, mumble. 'You couldn't have seen it because it hasn't been shown yet.' Trevor turns to the audience, 'There you are, you see. That's Americans for you. They congratulate you on performances they haven't seen!' It was a fair cop, even if it did leave those in charge of publicity sobbing into their pillows.

Between 1967 and 1970 Trevor Howard's biggest project was *The Battle of Britain*, in which he played Sir Keith Parke. It was a production studded with guest stars, including Laurence Olivier and Ralph Richardson, but the Thames remained flameless.

Then came an endurance test in a film directed by David Lean and produced by Anthony Havelock-Allan. Incredible as it may seem, the genesis of *Ryan's Daughter* was Flaubert's *Madame Bovary*. David Lean was visiting Naples and Capri when a script based solidly on *Madame Bovary* arrived from Robert Bolt with a note urging him to read it at once. David Lean read it, thought it was awful and cabled Bolt that he was not interested. Then he wrote a ten-page letter explaining why he didn't like it, and another cable went to Bolt: 'If you haven't sold Madame B don't stop wait for my letter.' He tore up the ten-page letter and wrote forty pages instead. The film *auteur* was hooked. He had made the subject his own although he disliked the book as much as he had disliked the script. Now it had become his – he could change it, modernize it and make it against a different setting. He considered placing it in India, and finally settled for Ireland. Nothing is as dangerous as the trap we set for ourselves.

The trap closed on all concerned for a long ten months on Dingle peninsula in south-west Ireland, an area noted for storms and 'soft weather', which is Irish for rain. The period chosen was 1916, the time of the troubles. Robert Bolt's wife, Sarah Miles, for whom the *Madame Bovary* script had been written, played the errant wife and Robert Mitchum suffered as the cuckolded husband. Christopher Jones was his rival while John Mills drew the role of the ubiquitous and mute village idiot. Leo McKern became Rosie Ryan's father whose active sympathies were on the side of the Irish rebels against the British. Trevor Howard was finally chosen to play a village priest. Finally, because he was by no means the first choice for the part. Flaubert didn't begin, leave alone finish, the race.

Apart from the unique length of time it lasted, the location was the most miserably unhappy period that many of those involved remember. Sir Anthony Havelock-Allan still winces fifteen years later: 'The whole thing was unfortunate. Mitchum and David didn't get along. Mitchum thinks, or affects to think, that film-making is a joke and should never be taken seriously, while for David films are life itself. It's a terrible trap, Ireland. It can be the dullest place in the world and then there is nothing to do but drink. All the actors had long periods of not working but they couldn't go away because if the sun shone they were needed.

'After the first week Trevor didn't drink at all, he just lived a very lonely and ascetic life. You'd see him when he wasn't working going for long walks and hardly seeing anybody. It was terribly tough on him and he wasn't happy – he loathed it. But he was wonderful. It wasn't a happy picture, nobody was happy on it.'

If Helen had been with Trevor life would have been easier for him but she was in a highly successful play, *Out of the Question*, at St Martin's Theatre, with Gladys Cooper, Michael Denison and Dulcie Gray.

Even during the shooting, the film showed signs of being over-long and unwieldy: top-heavy for the story it was telling. Sir Anthony attributes this to the pre-production rush to accommodate the programmes of Robert Mitchum and Sarah Miles. David Lean had no time in which to prepare his shooting script, which is akin to starting to build a house without detailed plans. The location was bedevilled by weather – and accidents. The magnificent storm sequence was bound to take its toll. It was shot over a long period of time, during every available storm, to capture enough footage. Trevor Howard and John Mills shared a scene in which they were out fishing in a little curragh. As there was some fear that it might not be visually exciting played on a calm sea, they had to play it during a storm: the fact that no Irishman would have attempted to fish in such weather was irrelevant. The curragh capsized, taking the actors with it, John Mills sustained a blow on the head and, being trapped under the boat, was in danger of being swept out to sea. Trevor managed to free himself and reach the surface of the water. They were both rescued with some difficulty.

It was later said that during this near loss of life, David Lean's main concern was that no footprints should mar the sweep of virgin sand that formed the foreground to his visual of the scene. This canard is unacceptable if only because, with such a tricky location on his hands, David Lean could have had no desire to recast two leading roles and start again.

That excitement had hardly died down before Trevor fell off a horse, injuring five ribs and his collar bone and landing himself in hospital. Helen was in a play at the time but she was very anxious to have a look at Trevor so on Sunday morning she chartered a plane from the nearby Elstree Flying Club and flew off. The plane landed at Killarney Race Course where she was given a grand reception. Everybody was delighted to see her, especially her bedridden husband. Then she flew back to London on Monday in time for the evening performance.

Shortly afterwards, Helen's break-date for the play came up, so she gathered up their much-loved poodle and went off to join Trevor in Ireland. Within days disaster struck again. The dog Mathieu – Matty for short – was taken by Helen for his last run of the evening. The dog sped into the pitch black night followed by Helen, who took one step too many and fell over the cliff. With the dog barking safely above her, she managed to crawl back to flat land and the house – but she was in great pain. The following morning the pain was worse and it was quite apparent that she had injured her coccyx. It was agreed that she must go to the hospital recently left by Trevor.

The story told is that Robert Mitchum was to hand, offering condolences and fears for her comfort on the journey to hospital, which he confided to Trevor: 'Jesus, she's going to be in agony. That road is packed with fucking rocks. Just think of it.' Trevor did think. He thought for quite a while, then he said: 'You're right. I don't think I'll go.' Whether Trevor went or not, Helen finished up in the same bed her husband had vacated.

The long location ground on, moving from site to site, as Sir Anthony says, 'This great cavalcade that looked like the Barnum and Bailey Circus going from one location to another – some twenty-five miles apart down narrow lanes. If we had gone to shoot rain, the sun was out, and if we wanted sun, we got rain. Nobody in their right mind would make a film without one studio shot in the south-west of Ireland at any time.' In final desperation the entire circus moved to South Africa to shoot in sunshine.

Ryan's Daughter was a long and costly experience for Metro-Goldwyn-Mayer, at a time when that company was already broke and selling assets. Had it been a true, if expensive, epic it might have made a fortune but it was at best too small a story for David Lean's magnificent technique; the canvas was huge, impressive and very beautiful but the matrix was too frail, and the film was too long.

Sir David Lean is full of praise for Trevor Howard's portrayal of Father Collins, 'I always gauge performances out of a hundred. A hundred, which you never get, is equal to the performance you imagined when you were working on the script. With most people, if you get fifty or sixty you're bloody lucky because casting is always a compromise. In *Ryan's Daughter*, Trevor as the priest I'd mark down at ninety-eight. He's the nearest of any character to perfection. And I only say ninety-eight because I'm frightened of saying a hundred. He's a terrific actor and I think he was absolutely wonderful. Use him again? Like mad! Oh, yes, immediately!' After *Ryan's Daughter* there wasn't much immediacy. David Lean's next picture was *A Passage to India* some fourteen years later, but he did regret that Trevor Howard wasn't young enough to play the schoolmaster in it.

Although *Ryan's Daughter* could be regarded as a compass error, it won a well-deserved Oscar for the photographer Frederick Young and another for John Mills' beguiling performance as Michael the mute natural. Sarah Miles received a Nomination. In spite of these awards the reviews reflected disappointment in a David Lean film. Of it, Alexander Walker wrote: 'Instead of looking like the money it cost to make, the film feels like the time it took to shoot.'

In order to promote a dubious runner, a small cavalcade set off for America to beat the drum. Although MGM claimed that five million had been spent on launching *Ryan's Daughter*, Sir Anthony recalls that the only visible publicity before the opening in New York, was the title of the picture stencilled on some streets beside the curb: 'Otherwise it was David, John Mills and Trevor appearing on chat shows that were glad to have us.' Such appearances are a bonus for the networks since they are unpaid; top stars in exchange for a word or two about the current offering is not the worst deal in the world.

During his numerous visits to America, either to work or to promote his films, Trevor has appeared, and re-appeared, on all the chat shows, great and small, across the country. He delights the audience with his unpredictability. If there is a musical group on the show he is liable to sing along with it, once giving a fine rendition of *Dinah*. This is great for everyone but the anchor man, who might sense that 'his' show is being whipped away from under him. Anchor men whose names are famous countrywide, are men of substance and stars in their own right. Upstage them at your peril lest you are struck off their list of free contributors.

Most actors tend to relate dates or periods of time to film or play titles, because it is so that their lives are governed. It isn't as precise as 12 April 1967 – it is rather the opening night of *Hamlet* or whatever. But Trevor Howard has crossed America and Canada so often that even these markers have become entangled and Helen can no longer remember exactly when she joined him in New York for the first time. She knows she met

Marge Guterman in the evening of her arrival and recalls that for a whole week their group, including Robert Mitchum and Sheldon Reynolds, met for drinks before a long lunch at 21, a restaurant and bar first famed during prohibition as 'Jack and Charlie's', the afternoon melting into cocktail time before going to El Morocco. She also remembers that Robert Mitchum's constant drink was Fernet Branca and that by the end of the week she felt very ill.

Although jazz is not Helen's favourite listening, she has accompanied Trevor on his round of the clubs and at one bar remembers meeting Coleman Hawkins. They chatted until it was time for Hawkins to take up his saxophone and play. Once he was on the stand Trevor found he could not see the group and moved to a table in another part of the room. From the stand Hawkins announced: 'I'm going to dedicate this to my friend Trevor – Oh, he's gone!' Trevor yelled, 'No, I haven't. I'm over here!' Hawkins smiled with relief and began to play, but Helen was struck by the hurt and sorrow on Hawkins's face when he thought Trevor had left: 'It was so moving.'

When Helen was unable to be with Trevor in New York for a première, she sometimes arranged to put him in the care of Marge Guterman because, as Marge says, 'Helen understands how lonely Trevor gets and also understands that some of us ladies are just plain friends.' Since Robert Mitchum was also one of Marge's 'plain friends', she occasionally found herself being squired by both him and Trevor, possibly with Sheldon Reynolds for good measure. At one time the gentlemen decided that instead of hiring a variety of cabs by day and night they would hire the same cab for a week. This worked very well for above five days and nights until they emerged from a restaurant in Greenwich Village to find their cab on fire. Trevor's reaction was immediate: 'See! I knew it. I knew it would happen. He wanted to get rid of us!' It was a self-punitive method of doing so, to say the least, but by then perhaps the driver was prepared to go to any lengths to get some sleep. Without his wife, Dorothy, Robert Mitchum also became lonely, which meant night-long merriment and demanding companionship. No one was allowed to sneak off and sleep. According to Marge, 'It was like Scott Fitzgerald.

Everybody loved them and both Trevor and Bob have said there would never be another time like it.'

The Metropole on Broadway was a favourite jazz haunt for Trevor: 'He'd go every night – up onstage to play and sing. Bob joined us one night but he got mobbed. People never did that to Trevor, he had a certain untouchable quality: he was a gentleman. They knew who he was but knew better than to interfere with him. Mitchum was one of their own.'

Marge Guterman finds the more serious side of Trevor very endearing: 'He's always good and kind to people who are having a rough time – and I was from time to time. But he's never promiscuous in friendship. If he doesn't like you, God help you.' It's not that Trevor attacks, or picks quarrels, with those he finds unpleasing – he just mentally and spiritually removes himself. He can be there, seated beside them, but he has the ability to create a quiet void, a defensive remoteness that cannot be pierced. When he is happy and comfortable with his companions, his eyes are alight with humour or interest, he is attentive or joking, loving to share laughter. When he is super-content and having a lovely time, the bull moose roar threatens to shatter glass. But alongside it all, he remains a very private man.

The nature of his privacy is nowhere better observed than among his friends in America. They do not form an interrelating group and some of them have no idea how he spends his time when they are not with him. His visits to P. J. Clarke's and his talks with Danny Lavezzo are almost sealed off from other interests; Danny Lavezzo learnt with amazement of Trevor's interest in jazz, and they have known one another for more than thirty years. Conversely, Danny Lavezzo has never met Helen, or any other lady in Trevor's company – although he was surprised one evening when, having greeted Trevor in the bar, he asked to be excused for a moment while he went to the back of the house to say hello to Liz Whitney. Trevor was delighted, 'Is Liz Whitney here? She's one of my dear friends.' Danny Lavezzo thought, 'My God. Those two are worlds apart.' He didn't know that Trevor and the Whitney's had shared a very merry Christmas as the Mitchums' house guests in Maryland.

The last time Danny Lavezzo saw Trevor they had a quiet chat in the bar and, as so rarely happens, Trevor talked about the theatre and acting. Danny was surprised that Trevor was so profound, so cerebral and articulate about his profession: 'He was amazingly technical – he knew his business. The most astonishing thing was that Trevor could get sloshed and the next morning he was on his way to Paris or somewhere to make another film. It never interfered with his work.' Allowing that he is no expert, Danny Lavezzo regards Trevor Howard as one of the finest actors in the world and believes that the best film Trevor has been in – and probably the best film ever made – is *The Heart of the Matter*.

Trevor places Lorne Polanski at the top of his list of friends in New York but although Lorne knows P. J. Clarke's – and who does not? – this is not their mutual playground. Here again the paths diverge and the one Trevor follows with Lorne leads to the jazz clubs and to capers invented on the spur of the moment. One of Lorne's girlfriends is a photographer called Theo. She had long wanted to meet Trevor and, above all, yearned to photograph him; so the three of them took a horse and buggy from outside the Plaza and drove through Central Park. Trevor lost no time in borrowing the driver's cowboy hat and Theo took pictures all the way to The Tavern on the Green, where they had lunch. Such a casual photographic session with a well-known and distinguished actor is not usually acceptable, and Lorne treasures Trevor's co-operation at the time as a mark of love and trust. It's correct that he should.

Another friend of Lorne's took Trevor to a function given by Mayor John Lindsay at Gracie Mansion, where Trevor had a wonderful evening listening to jazz. That was one of the rare occasions when Trevor did not join the band to sing or play! Lorne's favourite recollection of Trevor stems from a walk they took down Park Avenue. Suddenly Trevor put his hand on Lorne's shoulders: 'You know,' he said, 'I can't tell you how much I want you to come to England and spend a weekend with us . . . I only say a weekend because you'd find it so bloody boring for longer.'

Trevor and Helen are both very fond of Lorne Polanski. He is not only a delightful and funny companion, he is natural and sincere – qualities rarely found around artistes and so to be cherished. Affection for Trevor Howard in America is very real and takes many forms. Rock Hudson had a charming story relating to him, although they had never met. Rock Hudson's new houseman, or butler, was officiating at a large dinner party and, bottles in hand, he approached actress Claire Trevor, 'Red or white, Miss Howard?' he enquired.

CHAPTER THIRTEEN

Some actors who have drawing power at the box-office and a healthy portfolio at their brokers are self-generating from time to time. They buy options on books or plays and then work with a writer of their choice to develop a film script, letting it be known that they have it and wish to play in it. Sometimes it is a gamble that pays off, sometimes not, but the risk is not very great since any loss can usually be written off against tax.

Very uncharacteristically, Trevor had such a flutter just once. In 1963 he bought a script of *Kilo Forty*, which had been written by the author of the original book, Miles Tripp. Trevor still retains the rights and some twenty years later he began to think of the subject again, but he is far from being an entrepreneur so the project lies fallow. In truth, Trevor lacks the guile to be a wheeler-dealer. In such matters he is an innocent. Although he can be quite foxy when it comes to self-protection, the manipulative cunning required to set up a film is as foreign to him as Sanskrit.

When a successful independent producer was being discussed at a party, Trevor was full of admiration for his ability to raise film money. 'And do you know,' he cried, 'he gets it all from the laundries!' Somewhere, sometime Trevor had heard the term laundered money and he genuinely believed that the producer gathered his finance from the laundromats.

Thus it was possibly as well that Trevor Howard should have continued to accept the best roles he was offered. One that must have seemed hopeful at the time was that of Wagner in Luchino Visconti's *Ludwig*. Helmut Berger played the Mad King of Bavaria with Romy Schneider and Silvana Mangano also decorating the cast. Trevor found that working with Visconti was quite a new experience: 'Visconti never directed. He had four cameras but you never knew where they were, you never knew which one was on you – and they had different lenses. All you were told was, "You walk from here to there". That's all. He just told you where to walk. You never even knew when you were doing a close-up, but it was no good worrying about it.' When Dilys Powell learnt of this novel fashion in non-direction she nodded thoughtfully, 'Mmm . . . I thought it might be like that.'

Given the benefit of direction or not, as the great composer who enjoyed the patronage of the king, Trevor Howard made the picture his very own during the ten minutes or so he was on-screen. Vincent Canby wrote in the *New York Times*: 'There is one interesting performance in the entire film. Trevor Howard makes a rather British Wagner, but he is a profoundly interesting combination of self-absorption, craftiness, genius and vision. Because everyone else acts as if trying to make an impression during the eruption of a volcano, the comparative understatement of Howard's performance rivets the attention.'

While it is gratifying to receive such recognition and while Trevor Howard can rivet the attention in less than three minutes' screen time in the worst film ever made, such acclaim hardly equates with a well-written role in an interesting and well-made film which captures the audiences. But Trevor wasn't getting any of those.

However, he did make a film with Helen, which was an unusual occurrence and largely of interest because of a light it throws on Trevor's preparation for a role by the costume designer, Anthony Mendleson.

The film, *Eleven Harrowhouse*, was an American production made with James Mason, John Gielgud and Candice Bergen among the cast. Since it was a contemporary piece, clothes for the male cast were largely a matter of judicious shopping rather than design and tailoring. Mendleson had worked with Trevor before and had always enjoyed Trevor's warmth, fun and popularity: 'He wasn't mobbed or anything like that — it was just a lovely warm feeling; they not only knew him, they truly liked him.' It was also apparent that although Trevor gave the impression that he wasn't particularly interested in his clothes, he had in fact given a lot of thought to the appearance of the character he was playing. He might tender his views casually, almost modestly, but there was consideration behind them — and he was always right. Mendleson respected his judgement enormously.

So shopping for Trevor's clothes for *Eleven Harrowhouse* was a great pleasure: 'Everything went swimmingly and we had a lovely time – until it suddenly came to a hat. What the problem was I cannot remember, but I do know we went to an awful lot of shops and an awful lot of hats were tried on until we found what Trevor said was the right hat.' There was no problems with any other garment – just the hat.

When choosing clothes for the character he is playing, Trevor doesn't discuss, analyse or pontificate while choices are being made: 'But he has quite certainly an inner eye that sees exactly what the man he is playing should look like. Especially the hat.' That figures. In private life Trevor Howard reacts to hats as did the late Hedda Hopper. He collects them from all corners of the earth: straw cartwheels, fringed sombreros, rakish country tweeds, they are all worn at some time. One sunny morning, Trevor was talking about his great desire to play comedy, in an almost disembodied voice coming from under an immense battered straw hat that might have belonged to a down-and-out beachcomber. Helen regarded what she could see of her husband fondly: 'He's got to be a comedian – anybody's got to be a comedian who wears a hat like that.'

On a grillingly hot day in the South of France, Trevor arrived at a lunch party looking immaculate in a short-sleeved tropical suit, but wearing the rakish country tweed hat. Seeing the slightly bemused expression of his hostess as her eyes travelled over the hottest hat on the Côte d'Azur, he snatched it off: 'Darling, where can I put this? I don't know why I wore it.' The following season he sported a gift from Helen – the perfect panama banded with the MCC colours.

Trevor Howard could never be described as a snappy dresser because that kind of vanity is not in him. He takes very little trouble with his appearance but when the occasion demands he rises to it and, being courteous enough to make the effort, looks marvellous. Somewhat wryly, Helen remembers walking behind Trevor on their way to a beach restaurant in Portugal: 'He was wearing a funny hat, a tee-shirt, shorts and *boots* with no socks – and, of course, all the English people in the restaurant knew who he was.' Helen admits to hating it when Trevor fails to conform to such a degree, but she is embarrassed for him rather than by him. She is really very proud of Trevor and wants a better public 'image' for him: 'I know it's silly of me. Nobody else minds. The fault is with me that I mind.'

Meanwhile, Trevor is unaware of it all. He's comfortable. In his own words, he doesn't give a Mongolian damn.

In 1973 Trevor's Guardian Angel came out of semi-retirement, spun the wheel and up came a role that Trevor's Australian friends would have called a 'beaut'. Indeed, it was one of the best parts he has ever had – and it was in a television production. *Catholics* was scripted by Brian Moore from his own novella, directed by Jack Gold and made for American CBS-TV by Sidney Glazier, a man of great courage. The location was Sherkin Island, County Cork, and the cast included the lovely Irish actor, Cyril Cusack, and a brilliant young American, Martin Sheen.

Religion as a subject for prime-time television in any country was a bold choice; in America it was revolutionary. Brian Moore had set his vision of religious conflict in the future, when the Latin Mass had been abolished, private confession outlawed and theological liberalism and social activism replaced the old orthodoxy. The old Abbot of Muck Abbey – Trevor Howard – had upheld the traditional faith and continued with the Latin Mass, thus attracting believers from far and wide and satisfying the needs of his own gentle flock. But Rome must be obeyed, so Father Kinsella – Martin Sheen – is sent to put down the insurrection. The ecumenical battle for the new faith against the old is fought between Father Kinsella and the Abbot. But for years the Abbot had doubted his own faith and desperately tries to regain it by leading his gentle but rebellious flock in prayer. He fails. He is lost in the spiritual void, the null.

The production was a triumph for all concerned: beautifully directed and superbly acted, it was lauded from coast to coast in America and wherever else it was ultimately shown. In France, footage was added for distribution in cinemas. It is something of a mystery that, although *Catholics* won the 1974 Peabody Award, it attracted not a single coveted Emmy. Martin Sheen and Cyril Cusack received high praise for their performances and John J. O'Connor wrote in the *New York Times*: 'Trevor Howard's Abbot is nothing short of magnificent, a dominating figure of craggy gruffness and sophisticated humanity.'

It was one of Trevor Howard's happiest and most rewarding roles. When engaged in a personal rating of the many productions he has been in he has one word for *Catholics*, it is 'huge'. His performance gave rise to many letters in which the writers were questioning their own faith, even from priests and clergy: 'They don't realize you are an actor. They have been so moved by the performance, they feel you might be able to help. You get a feeling of deep humility because you cannot, of course, advise them at all. But it is warming and it does make you grateful for having a chance to do such things.'

A letter greatly treasured by Trevor was written by Graham Greene:

> *My Dear Trevor,*
>
> As I no longer live in London I missed your film *Catholics* until last night when I saw it on television. I can't describe how moved I was by your performance; there were tears in my eyes at the end and I had to take a pill to sleep. For me it was one of the two finest performances I have ever seen on the screen or the stage – and I write 'one of the two' only because otherwise you mightn't believe me.
>
> I write this with the cold wisdom of next morning, not in the flush of first enthusiasm.
>
> *Affectionately,*
> Graham

Some time after *Catholics* had been shown, the brilliant Peter Brook was discussing a production of a religious nature he had in mind with Trevor. Suddenly he wanted to know into which retreat Trevor had gone before playing the Abbot – and how much time he had spent there. When told that Trevor hadn't gone anywhere, including into retreat, before making the film, Brook was amazed. He had been so impressed by Trevor's performance he felt sure that some kind of spiritual preparation had been necessary before playing the role. Gently, Trevor pointed out that he was an actor, which puzzled Peter Brook a bit as far as Trevor could tell. However, Trevor realized that Brook was of a younger generation and probably believed in such a preparation for the part.

'I don't think they understand how the older generation works. The theory was that I had to go into a monastery to catch whatever it was the monks had got.' It would have been an unlikely sortie for Trevor Howard. As it was he approached playing the Abbot in the way he approaches playing anything else – not knowing how he does it. He accepted the natural order of things; the character was first a human being, then a man, then a priest. Of the last, magnificent scene he says: 'I didn't think about it. I was caught in the story, which helped me. I was a man who'd lost his faith, I had no lines and it was a close-up of me, holding it in because I was on the verge of crying – it was just despair. There was no retake. Of course, if you don't do it as well as that at once, you never will.' He makes it sound so simple.

1974 marked ten years since Trevor Howard had appeared in the theatre, not counting a brief appearance two years earlier in an excerpt from *Separate Tables*. This had been in a charity performance to celebrate Terence Rattigan's knighthood. February 1974 saw Trevor at the Haymarket Theatre playing in Anouilh's *The Waltz of the Toreadors* opposite Coral Browne. The play had its first English production in 1956 with Hugh Griffith and Beatrix Lehmann and some plays, like some wines, lose their bouquet after twenty years. However, the role of General St-Pé is nothing if not meaty; it is also very long, since the general is off for only a page and a half of dialogue throughout the play.

Although Trevor Howard's working roots were in the theatre, ten years away from playing a very big part in public and continuity was a hell of a long time. He was risking a lot, including loss of lines and reputation.

Much had changed in the theatre since Trevor's early years, both in content and directorial approach. Indeed, nothing was quite the same after John Osborne's *Look Back in Anger*. But Trevor Howard's name was never down for this new school, possibly because he seemed always to be making films. It was a pity because he had much to offer, as Tony Richardson discovered in *The Charge of the Light Brigade* – and Richardson was one of the masters of the new school. From time to time Trevor had been quoted as having plans to do *The Entertainer* but that must have been wistful thinking.

Since the only discipline acceptable to Trevor Howard relates to his work, he is at variance with too loose a form of direction as he is with dictators as opposed to directors. The former he calls fraying away: 'Another form of Stanislawsky stuff from the apprentices — and God help us if we're going back to that.' Equally alien are the dictators: 'The ones who put you in corsets, or ride you like a horse because their own vision has to be met. They're so certain of it. And you never know in the theatre. You know in a film because you fiddle around with it until you've got what everybody wants. In the theatre, once it's set, you've got it for however long it lasts.'

His ideal director is the one who works with the cast in a spirit of enthusiasm but 'some don't even speak to the cast apart from "Do this or do that". No sort of keenness about it.' Certainly actors are unlikely to give of their best if they are robbed of stimulation and treated like pieces of machinery. Not that this applies only to actors. It's a little accepted truth that everybody needs an audience; the dog for whom a stick is thrown, the housewife who has laboured over a delicious dinner, the artist, the musician, the plumber and his mate, as well as the fine actor playing Hamlet. Everybody needs appreciation or informed criticism.

Many of Trevor's contemporaries assimilated new plays and young directors with greater ease because they worked more frequently in the theatre than in films, but the gaps had been too frequent and too long for Trevor. *The Waltz of the Toreadors* was an unhappy experience for him and he doesn't think anybody enjoyed it very much. Also he was scared: 'I don't think one feels one will be, but I was nervous because I wasn't happy somehow. Of course, if you've once learnt to swim you won't drown. You never really forget and I've never really been frightened, but I just didn't enjoy it any more. And I'll never go back again.'

In spite of Trevor's miseries and fears, one reviewer who found the play had aged wrote: 'Trevor Howard plays General St-Pé most engagingly. Unable to suppress his immense natural charm and humour, the actor takes an amused, sidelong glance at the old reprobate, endows him with crooning cadences reminiscent of the great and unforgotten Wilfrid Lawson ... Only the flicker of lechery keeps him going.' It was a case of 'Up the back stairs and the best of luck,' as the general says in the play.

The run of *The Waltz of the Toreadors* was over when, in the last week of July, Trevor's remarkable mother collapsed. She had been cared for to the end of her days by Merla and although her sight had failed, her mind remained crystal clear. She finally died on 30 July 1974 and was cremated at Golders Green. Since she had trafficked with her age as a young girl, neither Trevor nor his sister could be certain of it exactly but Merla knows that their mother was well into her nineties. She had had a long and rewarding life.

After a couple of small parts in dull films, Trevor Howard entered into his first cinematic romp, *The Bawdy Adventures of Tom Jones*, directed by Cliff Owen, and purporting to be a musical version of the original story. Among an interesting cast was the redoubtable Joan Collins, playing Black Bess for all she was worth. Trevor found that playing the Squire was huge fun, he sang and romped and loved it. Douglas Slocombe, one of that small band of superb cameramen who don't want to direct, had first met Trevor in Palermo when Helen was making *His Excellency* for Ealing Studios in the early Fifties. Trevor was there to be with Helen, not to work, and he found himself in excellent drinking company with the brilliant but self-destructive Robert Hamer, and Douglas Slocombe, who remembers that the unit had taken over a pleasant hotel overlooking the sea.

Trevor and Slocombe had met fairly constantly when both were working in the same studios but on different films. Slocombe found Trevor to be a delightful friend and always loved seeing him. Until *Bawdy Tom Jones* they had never worked together, and although Slocombe has no affection for the film he says: 'Trevor is an amazing man – he has extraordinary quality. Even in that terrible Tom Jones thing, what he did was quite wonderful. The only reason to see the film would be to see what he did. It was ghastly material but he's such a remarkable pro that even if he doesn't really like the script, if he says he'll do it he gives it everything. He's got tremendous humour and warmth but he never curries favour.'

Douglas Slocombe feels that, as one of Britain's great actors, Trevor Howard has been sadly underrated. He also thinks – as does Trevor – that every studio had its own list of runners. There was a certain loyalty to people who 'didn't cause too much trouble', who were known qualities even if dull. This is quite true, as anyone who has sat in on casting sessions could attest. By virtue of his métier, the cameraman has the sharpest view of a film being made and can rapidly assess an artiste's calibre: 'Trevor is a very generous performer – he'll downstage rather than upstage.'

Apart from the sport involved in the playing, *The Bawdy Adventures of Tom Jones* did little for Trevor Howard except to cause lifted eyebrows and wonderment that he had accepted such a role in such a film. It was the old story: there was nothing better on offer.

Although Christopher Lee had known Trevor for many years and had played with him in one scene in *Cockleshell Heroes*, which amounted to a salute and a handshake, he had never worked closely with him until they came together in Rhodesia to make *Death in the Sun*. As far as Trevor was concerned it was 'a few days work and a new place to go'. For Christopher Lee, actually sharing Trevor's scenes amounted to a revelation: 'I couldn't take my eyes off him and I came very close to drying because I was so absorbed by the skill, the thought and the dedication that Trevor brought to his work.' Hitherto, Lee had known Trevor as a kind, charming and very good friend, a man without malice with whom he had spent much time talking cricket and meeting at Lord's. Seeing Trevor in action was a mouth-opener – Lee nearly found himself gaping.

Apart from wearing fangs with great effect for Hammer Films, Christopher Lee is a cultured, erudite man with a gift for languages. He has a highly developed critical sense and is not given to fulsome praise in order to please. He regards Trevor Howard as the finest British film actor of his time – this without any doubt. Apart from Ralph Richardson, Trevor is the only actor he can think of who can take the ordinary and make it extraordinary. In every role Trevor has played he *became* the character, never Trevor Howard *playing* the character. In everything that he and Ralph Richardson have done, they have vanished into their roles. Lee sees Trevor as a man of unusual skill as an actor, with enormous intensity and integrity 'who would quite cheerfully do one day, one week, one month or one year in a film'. The year might be stretching Trevor's cheerfulness but he has certainly proved that he can make his mark in one day.

Trevor's next near-award was an Emmy Nomination for a television production made in Rome. He played an old man, a long-time prisoner in the Château d'If, in *The Count of Monte Cristo*.

If newspaper headlines were to be believed, Trevor was in danger of being incarcerated elsewhere and much closer to home on an Income Tax charge. Although Trevor could not, at the point of a gun, have explained his actual tax position, he was swift to add fuel to the flames for the benefit of the daily readers; if he wasn't facing a prison sentence he was certainly about to become a bankrupt, and the news was as big as the headlines. It was also beautifully inaccurate, but rather unfortunately Trevor's man of affairs, Bernard Kimble, was on holiday at the time, so the sorting of fact from fiction had to await his return. Bernard Kimble is very lucid on the difference between tax avoidance as opposed to tax evasion: the former being the favourite dish of bright accountants and the latter totally illegal. Since he guards the well-being of many artistes and since the diligent Inland Revenue have ways of transforming avoidance into evasion overnight, Bernard Kimble is honour bound to evolve the best possible plans to safeguard his clients. When one plan is put out of court, by something like Section 28 or a gear-change by the Inland Revenue, another takes its place. However, since tax is retrospective, the validity of the former plan often has to be argued in court.

Such was the case when Trevor Howard hit the headlines in 1975 and, although he didn't know it, his was one of many being guided by the estimable Bernard Kimble who arrived at a reasonable settlement with the Inland Revenue very quickly. Far from being rendered bankrupt, Trevor felt no financial pain at all. Not being the last of the big-time spenders his tax was met by accrued interest – and Bernard Kimble went on to make other plans. His attitude to an artiste's use of money is that if they could be persuaded not to be extravagant when the money is rolling in, by the time their tax is negotiated the sum due can be paid out of growth – since it usually takes several years to reach an agreement with the Inland Revenue. This is an accurate assessment, and a lovely dream. Trevor Howard is probably unique among his peers in causing Bernard Kimble's dream to come true; he has to be exhorted to spend money, not to save it. He has never sought a tax exile and if he had a second's doubt that his income tax lay unpaid, he would be the unhappiest man in the world. With Bernard Kimble attending to the mysteries of his business affairs he knows himself to be secure from penury, prison or bankruptcy.

Nevertheless, one of his statements to the press followed him to Australia in May 1975: 'In a lifetime of work for the British film industry I have never left Britain and now I'm going to find myself practically bankrupt. I may have to go to prison.' Quizzed on this quote, he shifted ground: 'There's no truth in the fact that one's in trouble. It was just me blowing my top and that's all there is to it.' And so it was, but it might be suspected that he had momentarily rather enjoyed the idea of being victimized and imprisoned for non-payment of tax. The reality would have been quite a different matter.

This visit to the other side of the world included a tour of Melbourne, Canberra, Sydney and Auckland, New Zealand to promote *Eleven Harrowhouse*. Again, he was in the capable and friendly hands of Bill Band. Band's report of the press interviews, television appearances, civic engagements et al covers five closely typed sheets of Twentieth Century Fox paper. It is an itinerary that could have felled a man half Trevor's age and in no way reflects the supposed habits of a much-vaunted hell-raiser. Rather it is the all-out effort of a travelling salesman honourably flogging a dubious product. Bill Band notes in his report: 'Although the figures for 11 Harrowhouse are not spectacular, the film would not have got off the ground but for Trevor's visit.'

It might cause wonderment that an actor of Trevor Howard's stature should be willing to follow such an exhausting trail in order to promote an unwarrantable film. The reason could be that Trevor never dwells on his 'stature' — that can be left properly to others. He also loves Australia and his friends there and he had nothing better to do. If he is not working he would accept a commission to go and sell ice to Eskimos — just give him a ticket and book his hotel.

However, more was achieved than publicity on that visit: Trevor engaged to make an Australian film the following year. This was *Eliza Fraser*, with Susannah York and Noël Ferrier. Trevor returned to Australia in the spring of 1976 for pre-production interviews, costuming and chats with the director, Tim Burstall. The story of *Eliza Fraser* was based on fact. In 1836, a tea-clipper, called the *Stirling Castle*, was wrecked off an island on a voyage from Sydney to Singapore, Captain Fraser was killed by Aborigines and his wife taken captive but survived to marry again. The wrecking island is now known as Fraser Island and the story has become part of Australian folklore. Sidney Nolan, the great Australian artist, has painted pictures commemorating the tale.

While waiting to start location work, Trevor stayed with his friend Bill Band — or Handholder, as Trevor called him. During the Easter weekend, Trevor expressed a desire to visit Googie Withers and her husband, John McCallum. Bill Band made arrangements for them to go to lunch and, thinking to give pleasure to all concerned, also arranged for them to pay a visit to his friends, Gilly Stone and his family, on the way. The Stones were delighted to be meeting Trevor Howard and gave him and Bill Band a fine welcome. They arrived to find a splendidly cosy atmosphere with a log fire burning and jazz playing. First crack out of the box Trevor caught the music and yelled, 'That's Eddie Condon! You people can't be all bad if you play Condon.'

They all had a drink or two and then Bill Band thought they should be moving on to their lunch date. 'To hell with that,' said Trevor. 'We're staying here.' And stay they did, right through the day and into the night.

When they left around midnight, plans had been made to see John and Googie the following day. Relating this tale, Gilly Stone chuckled with remembered pleasure: 'Damn it if next morning at ten o'clock there wasn't a knock on the door and there stood Bill and Trevor, who wanted to hear a bit more music and have one Bloody Mary before going off to see John and Googie. And they stayed all that day too – and the night.' The unexpected visitors were furnished with razors, pyjamas and breakfast. After the last cup of coffee Trevor looked at Bill, 'One drink, Bill and we must go. We've really got to get there this time.' But they stayed that day too, and that night, totting up three days in a row. As Gilly Stone said, 'If Trevor enjoys something, he wants plenty of it.' Gilly also allowed that his guests finally went away, and finally got together with Googie Withers and John McCallum.

Trevor was just having a lovely time, enjoying the music and the cricket talk. The Stones' children were around fifteen and sixteen at the time and naturally asked Trevor all manner of questions about the actors he had worked with. Their father was most impressed: 'He never made one cruel remark about any of them.' During that Easter weekend a strong and fond friendship was formed between Gilly and Janice Stone and Trevor. It was to embrace Helen when she arrived on her first visit to Australia.

Helen recalls her flight to Australia with pure delight. The Air Malaysia plane was far from full and was scheduled to go right through to Sydney. But then they were put down at Kuala Lumpur and told to leave the plane: it was not, after all, going to Sydney. Hotel accommodation had been reserved for the passengers and while Helen was waiting for a taxi, she was joined by a charming lady wearing jeans, tee-shirt and a camera. They naturally shared the taxi and Helen confided to her new friend that she was looking forward to a bloody great drink. Her companion was all for that, she was also all for the hotel which she thought was marvellous, being delighted to find she had her own bathroom and other facilities that most travellers now take for granted.

Enquiries revealed that the passengers were to be held up for two days before catching an onward flight to Singapore and Sydney. As Helen knew nothing of Kuala Lumpur, her companion, whose name was Mary, volunteered to show her around. They had a marvellous time going all over the city by bus, seeing the sights, examining the batik and so forth. Helen thought Mary had been so kind to her that it would be a nice gesture to take her to lunch at a good restaurant instead of constantly eating at the hotel as guests of the airline. They shared a bottle of Niersteiner after an aperitif or two, dined and spent the evening together, and went off the following morning to fly to Singapore where they were to change flights.

While they were waiting for the plane to Sydney, Mary went off to the Ladies – and returned dressed in a nun's habit. 'I thought I'd better get dressed before I meet my people,' she said to a totally dumbfounded Helen, who was busy trying to remember which four-letter words she had let slip during the last forty-eight hours, and how often. Luckily their flight was called and Helen had time to rejig her thinking. As they journeyed towards Sydney, Helen learnt that Mary was a teaching sister working in New Guinea. Helen had been in first class on the plane from London so she offered Sistery Mary the gifts that were a prerequisite for travelling up front. The eyeshades were very welcome – the Bishop had once given some to Sister Mary but they were now worn out. The soft slippers were also a joy but when it came to the scent Sister Mary smiled: 'I really don't think that's much use to me, dear.'

Helen was enchanted by her: 'She was such a lovely lady – we even corresponded for a while.'

On arriving at Sydney, Helen was met by Bill Band who had met every flight since the non-arrival of her original Air Malaysia plane. Trevor had already left for work on location and, as Bill Band lived alone, it was thought to be unsuitable for Helen to stay with him. So she was invited to stay with Gilly and Janice Stone. Helen loved them: 'They were so marvellous to me, a total stranger. They could not have done more for me or been kinder to me.' She was fascinated to learn that Gilly Stone held a high position with Rothmans in Sydney although he was a non-smoker. She thought the appointment might have presented difficulties. Gilly Stone laughed and told Helen what he had told Rothmans: 'My job before this was selling sheep dip.'

Although Trevor Howard was originally offered a leading role in *Eliza Fraser*, he chose to play Captain Foster Fyans, the commandant of the prison camp at Moreton Bay. His own given reason for the choice was that Fyans was the more interesting character: 'He was a bigger sod.' Ossie Bates is pretty sure that

Trevor had looked over the fixtures and saw he would be missing a lot of cricket if he took the larger part; playing Fyans he had about two weeks' shooting out of fourteen. During the location, he acquired not only a convict's cap but also a sweatshirt with 666168 HM State Prison printed large across the chest, and wore both with great delight. Helen was not terribly enthusiastic about either garment.

For a while both Helen and Trevor stayed with Bill Band, who had a huge tame duck. Keith Miller, the Australian cricketer, had presented the duck with a mirror so that the bird wouldn't feel lonely. As it was a quackless duck, Helen spent some time teaching it to quack successfully and Trevor kept the mirror brightly polished. It's little wonder that both Helen and Trevor are adored in Australia. Gilly Stone is much impressed by Trevor's lack of side or 'being difficult'.

Jack Lee is an English director now living in Australia. He never worked with Trevor in England but they used to meet at various studios occasionally and Lee regarded Trevor Howard as an actor of such calibre that he was really in awe of him. They remet at a cricket match in Sydney. Lee is another observer who finds Trevor to be very un-actory: 'They're mostly so bloody neurotic, they go poncing about the place spending money. Trevor doesn't do that. He's not the kind of actor who goes around buying things all the time. And he never chased women. He chased a much more sensible thing – cricket.' Lee's delivery is as staccato as machine-gun fire and just as positive. He laughs as he quotes J. B. Morton (*Beachcomber*) on the subject of cricket: 'Cricket and bigamy go hand in hand.' Not always they don't.

In Sydney the term 'a clean skin' is applied to Trevor just as it is by Danny Lavezzo in New York. In Sydney it means that no scandal of any kind has touched him: 'He is the epitome of a gentleman', is the way Ossie Bates puts it.

For reasons best known to the distributors, *Eliza Fraser* was never shown in British cinemas but it did get a late airing on television during the autumn of 1985.

Sadly, 'Handholder' Bill Band is now dead but 'Sportsman' Gilly Stone remains in Sydney, eagerly looking forward to Trevor and Helen's next visit.

A story about Trevor Howard that pleases his Australian

friends, might just be true. When undergoing a routine medical check before a production, Trevor was given a test tube and shown into the relevant cubicle in order to present urine for analysis. Either through inability, a pressing engagement or plain boredom, he borrowed a little from several samples already lined up, stuck the label bearing his name on the illicit cocktail and went away. Returning a day or so later to learn the result of various tests, the doctor regarded him with some interest and said, 'I'm happy to be able to tell you, Mr Howard, that you are not pregnant.'

Although this smacks of a golden oldie invented in medical school, it is also a ploy which would be characteristic of Trevor Howard.

When Trevor and Helen returned from Australia it was to a pleasing domestic project. For years they had spent holidays in the South of France, either at their favourite hotel in Villefranche or in an apartment belonging to Euan Lloyd. For some time they had circled around the notion of finding a house of their own up in the hills behind the coast. Their long-time friend, scriptwriter Jack Davies, finally found them a little charmer just below Les Hauts de St Paul, where Jack and his wife Dorothy lived before moving to California. The purchase was completed in 1975, and they had started the process of sinking a swimming pool in the garden. Although the idea of a pool might seem like sybaritic luxury in northern climes, in the hills of the Alpes Maritimes it is virtually a necessity. The summer heat is intense and the journey down to the crowded coast is what golfers call an unplayable lie.

Despite the modernity of the house, it was designed with imaginative care and quite resembles an upmarket shooting lodge with a large fireplace and a high ceilinged, galleried main room. Just as their house at Arkley is not a film star's set, this is not a film star's villa.

When Helen had completed the decoration and furnishing of the house, they cast about to find a title by which it could be known. The garden contained a picturesque old well and it was also flanked by a vastly wooded hill in which wild game, including boar, were hunted before development and enclosures. They were reminded that this had been so on one of many visits to a family-run and excellent restaurant in nearby La Colle, Chez

Hubert. In his day, Monsieur Hubert had been an enthusiastic hunter, as had every male from growing lad to grown man in the area.

One evening Trevor and Helen were seated at dinner beneath one of Monsieur Hubert's trophies, a mounted boar's head. Madame Hubert drew their attention to it with some pride, explaining that it might even have been hunted on the very hill beside which they lived. Then lightning struck and their house became known as *Le Puits du Sanglier*. Although Monsieur Hubert has, alas, gone to supposedly happier hunting grounds, Madame carries on with the help of her daughters, and Trevor and Helen continue to enjoy their favourite local restaurant.

As in Arkley, in France Helen does the work and Trevor occasionally murmurs, 'I'll do that', without moving a muscle. Their favourite morning drink is the delicious mixture of champagne and orange juice known as Buck's Fizz in Britain and Mimosa in France. One morning Helen had nipped off to the village on some errand, leaving Trevor and their guest with charged glasses. As time went by, the glasses were emptied and Trevor wandered off to the kitchen, only to return disconsolately – without the orange juice. When Helen returned, seconds later, he looked at her pleadingly: 'Henny, darling, I couldn't find the orange juice . . .' Helen smiled, 'I expect that's because it's still in the oranges.' And she went off to squeeze them.

Trevor is happy in France, he enjoys the house, the swimming, the sun and – above all – the constant presence of Helen. In England, even if neither of them are working, Helen feels the need of 'air'. Her interests are wide and catholic and her friends numerous, all taking her off to London for a day fairly often. In France her time is exclusively for Trevor so even her absence on a domestic shopping foray leaves him twitching with muted impatience until her return.

Although Trevor is happy in France – he can even listen to the cricket and watch Wimbledon – unless he knows with certainty that there is a production awaiting his return, he becomes restive. He can almost be seen to be listening for his agent's call, and as days pass without one he becomes more than restive, he becomes patently disgruntled. This could account for his appearance on several films that are best forgotten, including another romp, *The Last Remake of Beau Geste*. Of such he says, 'These were the joke films that would never be seen and were such fun to make.' They also fed his yearning to play comedy, even if not in the ideal genre. But few first-rate film-makers can erase their image of Trevor Howard as a powerful British actor with stern and tragic overtones. To them he was always a straight and true actor with no time for comedy so, as Helen says, 'Trevor has never had the opportunity to play the sort of comedy that he'd be so marvellous in.' She is quite right, as the occasional flashes of wit that Trevor has been allowed on screen or stage bear witness.

Certainly there was nothing much to laugh about when *Slavers* was released. The film was made in Africa and directed by Jurgen Goslar. As always, Trevor gave of his best in what amounted to an unambitious pot-boiler. Christmas 1976 found him, somewhat astonishingly, in the Royal Alexandra Theatre, Toronto, Canada. He was there to play an alcoholic scriptwriter, d'Anthac, in *The Scenario*, by Anouilh. Earlier, he had been invited to Toronto to appear in a play of his own choice but through modesty, indecision or plain idleness, he had failed to offer a personal choice and therefore took what he was given. With Trevor Howard's name and also that of Anouilh, the piece was a sure-fire success for its month's run. Also the producers, Duncan Weldon and Louis Michaels, were no strangers to success.

For Trevor, the puzzle was the play. Even before playing in *The Waltz of the Toreadors*, he was no stranger to the works of the distinguished author – no actor was – but here he found loose ends and strange construction. He came to a conclusion which he has retained, namely that it was an old play which had lain long at the back of a drawer and could now be aired under the flag of Anouilh's current fame. By Trevor's standards, it wasn't quite good enough.

Helen Cherry was also in *The Scenario*, which was splendid for Trevor but although Helen enjoyed working instead of just being there, she found that the pleasure of playing with Trevor in the theatre had dimmed because she was regarded less as an actress than as the star's wife.

Wives of the famous often feel they have to fight for their corner if they are to retain a sense of personal identity and often the battle becomes very unattractive, resulting in diminished returns. But Helen Cherry is also a professional and very much her own lady. She remembers a dinner party given by a maharajah in Bombay. Helen was seated next to her host who wanted to know why she was not beside her husband. Delicately she explained that in England it was not customary *placement* for husbands and wives to sit together at a formal dinner, and asked whether this was the custom in India. Always, she was told, because then the wives have some identity. Helen replied that the only way she retained her identity was when she *didn't* sit next to her husband. This was not quite accurate for a lady of Helen's charisma, neither is Trevor a husband who enjoys overshadowing his wife. Such husbands exist but he is not of their number, he is far too fond and proud of her.

During the next two years Trevor Howard worked occasionally, but not often enough to satisfy him. Either the roles were not there or they were not offered to him and he still drew the line at appearing in blatant rubbish. He had time to visit Helen in South America, where she was touring in a play, and he went to Cairo where he was chairman of the jury at a film festival. He also made a rare appearance on British television playing Chief Inspector Mavor, a tough hard drinking character, in *Easterman*, a play in a group of five called *Scorpion Tales*. He was a natural for the part and although his performance was appreciated, *The Times* noted: 'A pity that Trevor Howard , in a much too rare television appearance, is yet another controversial policeman.' Thereby proving that nobody can win them all.

Trevor also accepted small roles in three supposed 'large scale' films – *Meteor*, *Superman*, and *Hurricane* – and claimed he had trouble distinguishing one role from another. His opinion of spectaculars which rely heavily on special effects is that the actors don't really matter. Their names might attract the audiences but, once inside the cinema, it was the metaphorical thunder and lightning that captured them rather than fine performances. *Hurricane* was shot on Bora-Bora, to which Trevor adds the prefix Boring, and was engineered by Dino De Laurentiis who had built a settlement on the island to house the crew and artistes. In fact, the settlement was destined to become an hotel, which led Trevor to grant De Laurentiis full marks as an entrepreneur while feeling that he cared very little about the film.

James Michener has described Bora-Bora as the paradise island of the world and Trevor Howard thinks he must have seen it from an aircraft. 'There's a Chinese store and a rock – and that's it.' Helen, who was with him on the island for six weeks, thoroughly enjoyed it. She liked the sun and the swimming and made friends with some of the local inhabitants, such as the doctor and his wife. The pace of life there suited her and she visited the Club Méditerranée 'where they had champagne you could put on your credit card. Little comforts like that.'

Trevor and Helen returned to England by way of Los Angeles, where Helen arrived sporting a beautiful black eye and a bruised jaw, the results of a fall in the shower. Trevor speedily claimed credit for both injuries, seeking the tag of wife-beater, on the well-used grounds that it 'made a better story'. They were also in Los Angeles to attend the opening of *Stevie*, a film that had been made in England.

Stevie had been adapted by Hugh Whitemore from his stage play and directed by Robert Enders. It deals with the life and works of the poetess, Stevie Smith. Glenda Jackson played the name role with Mona Washbourne as her aunt. Trevor Howard played The Man, a character embodying a number of Stevie Smith's literary friends and admirers, forming a link between the film and the audience whom he addresses directly through the camera.

Although Trevor has said he didn't really know what he was doing in his role, he found relief in playing a production that seemed to him worthwhile at last. 'It was a very special, different picture and it was a real pleasure to work with Glenda. She was marvellous.' He also much admired Mona Washbourne's performance and thought she warranted an Oscar for Best Supporting Actress.

When *Stevie* was released, Trevor Howard was approaching his sixty-second birthday. He had long proved himself to be a great actor with a vast, seemingly limitless range. He had no physical disabilities, his presence on-screen had strengthened rather than diminished and his voice was even more compelling than in earlier years. Yet he was driven to feeling gratitude when he was offered a telling cameo role in a decent production. He was not only underrated, he was overlooked. But not by the press. Interviewers in Britain, America and Australia wrote of him with respect and affection. By now he had become 'that great veteran of many films' or 'Britain's much-loved character actor', but none expressed the belief that his long song was almost finished or that he was nearing retirement. They were wise enough to know that actors seldom retire, they like to take their place on the celestial stage already made-up.

At last Trevor's idling Guardian Angel realized that he was still protecting one of the most able actors on earth and placed a small package containing true worth in his path. This was Antoine de Saint-Exupéry's *Night Flight*, and it was a very small package indeed, since it was planned as a twenty-two minute television special; or thirty minutes including the commercials.

The support for the production came from a quite unusual source: the Singer Company, famous for its sewing machines but perhaps less known for its long association with aviation. Saint-Exupéry's marvellously moving story is widely held to have been autobiographical since it is about the early days of aviation, around 1930, when a small French airline operating in South America was striving to establish the reliability of airmail. Saint-Exupéry was a French airmail pilot who was killed during the Second World War, flying reconnaissance missions. He was also a superb writer.

Night Flight was shot in Montreal and directed by Britain's Desmond Davis. Bo Svenson plays the doomed pilot, Fabien, and the Canadian actress, Céline Lomez, the wife who waits until waiting no longer applies. The centre of the structure is Trevor Howard as Rivière, a veteran flyer who is now the hard-bitten master of the fleet which operates out of Buenos Aires. Fabien is on a night flight from Paraguay, flying through a storm in his open-cockpit plane, while Rivière tries to guide him in by radio from the operations office. Their only hope is the radio – and it fails.

Today air travel is commonplace, fifty-five years ago it was an adventure, filled with dread or an almost holy joy, elevating the flier beyond recognition of certain disaster. It is the joy that Saint-Exupéry celebrated: 'They flew in submission to those elemental divinities – day, night, mountain, sea and storm.'

Desmond Davis and his cast captured the very essence of Saint-Exupéry which was no mean feat, and even the music reflects his dedication to the air.

The scenes between Trevor Howard and Céline Lomez are remarkable for their intensity, their spoken thoughts being intercut, both striving for self-knowledge in the face of tragedy. Here Trevor Howard has some of the best lines of his screen career: 'I believe that human life is precious. But my pilots and I believe there is something more valuable than our lives. What that is I don't know. The future perhaps ... we are not asking to be eternal. All we want is that the objects we live by do not lose their meaning.'

Night Flight might have been a small package, but it proved yet again that small is beautiful. Céline Lomez paid Trevor Howard an elegant compliment: 'It's lovely working with Trevor – like a waltz with a great partner. He carries you.'

American critics welcomed the film with the acclaim it deserved. In the *New York Post*, Tom Topor wrote: 'At bottom, it is about the conflict between a "normal" life and the seductions of living – and dying – in the air. This is not an easy conflict to get across in a 30-minute film but the Singer Co hired a secret weapon, and his name is Trevor Howard ... he manages with a few inflections, and a few expressions, to deliver both a man and a theme.'

Trevor and Helen were briefly in America for the press shows of *Night Flight* in January 1979. They then returned to England where Trevor was signed to play in *The Missionary* with Maggie Smith. The script had the kind of ironic overtones that pleased Trevor as it told of a young man who had been sent back to England from Africa, where he served as a missionary, in order to study 'fallen women' in the streets of London. His natural involvement with them being the nub of the story. Trevor loved making it and thought it was very well and tastefully done.

He then had a sportive time playing in *The Shillingbury Blowers* for ATV. As Old Saltie, the conductor of the Shillingbury Brass Band, he manages to get the better of a pop musician and his wife when they become involved with the opposing side in the brass band contest. It was the stuff of which Ealing comedies used to be made, and in America, it was felicitously retitled *And the Band Plays On*.

CHAPTER FOURTEEN

So far, the present decade has treated Trevor Howard well. There is a welcome aura of renascence around the strength of his roles. Apart from their infinite variety, some have been counter to his previous public image, but that's as may be; Trevor revels in metamorphosis as does any world-class actor.

Admittedly *The Sea Wolves* rang no change but it meant a far-flung location, Goa, and a distinguished cast of friends – Gregory Peck, David Niven and Roger Moore. The film didn't do a lot for anybody, but it was highly pleasing company.

In terms of entertainment available on both sizes of screen, the early 1980s might well become known as the Indian Period. Such a plethora of subjects with an Indian background could have arisen from increasing interest in the works of Paul Scott since the publication in 1966 of *The Jewel in the Crown*, the first volume of the Raj Quartet. In 1980, his coda to the Quartet, *Staying On*, was made in India for British television with Celia Johnson and Trevor Howard. It was their first appearance together since *Brief Encounter* and it was a *tour de force*. It seemed nothing short of genius to have cast the two lovers of the earlier film in a story that almost suggested what might have happened had their encounter not been brief but enduring. However, no genius was at work because the role of Lucy was originally to have been played by Dame Wendy Hiller. Indeed, the very idea of dramatizing *Staying On* emanated from Wendy Hiller, or, to be quite accurate, her brother.

Dame Wendy's brother had urged her to read the book, which she did. She also understood why he had so advised her. 'This will do nicely,' she thought and her husband, playwright Ronald Gow, agreed. Later she realized she should have bought the rights straightaway. When Warriss Hossein, a director for Anglia TV, rang her to suggest a revival of *A Passage to India*, she countered with the more up-to-date *Staying On*, luckily leaving E. M. Forster's work to a wider screen and Sir David Lean.

Anglia bought the rights, Hossein and Dame Wendy met to consolidate the shooting dates and then Hossein suddenly discovered that the dates agreed could not be met by him. He had some episodes of another programme to complete. Loyally, Dame Wendy said, 'Oh, well. I suppose we can accommodate you.' Later she added, 'I tried to accommodate him, Anglia tried to accommodate him – and the way he accommodated us was to get rid of a very good scriptwriter, take the property away from Anglia and get it to somewhere else. Then came a great television strike.' The 'somewhere else' was Granada Television.

The next blow for Dame Wendy was the grapevine news that Trevor Howard wasn't interested in *Staying On*. This was really bad because as far as Dame Wendy was concerned there were lots of ladies who could play Lucy, 'but there was only one Tusker and that was Trev'. So she sent him a copy of the book and a note, written large and clear:

> *Dear Trevor,*
>   Don't be stupid. You must have got an off-putting script or you can't have read it properly. I'm doing you a favour. Read this.
>
> > *Love and kisses,*
> > Wendy.

'Right,' says Trevor. Having read the original story of course he wanted to do it.

Then Dame Wendy's agent took a hand. His view being that she had waited far too long for *Staying On*, there was a part for her in *Elephant Man*, and a film in the hand ... and so on. So Dame Wendy accepted *Elephant Man*, 'and then most of my part was cut out of the picture. In the beginning I had quite a nice role. It was the only time I've sat through a film and been really annoyed. I don't often sit through them – leave alone get annoyed.'

It was all very rough on Dame Wendy and, ironically, Celia Johnson wasn't too enthusiastic about working on location in India. Although Trevor makes no such claim, it's most likely that he was the persuaded who turned persuader. Thus it was that televiewers in Britain, America and elsewhere were able to marvel at the well-remembered lovers, Celia Johnson and Trevor Howard, in *Staying On*, finally directed by Silvio Narizzano.

It is no slight to Dame Wendy Hiller that Trevor revelled in playing with Celia Johnson again. He has great affection and respect for both actresses but, after all, his first screen triumph was with Celia Johnson even if he does wince when he appears to be remembered only for the film *Brief Encounter*. He has always been discreet when asked to name his favourite leading lady but, if backed to the wall, his answer is always Celia Johnson.

There is a great distance between India and Salt Lake City, but the span between the roles of Tusker and a Cheyenne warrior is even greater. As disparate parts go this was Trevor Howard's biggest and boldest leap yet.

In *Windwalker* Trevor Howard plays the title role, an octogenarian Cheyenne chief. The film is set in 1979 and is based on a novel by Blaine Yorgason. It tells the story of Windwalker who dies of old age but is brought back to life by the Great Spirit to be reunited with his long-lost son, and to help his family to do battle once again against their born enemy the Crow tribe.

Trevor was the only member of the cast of sixty who was not a native American; it included Nick Ramus, Serene Hedin, Dusty Iron Wing McCrea and Harold Goss-Coyote. The film was shot in the High Uintas mountains and Salt Lake City, under the direction of Kieth Merrill, a young man who had already won an Academy Award for a documentary, *The Great American Cowboy*. The producers were Arthur R. Dubs and Thomas Ballard and the production company, Pacific International Enterprises, represented the new genre of film-makers. They didn't operate out of Hollywood or New York, they were to be found in Medford, Oregon. They were independent producers, in the true sense, and *Windwalker* was their most ambitious production to date.

As far as Trevor Howard was concerned the proposition 'just came out of the blue'. It was different and it was certainly a challenge, so he agreed, Helen packed, and off they went to Utah.

During the first day of shooting he realized just how great a challenge it was. He lay on his funeral pyre in blazing sun wearing contact lenses for the first time in his life. When he could no longer bear the agony, it was agreed that he had better play Windwalker as a blue-eyed American Indian, 'as many of them were', he points out.

In the course of the production Trevor climbed mountains, wrestled bears and fell through ice. Physically, it was a tough location for a man of his near-sixty-four years – and he loved every second. Much of his dialogue was in Cheyenne, and he spoke it, it wasn't dubbed. In all, *Windwalker* stretched even Trevor Howard's unbounded talent as it had seldom been stretched before. He saw his role as 'an Indian King Lear' and he was not far wrong. When Kieth Merrill was asked why he had cast Trevor Howard as an American Indian, he replied that he wanted the best actor he could think of.

One of the problems besetting such an independent production is distribution. Having no vast, established machinery behind it, it has to be sold, as it were, by hand. Wherever *Windwalker* was shown, the critics applauded it. *Film Bulletin* called it 'one of the year's five best films'. *Screen International* believed that Trevor Howard's performance was an Oscar certainty, as did the *Detroit Free Press*. The cameraman and the composer also received particular notice: 'Reed Smoot's photography of the beautiful Utah mountains and valleys will win an Oscar Nomination for sure.' Merrill Jenson's music was also cited as having good Oscar potential.

This was a film that needed an Oscar, or even a Nomination; either would have ensured world-wide distribution. *Windwalker* failed to classify as a foreign film because it was released after 31 October – the deadline for foreign entrants – and it was unacceptable as an American film because of the Academy ruling that any film with a basically non-English sound track is foreign. It was a classic example of Catch-22, since a film about American Indians could hardly be more indigenous.

In Hollywood the major film companies were having their own problems, making high-budget films that failed to attract audiences. Many millions of dollars were going down the drain so it has to be supposed that the powers-that-be – or were – had to protect their own.

The lack of an Oscar would never haunt Trevor Howard and he still regards *Windwalker* as one of the best roles in one of the best films that has ever come his way.

While *Windwalker* was struggling for recognition in its native land, the old Cheyenne warrior could be seen on British screens wearing black face, a wig and riding a unicycle clad in spangled drag. Breadth of range could hardly have gone further.

'I don't know what I want but I want it *now!*' yells Trevor Howard as Sir Henry in *Sir Henry at Rawlinson End*. Whatever it was, he got it and plenty more from Vivian Stanshall, the eccentric genius who was behind – and in – the film. *Sir Henry* was first born of Vivien Stanshall on John Peel's radio show in 1977: a permanently pissed feudal jingoist whose motto is *Omnes Blotto*, who plays war games with German prisoners of war kept as pets on his estate, and who protects himself from his wife's advances with a barrier of barbed wire around his bed. As a kind of musical event, this lovable character became a popular album, a book and, as a film, the most anarchical British comedy ever. No *Lares* or *Peanates* remain intact, no shibboleth rests unturned, no joke is too old to be revamped, and if some of the new ones cause Aunt Hettie to wrinkle her nose, they equally give Uncle Bert a belly-laugh. The line 'If I had all the money I've spent on drink, I'd spend it on drink,' finds its way straight to the hearts of the faithful.

As the outrageously eccentric aristocrat with his id firmly mired in the past Empire glories – 'Never met a man I didn't mutilate' – Trevor Howard was in a brand-new comedic element, visually and vocally. Vivien Stanshall, who shared the script-writing credit with the director, Steve Roberts, thought of *Sir Henry* as sur-Ealing comedy. Many critics thought of Monty Python or the Goons with overtones of James Joyce and Dylan Thomas; they also saw a film that might become a cult. Since it was shot in black and white in three weeks and cost less than half a million dollars, it certainly deserves a place in any film history of its time.

Vivien Stanshall's first reaction to Trevor Howard as Sir Henry was that Trevor was too upper-crust and wouldn't do at all. It is a measure of Stanshall's integrity that he didn't seize upon such a famed actor, right or wrong. When the film was finished he found that Trevor was more like Sir Henry than his own creation.

By rote, eyebrows were raised at the very idea of Straight-bat

Howard appearing in such an esoteric jape and he knew it: "Why on earth is he doing that film?' they'll say, and the answer is, because I want to do it. I might never get the offer to do such a thing again.' And he didn't, because there never was quite such a thing again. Trevor thought the film highly comic and a film to see more than once, 'People want to see it again and again because you can't grasp it all at once. It's *wild*.'

Dilys Powell appreciated Patrick Magee as the Reverend Stodden and J. G. Devlin as Old Scrotum, the butler: 'But on the whole this is a jest to be heard, not seen, except for Trevor Howard as the shoot-the-lot reactionary. Mr Howard offers a caricature. But it is jolly caricature, enjoyable. He enjoys himself.' And so he did.

Tom Buckley, in the *New York Times*, makes mention of a 'comically inflated narration that suggests at various times Fielding at his most orotund, Ezra Pound and T. S. Eliot.' Add them to some British critics' choice of James Joyce and Dylan Thomas, stir well and there's a very heady mixture in the punch-bowl.

Although American television had given Trevor Howard excellent chances to show his worth for many years, his home market had been lagging behind. Possibly *Catholics* and *Staying On* prompted his being cast as Jonathan Swift in BBC 2's *No Country for Old Men*, with Cyril Cusack, one of Trevor's favourite actors.

Swift was a particularly difficult character to get inside and Trevor has always been meticulous when depicting historical reality. It helped when he could recognize certain quirks which he shared, such as Swift's unwillingness to be understood, his need for secrecy — and his sadness. All are in Trevor's own nature.

The Times showed awareness that American television had been getting the best of Trevor Howard: 'But British television is now getting the message. Jack Gold's superb *Catholics* . . . Paul Scott's *Staying On* and Tristram Powell's *No Country for Old Men* have brought Howard to our small screens with gratifying regularity and consistent distinction.'

On 19 May 1981, a Franco-Swiss co-operation, starring Trevor

Howard, was shown at the Cannes Film Festival. This was the full evening dress, studded-with-stars showing; a few days earlier it had been shown to the Festival Jury at eleven o'clock in the morning. As jurist Douglas Slocombe emerged from the dark theatre into the Côte d'Azur sun, he heard a familiar bull moose roar and there was Trevor. Slocombe greeted him with the news that he had just been watching Trevor in *Light Years Away*, and thought he was wonderful. 'Tell me,' said Trevor, 'what was it about?' Slocombe reflected that if Trevor hadn't found out in three months, he certainly couldn't find out in two hours.

The script of *Light Years Away* had been given to Trevor by the Swiss director, Alain Tanner, the previous year when he had visited Trevor and Helen in France. Later Trevor said, 'I thought when I read it that this seemed like lunacy, so let's do it. I do love to take risks.' The film, based on a novel by Daniel Odier, *La Voie Sauvage*, was scripted and directed by Alain Tanner and shot in Ireland. Trevor Howard plays Yoshka Poliakoff, an old Russian immigrant, a hermit sage, a mystic dreamer – or a mad old coot, depending on the viewer's susceptibility. His young protégé, or pupil, Jonas, is played beautifully by Mick Ford and Trevor more than deserved the 1982 Best Actor Evening Standard Award which he received; just as the film fully warranted the Special Jury Prize it received at the Cannes Film Festival.

The film has all the magical quality of an ancient legend: the Wise Old Man testing the young neophyte with imponderable task after task until he proves himself worthy to share the Old Man's secret dream – that man can fly as a bird. However, the protagonists are not clad in samite but in cloth caps and ragged tweeds, or old jeans and tee-shirts. They live today, thus the film plants seeds of reassurance that man is still entitled to dream.

In *The Times* David Robinson wrote; 'The old man, lurching between senile crabbiness and beatific serenity, is Trevor Howard, whose vasts gifts British films consistently squander.' Dilys Powell recalled the film with joy: '*Light Years Away* was a ravishing picture and I thought Trevor's was a wonderful performance. A mad, beautiful performance. There again, in his best there is the accent of tragedy. He must attract tragedy really. It was a perfectly graded performance – the rejecting of the boy and then the embracing. And, of course, you thought he *ought* to be able to fly.'

Devoted as Trevor Howard will always be to his game, his hobby – as he calls his work – he has had to come to terms with the change of pace in shooting for both large screen and small. Inaudible hurry-music haunts sets and locations; films are shot in weeks instead of months or years, and television schedules are a matter of days. No longer can director and cameraman wait for the passing of a cloud. It all makes great economic sense, but it is hard on old-timers who have become used to more leisurely ways. Cameo 'guest star' appearances are in another category but are often no easier for the player. As Judge Broomfield, Trevor Howard worked for two days in Sir Richard Attenborough's *Gandhi* in 1983. Because Trevor wasn't immediately available, Sir Richard was prepared to wait for him: 'You name the date and we'll do it on that date, I said, because I wanted him just desperately. The Judge was a very remarkable man and he had about forty words, or less, to present in that one scene, all that had to be said of the greatness and stature of the Indian Civil Service. That was not the story, the film was *Gandhi*, which highlit many faults in colonialism. But tribute had to be paid to the great British figures who had contributed so much to India's past, to the great compassion of those figures.

'If the performance of the Judge had been anything less than great, that whole element in the film would not have been satisfied. My conscience in regard to the people who thought the film too critical of the British is totally clear in view of Trevor's performance. Now, there's almost no other actor on earth that I can think of, who was capable of doing just that.'

As an actor, Sir Richard feels that nobody knows the difficulty or the terror of playing a small part and greatly admires British character actors because they are prepared to give as much as they've got to a cameo role: 'They have the courage to go on the set without any of the preparation or discussion that the stars have had and present their wares magnificently.'

Trevor had rather more than two days as Professor Tessonow for *Inside the Third Reich* – he had ten. This was for American television and it was made in Munich with John Gielgud and Derek Jacobi. Then it was Guardian Angel time again, working with George Schaefer in *The Deadly Game*. This Dürrenmatt story had been a favourite of Trevor Howard's for years and at last he was not only in it but directed by George Schaefer, whom he loves. Also, although it was made for American cable television, it was shot in the BBC studios.

It is an excellent upmarket television tale about a young man lost in the Swiss snows. He is rescued by four men who relive their former careers – a judge, prosecuting counsel, defence counsel and a hangman – and they accuse the young man of having murdered his wife.

Robert Morley played the judge, Trevor the prosecutor, Emlyn Williams was for the defence and Alan Webb the hangman. George Segal was the accused. George Schaefer enjoys working in London: 'But we were working under pressure. Frankly, it is not easy now for Trevor to retain those great quantities of words and the back and forth question and answer. He worked so desperately hard and I hope he's as fond of me as I am of him. The show did wonderfully well here in America, and I'm told the ratings were very high in the UK.' With a cast like that they should have been high. In America, *The Deadly Game* won nominations for Achievements in Cable Excellence for George Schaefer, Trevor Howard and George Segal.

During 1983 Trevor Howard was again summoned by American television but this time he went to Washington to play Lord Thomas Fairfax in *George Washington*. It was one of those productions that Trevor describes as being 'un-family': the cast was never all gathered together at one time.

Douglas Roberts is a young actor from Baltimore who played the Auctioneer in *George Washington*. He had been fascinated by the stories going around at the time of *Mutiny on the Bounty*. He also attended the première of the film in New York and it was his very first première – the spotlights and the stars, wow! The stars were all making their grand entrance and he thought the people were so rude: 'They were all Hollywood show-bizzy people and when Brando came in they booed because he had cost their business so much money with his whims and fancies.' Roberts found he was embarrassed for Brando. Although Trevor Howard wasn't present at the opening, when his picture came up on the credits: 'He actually got applause from this arch 3,000 people.' Roberts knew that Trevor Howard was very highly respected, but he thought Brando was held in respect, too: 'But not this time. He'd cost them too much money. They booed again when he made his entrance dressed as a fop. To an American audience that meant queer. Fifteen minutes later Brando left the theatre.'

Douglas Roberts's observations were made twenty-one years after the première of *Mutiny on the Bounty* and he was still embarrassed for Marlon Brando. During the filming of *George Washington*, Douglas recognized Trevor Howard in the dining room and noticed other members of the company going over to pay their respects. Although he was dying to meet an actor he revered and respected, he was too diffident to join them. Then, while he was in the trailer being wigged, he was left alone while the lady wigger went off to fetch pieces and switches – and in walked Trevor Howard. He sat at the other end of the trailer and there they were alone – in dead silence. There was nothing to read and the silence grew considerably louder. Finally Roberts broke it: 'Hi, how're you doing?' Trevor smiled, 'Fine'. They chatted for a while from either end of the trailer until Roberts said, 'I'm going to move down so we don't have to scream at each other. Would that be all right with you?' Trevor agreed that it would be perfectly fine.

Then the chat really began. Roberts observes that English gentlemen always wind up doing the interviewing. There were all the things that Roberts was dying to ask about *The Bounty* and instead he was answering questions about his own life. After ten minutes, Trevor Howard knew exactly why Roberts was there but Roberts was no further forward than when they started chatting. But he watched and observed. He was amazed at Trevor's interest in everything going on around him: 'It was like watching a twelve-year-old looking around at the wigs and make-up sketches. It was almost as though it was his first time around – that wonderful inquisitiveness that some of the great ones have. They never quit studying and finding out what's going on and he had all that. His eyes were just so alive. He treated me with all the graciousness and courtesy of his leading man – instead of the guy who was in from Baltimore to play the

Auctioneer, the scene that would probably be the first one cut out of the movie.'

To Roberts, it looked like Trevor Howard's first day for wigs and fittings. There were masses of people around him with tape measures, the lot: 'More than God really needs', but the movie was financed by MGM.

Roberts and Trevor never played together and Roberts never had a chance to watch Trevor at work. Finally Roberts said that, although he would have given much to have had a scene with Trevor Howard, he felt he had been better served by the twenty minutes tête-à-tête he had with him in the make-up trailer.

None of Trevor Howard's tasks in 1984 were lengthy engagements, but the subject matter ranged far and wide. To his agent's dismay, he insisted on accepting a part in *Love Boat*, the American soap opera for American televiewers, and some others. Having used Californian waters to the limit, the producers of *Love Boat* thought to cruise European waterways for a change of scene so Trevor missed out on Bahia California, and was only obliged to travel as far as Southampton. He was teamed with an actress he had long admired, Colleen Dewhurst, and he enjoyed every second: 'Happiest time I've had for years, Colleen Dewhurst was wonderful. I don't think our bits were written as comedy, but we chose the style between us. The writer lost out on that one – he was in America.'

Trevor's next stop was Vienna, to play Sir Isaac Newton in *Peter the Great*, then on to Spain to play Le Père in *Dust*, a Belgian production directed by Marion Hansel. The script was based on a book by the South African writer, J. M. Coetzee, and is set in his country. Essentially, the film has four characters, Le Père, and his daughter Magda, played by Jane Birkin, and their native foreman and his wife, Hendrik and Klein Anna. Magda suffers the frustrations of an old maid's virginity and an Oedipal obsession for her father. When he seduces the young Klein Anna, his daughter kills him and buries the body secretly.

This was very unusual material for Trevor Howard and, at the time of writing, *Dust* has not yet been released. However, the film was awarded the Silver Lion at the 1985 Venice Film Festival.

From his co-star, Jane Birkin, Trevor received the following message, written on the back of the title page from her script:

San Jose. 16 Oct 1984
'Dust'

Very dear Trevor,

I can't tell you how happy you have made me. What a sweet companion, wonderful fun, moving and truly inspiring.

Father, thank you for being you and for giving me such a dear part of you. I will stop now so as not to be soppy! But I am so *fond* of you, so what can I do?

With my love,
Jane.

Please accept this unsentimental ham – given with affection to you and Helen ... if uneatable bury it in the garden!

Trevor rounded off the year as Handel in *God Rot Tunbridge Wells* for Tony Palmer. Sadly, all concerned with the production, with the exception of the cameraman, Nic Knowland, were soundly trounced by the critics, but Tony Palmer appears to be a survivor. His comments on working with Trevor Howard are touching and perceptive.

Tony Palmer was born in the year that saw the making of *Brief Encounter* and it somehow became one of his earliest film memories. As he grew he saw more of Trevor Howard on the screen and determined to work with him one day. When discussing *God Rot Tunbridge Wells* with John Osborne, who wrote the script, they both agreed that there was only one choice for the name role – Trevor Howard. At the beginning Palmer had difficulty in getting a decision from James Sharkey, Trevor's agent, who asked how long Palmer would need to film the very long role of Handel. Thinking that Trevor was pressed for time Palmer replied, rather grandly, that he could probably wrap it in four or five days. Then a meeting between Trevor and Palmer was arranged, with Palmer immensely nervous about meeting one of his heroes. It transpired that Trevor wanted to play Handel very badly, but knew there was no possibility that such a part could be shot in five days.

Then Palmer realized there was a certain amount of nervousness about the retention of such very long speeches. Palmer rapidly solved that problem. As he says, 'Mrs Thatcher has the boards so why shouldn't Trevor Howard have them? He's a much better performer.' Having found a way to do it, Trevor Howard agreed, and they did it in four days.

Once they started shooting, Trevor Howard wouldn't stop. Everyone else felt the day was done by five-thirty, but there was no break until Trevor had done what he thought he could do that day. So they worked on until eight-thirty or nine. Eventually it was Palmer who had to flag him down and point out that the unit was getting a tiny bit tired: 'He got rather grumpy when we stopped – a kind of lighthearted grumpiness – because he just wanted to go on. We were falling by the wayside – but not him.'

As a director, Tony Palmer found Trevor Howard, 'one of the most delightful, really professional people one has ever worked with. He doesn't disappoint in any way.' Like other directors, he was impressed by Trevor's habit of changing the pace of a sentence so that, at the time, it sounds totally bizarre, but seen on screen it is completely enriched. Looking back in all the films that Palmer has seen Trevor in, he remembers the special quality he brings to them: 'Even in *Gandhi* – that tiny part is a show-stopper for me. That's the hot spot of the film. You are seeing great acting there, with about three words, two nods and a wink.'

When Trevor Howard finished *God Rot Tunbridge Wells*, he had an instinctive feeling that he had gone over the top, and the critics appeared to agree with him. Tony Palmer, however, flatly denies that it was so – and he's a young man with more than the courage of his convictions.

Trevor was in three other television productions: *Sharka–Zulu*, which was made in Durban and Capetown with Edward Fox and Christopher Lee; *This Lightning Always Strikes Twice*, with Charles Dance for Granada; and *Time After Time* which was made in Co Wicklow with Sir John Gielgud, Googie Withers, Brenda Bruce and Helen Cherry. As a valediction to 1985 he played Dr Stirrup in the film *Foreign Body* directed by Ronald Neame. This is a comedy scripted by Céline La Frenière and Ronald Neame from a novel by Roderick Mann. With Trevor Howard are Victor Banerjee and Warren Mitchell.

Of the cameo parts that Trevor has played, none were smaller than his appearance as Hippo in *Time After Time*, but it was a personal choice; Helen had a lovely part and he wanted to be in Ireland with her. It was the work of a young director, Bill Hayes, who enchanted Helen one evening at dinner with an on-rush of enthusiasm: 'I'm so happy you and Trevor are playing together in this,' he said, 'because, after all, you are getting on — it might be the last thing you do.' He appeared to have overlooked the fact that another distinguished member of his cast, Sir John Gielgud, was eighty-one years of age.

Certainly James Sharkey, Trevor Howard's agent, sees no likelihood of Trevor drifting into voluntary retirement. During the fifty-two years since Trevor Howard first appeared on the stage and the forty-one years since his first film, he has been on the books of several agents. With James Sharkey he has almost returned to base, since Sharkey was Al Parker's associate for ten years. Sharkey not only knows every phase of Trevor's career, he is intelligent, articulate and recognizes the winds of change that have blown through every aspect of show business. He is sympathetic to Trevor's passion for work — even though he was against *Love Boat* — and is very aware of the hazards of instant stardom: 'If you get a coup like *Brief Encounter*, you might be lucky and get other good pictures. Or you are offered rubbish and have to decide whether to refuse it, and have no work, or do it and deface your own currency. If you go to the top in one and then refuse all offers unless they are exactly what you think you should be doing, the chances are that you just become a fable in your own lifetime.'

James Sharkey's general views are germane to Trevor Howard's working history; many actors suffer an up-and-down pattern between very good, not-so-good and dreadful productions, the overriding factor being that the function of an actor is to act, hoping to be remembered by the good ones while the rubbish lies forgotten. He acknowledges Trevor's very high standards and feels it must be very galling to try for the best alongside mediocrities in the form of actors and scripts. Once started, the actor is on a treadmill and it takes great courage to call a halt and refuse to do anything that isn't first-class. 'Ally that to Trevor's passion for work and only the Almighty could stop him.'

Ironically, although many Trevor Howard watchers claim that his great talents have been neglected, underused or even badly used during his career, there has also been the view that he has chosen wisely and well. This has been expressed in somewhat envious tones by other actors in the belief that Trevor Howard would starve rather than accept a bad film or a role that was less than his due. The feeling was that he could pick and choose — and did. This could be because he has never accepted anything below the mediocre, which he uplifts, and because he has brought a luminosity to the smallest of parts.

Now Sharkey is trying to reverse the cameo aspect of his career. Apart from other considerations, no matter how high the quality of performance, unless the production is a fiscal success even the cameo player loses out. This is particularly so in America: box office returns equal bankability for all concerned. Although he is trying to arrest the trend, Sharkey does not think Trevor's small parts, or cameos, have been a bad policy by and large because: 'With that marvellous face and extraordinary talent, that picture-stealing quality, he has become much more marketable once again.' He also believes that careers tend to be cyclical and the dips registered on Trevor Howard's working graph are not peculiar to him. Many artists are forced by circumstances to accept less than they would wish because the alternatives don't exist.

'The thing about Trevor is that when he's on-screen he takes over, not in an unbalancing way, just his ability, his persona; not theatrical panache, but the truth and honesty of his talent. He was wonderful in very good films, he's also been wonderful in mediocre films — and in some quite bad ones.' It's also fair to say that a mediocre script can become quite a bad film in the making.

Sharkey appreciates Trevor's complete professionalism, that he reads scripts as soon as he receives them and is quick with his reaction. Usually it's a very positive reaction and he's usually correct in his assessment. If he's not sure, he reads it again and then gives an answer, often by telephone. During one such call Sharkey made the Freudian slip of a lifetime. Trevor sounded a little 'overtired' so Sharkey said, 'Don't let's discuss it today, let's discuss it tomorrow when you're not feeling so well.'

Having known Trevor for so many years, Sharkey remembers the past: 'In the old days Trevor had the reputation of being a hell-raiser, along with a lot of other people, but he was younger then and, anyway, what's the point of being a movie star if you can't raise a bit of hell?' Sir Richard Attenborough put it rather differently, 'If it was necessary for two people to get pissed every now and again in order to give the performances that emanated from Trevor Howard and Wilfrid Lawson, I'm for getting pissed.'

Quite so, but was the reputation damaging? Sharkey thinks it was. He thinks that it did militate against Trevor and may be one of the reasons why his career didn't always flourish as it should have done. It's a lively possibility, but it's a stone-cold certainty that Trevor Howard would be the same all over again. He gave his very best to his work, but his private pleasures were, and remain, his own affair.

However, it seems that even now there are newer directors who have never worked with Trevor and have never met him, who question his reliability because of that reputation. If the quality and range of his recent work has done nothing to reassure them, it is possible that their reluctance is more nearly rooted in fear of working with so seasoned an international player. A sense of personal inadequacy in directors has been known vis-à-vis star names. But they are counter-balanced by young directors such as Marion Hansel and Tony Palmer who were delighted with their star and with whom Trevor Howard much enjoyed working.

As Sharkey says, 'Trevor is learning to work with new and young directors and enjoying it. He has realized that you don't have to be an old master – you can be very talented at twenty-five. Trevor gets on perfectly well with anybody, providing he can see they know what they're doing. He would certainly find it tiresome to walk on a set and find an inexperienced young idiot director – and some are.'

To some degree this answers a doubt expressed by Dilys

Powell. While she feels that there is 'a great big film in Trevor somewhere', she also wonders who might direct it, fearing that young people might not understand him. It would seem that some do and some do not – but that might be equally applicable to some of the older hands.

Although James Sharkey can rationalize Trevor Howard's career he also feels that he could have played in less of the mediocre and more of the good with the right voice behind him; he did lack the right guidance and did deserve a far more illustrious career. But it would have been a hard task to curb his impatience to work every possible day, since work, and Helen, are his entire life: 'Hard to apportion blame, but it's sad that there wasn't somebody who could have persuaded him to be a little more selective, because he could well have afforded to be.' When it came to the rate for the job, Sharkey shares Bernard Kimble's view of Trevor's attitude towards money: he expects to be paid, but isn't greedy. 'He won't do rubbish for nothing but he'll do better than rubbish for less than he would normally command because it's worth doing.'

Sharkey thinks that Trevor receives admiration and respect from so many people because of his background. He sees him as one of the few English actors who belong to the equivalent of the great Hollywood days – an international star. On the street, in a restaurant, he is recognized with affection, but always with respect.

While others are picking over the vast number of roles he has played and claimed on his behalf that his great talents have not been used to the full, Trevor keeps his own counsel and voices few regrets. He is far more interested in the role he might be playing tomorrow than in the one he played the day before yesterday. But he does wonder. He wonders about two facets of his roles that have been a constant puzzle throughout his long years as a leading man. He wonders why he has never, ever won the girl in the end and why, since he's supposed to represent the epitome of the British male, practically all his leading ladies have been foreign. He did win the girl once. He was linked inexorably to Aissa at the end of *An Outcast of the Islands* – by which time he loathed the sight of her.

Throughout the years, Trevor Howard has suffered very few

cool reviews and no downright bad ones, but he has never courted critics, has never forged personal friendships, through correspondence or hospitality, but has just been courteous and friendly when the occasion arose. In this he must be almost unique, but his reasoning is sound. He doesn't care for good notices that might be tempered by friendship. He wants straight, uncontaminated, professional critiques of his work. Dilys Powell respects this view and shares it. She feels as deeply as Trevor that there can be no easy meeting place between actor and critic and has often refused even to meet actors, 'because it's so difficult if you meet somebody and you think they're awfully nice – then you go back and write that they act like a starfish. It's painful.'

Dilys Powell is often quoted in this book, not only because she is our most distinguished film critic, but because her career and that of Trevor Howard have passed through the same years, the same films. But she and Trevor are not close, personal friends. They have met, in warm and friendly fashion, at film festivals abroad and film showings at home, but that is all. Therefore the last words on Trevor Howard from Dilys Powell are ones to be treasured by him: 'I'm a fan, not only an admirer, a critical admirer. I'm a fan, really.'

CHAPTER FIFTEEN

It has been quite a while since Helen or Trevor Howard received a call from Fleet Street asking if one had left the other or whether they were just discussing divorce. Presumably, after more than forty years of marriage, either the answer is no longer of vital interest or the enquirers have despaired. In fairness to those whose task it was to ask, many of Trevor's former antics and peccadillos could have given rise to such suspicions. The so-called hell-raising was not very serious in marital terms — he never left a face on the bar-room floor, not even his own — but he was unpredictable in ways that many a bride would have found intolerable.

Jack Davies recalls attending a party at Arkley where Helen greeted the guests with her customary warmth and charm but where there was no sign of Trevor. When Jack asked where he was Helen smiled. 'I don't know,' she said. 'I think somebody invited him to Paris for a drink and he's gone.' And so he had, with Kenneth More and several other merry-makers. Spur-of-the-moment adventure brought a light to Trevor's eye that only a good script could equal. He once took off, at a moment's notice with friends in a private plane to Capri for breakfast and was surprised to see the jaunt reported in the press. He saw nothing odd in his actions: when not working, his time was his own, he wasn't a nine-to-five fellow, so what was the matter with going to Capri for breakfast? He was game for anything and everything outside the boring normal was a game.

In Trevor's case the onlookers didn't see most of the sport. They saw a man they thought to be testing his marriage to the limit; no wife could possibly put up with Trevor for long, she would have to be a saint. As time passed and the marriage endured they decided Helen *was* a saint. However, rumours of her canonization were greatly exaggerated. Helen is not a saint, but she is a truly remarkable woman who has never doubted that she married the right man, that is to say, right for her. Life with

Trevor may have been exacting — and remains so — but it has also been exciting and never boring. Helen cherished his unpredictability because she is very much her own woman, with her own interests, her own work, her own foibles and an independence of spirit, apart from things material.

Like many a full-blooded man — and a lot of women — Trevor can never be wrong. He might make a few mistakes, but he can't be wrong — it was somebody else, not him. Even so, he has been heard to wonder aloud why on earth Helen put up with his early shenanigans, just as he avers that the best thing he ever did in his entire life was to marry her. And so it was. For all his adventures, Trevor has always had a strong homing instinct, expecially when far from it. Buried somewhere in his subconscious must lie an image of Helen and home, which manifests itself in strange ways and unlikely places.

Christopher Lee has vivid memories of flying with Trevor to the first Panama Film Festival. They sat together on a nine-hour flight to Miami talking about everything under the sun, but not drinking as far as Lee can recollect. Trevor was in good form when they put down in Miami, with an hour and a half to wait for their connection to Panama. They wandered around the airport bars and shops before returning to the Clipper Club.

By then Trevor was feeling no pain so he continued to take his medicine like a man during the next flight. While there was no pain, there was much voice and a certain amount of action. Trevor wanted to stand up and the hostesses wanted him to sit down for the landing. So far as Trevor was concerned, this meant they were not on his side — and he told them so, because not to be on Trevor's side is kissing cousin to a mortal sin. Watching the cabaret, Christopher Lee reflected that the meeting with the reception committee would be interesting. It wasn't because by good fortune there had been an error and the British contingent was thought to be arriving the following day.

Somebody made a telephone call and a fleet of cars arrived. Trevor was pressed into one and promptly fell asleep. By now it was night. A few miles outside Panama city, Trevor woke up. He gazed wildly around, opened the window and peered out, then gave a despairing cry, 'This isn't the way to Barnet!'

There are several variations on that theme from around the

world. They all indicate Trevor's basic need in time of stress — Barnet, or home, which means Helen.

During the early years of their marriage, Trevor and Helen were frequently separated by work. Then came a time when Trevor's contracts included a clause enabling Helen to join him on location at will. As Trevor says, 'If you're stuck half way round the world for weeks or months ...' Since Helen enjoys travel and new countries as much as Trevor does, she has always film-followed whenever possible. She has also accompanied him to film festivals from time to time, including one in Mar del Plata. It was held at the same time as the elections and Helen was astonished to see numerous posters of the long-gone Evita urging the populace to vote for Perón. She was even more amazed that such blatant usage won votes.

Although Trevor loves to travel and has enjoyed adventures, he now likes to be properly organized. He has travelled so far and wide on locations that he is accustomed to having his flights arranged, to being met in style and to know that a comfortable hotel expects him. Helen rather yearns to take off into the blue and take whatever is available as they find it. She hasn't won that one yet.

Because holidays are governed by work, dates are hard to pinpoint when looking backwards, but friends, places and jokes remain sharp in the memory. To Trevor and Helen ski-ing in Switzerland means Dr Fred Auer and his wife, Heidi. Helen had met them first when she went to ski in Engelberg, they became close friends and Helen is godmother to one of the Auer children. When possible Trevor and Helen stayed with them and skied in Engelberg and when Fred and Heidi moved to St Moritz the holidays continued there.

Other jolly times were spent in the Bahamas with much-loved friends, Bill and Penny Turtle, or at Hammamet in Tunisia where the Howards revelled in Jean and Violet Henson's house which was set on a beautiful stretch of deserted beach.

As Helen is a superb co-driver, and hates to travel anywhere without a dictionary, an atlas and a encyclopaedia, motoring holidays have been the most frequent. They were once driving towards Florence and decided to spend the night at Fiesole, thinking to stay at a former monastery, the Villa San Michele.

On arrival they were told that a room was available but, 'Would you mind waiting while we put the furniture back?'. They didn't mind, but they were curious. The explanation was simple. Sir Alec Guinness had just vacated the room and he preferred it to be stripped down to cell-like sparseness — hence the replacement of the furniture.

In France, a far less spiritual atmosphere was engendered by Trevor at Cassis, a favourite overnight stop. They arrived towards evening and there was every sign of a storm blowing up at sea. Before going down to have their routine drink on the quay, Helen attended to some unpacking while Trevor looked up a word or two in the dictionary. His French was rather shaky but he wanted to have something to say, particularly as there was a storm brewing. He sorted his dialogue out and they went off for their apéritif.

The regulars and the old men with pipes were in their customary places, *Bonsoirs* were exchanged and Trevor waited for his cue — which was thunder and lightning. Then he seized a gap in the general conversation and was on: '*Je pense qu'il y aura un peu de zig-zag ce soir,*' he announced. There was dead silence until an old salt gave voice to a rich 'Ho-ho-ho!' when everybody roared with laughter, which gave Trevor a clue. In local parlance, he had opined that, 'I think there'll be a little fucking tonight.'

A few years later Trevor and Helen were back in Cassis and were strolling beside the port looking for the boatmen who used to take them out. As they neared the café some youngsters appeared, stared at Trevor and at once raced into the bar calling, '*Venez, venez — Monsieur Zig-Zag est venu!*' That's folkloric fame.

For the last ten years holidays have generally been spent in their own house in France. When they are coming to an end, Trevor can be found poring over maps and guidebooks, plotting their homeward course. This is a very private task because it has to be a day-to-day surprise for Helen as they take their time, sharing the driving, across country towards the Channel.

Currently they make the journey in a Mercedes 350 SL, a fairly recent acquisition which Trevor felt, rather shyly, was an extravagance — until he got a friendly nudge from his wife. Now he admits to enjoying a car which 'practically drives itself'. Years ago Trevor drove a sporty Bristol, in racing green with tomato-coloured upholstery. Once, when accompanying Helen to the Motor Show, he fell to chatting with a Bristol salesman who turned out to be an Old Cliftonian. His name was Anthony Crook and he took lively pride in his lapel button which read A. Crook. This so delighted Trevor that he actually bought a very large, limousine-style Bristol. After a few months Trevor sold it again on the ground that it was too pretentious, it wasn't his style and, anyway, he was due to visit Australia. Status symbols and Trevor have little in common. Neither is he likely to emulate a film director with whom both Helen and Trevor have worked. This one bought his wife a Rolls-Royce Corniche to celebrate their twenty-five years of marriage, discovered they had only been married for twenty-four, so decided to keep the Roller for himself.

Trevor and Helen not only relish that story, they also recall being weekend guests of the same director. It was a large house party, reeking of opulence and grandeur. Helen went up to bed before Trevor and was somewhat surprised to find that she was trying to nestle between starched damask tablecloths in lieu of sheets. Sleep was not easy and when midnight came with no sign of Trevor she set off to find him, creeping carefully around a vast and strange house. Trevor was found, not quite stretched out on a settee and very far from comfortable. Nobody had thought to show him to their room and he wasn't about to go round knocking on every door.

The following morning Trevor went down to breakfast quite a while before Helen. When she finally descended she found her husband sitting bolt upright on the same settee looking highly embarrassed. Their practically naked hostess was draped all over him, drinking whisky. It became apparent that the name of the game was to 'go Hollywood'. By the end of the day the entire party had forsaken their clothes, with the notable exception of Trevor and Helen. As Trevor says, 'You don't get laughs like that any more.'

Neither did they attend such parties very often; show-bizzy gatherings have never been their favourites. They both enjoy jollies and Trevor has often been quoted as always being the last to leave them, 'I'm always afraid I might miss something. Just something.' But that mainly applies to parties of people with whom he is at ease, whom he likes and finds interesting or amusing. Helen is more gregarious and is sometimes hospitable to people for whom Trevor has little time, or with whom he had nothing in common, but such occasions are never a cause of conflict. Either Trevor stays and is quietly polite, or he just ups and goes elsewhere.

Although Trevor and Helen have many friends in many countries, their affections are not always vested in members of their profession. Trevor is always drawn to people who have created a niche for themselves, who have chosen to succeed in something that is not commonplace.

But there was one actor whom Trevor describes as about the greatest gentleman he ever met. Although the actor was firmly based in Hollywood he always refused to film during the English summer because then he returned home to watch cricket. Trevor used to sign him in at Lord's every day a match was playing, loved his company and thought him a very handsome man. Helen was equally devoted to him, finding him attractive and very intelligent. This was the actor known as Boris Karloff, born William Pratt in England. He fascinated Trevor as a man who had chosen his particular genre of role and style of acting and had never stepped aside from it.

Pressed to name his truly close friends, Trevor shakes his head, thinks a while and murmurs, 'Just Helen really.' It sounds unbelievably sad, to the point of being melodramatic but, by Trevor's standards, undeniably true. He is too private, too secret a man to have close confidants. He wouldn't trust any other human being with his entire self. But he has many friends, in the more loosely used term, all over the world and they are all on his side – although he often suspects they are not. Then he feels betrayed and can become savagely critical of them.

He claims to be puzzled by references to that strain of sadness that seems to come from within: 'Lots of people say it. But I don't know what I'm sad about – boredom, I suppose. You can't be jumping up and down laughing all the time. I've done enough of that and it was called hell-raising.' He is now tired of that tag and would prefer to be recognized as an eccentric – a term with which most of his friends would concur although it is at total variance with those polished performances, if not with romps such as *Sir Henry*. But as that old rascal Trevor reckons he was just being himself.

As an eccentric, he feels somewhat cut off from the action nowadays. He rarely visits friends in London so, unless he is working, he says, 'There's no one to be eccentric *with*, except Harry. He's got a bit of it.' Harry Poole, the landlord of The Gate, is a good friend and a visit to his pub is now regarded as an outing.

Trevor's belief in his Guardian Angel, to which he clings, is the closest he comes to admitting a religious belief, but this is probably part of his iron-clad privacy. Helen is slightly ambivalent about religion but there is a little Catholic church in Maiden Lane which she used to visit, to pray and light a candle when her brother was desperately ill. Ever since, she has arranged her appointments in London to have time to sit a while in the church, which gives her great comfort and pleasure. But she is unsure, she doesn't know whether her actions are born of faith or superstition. She just knows it is something she does privately, as opposed to attending the local church wearing a new hat. She does, however, collect funds for the local church as well as doing other good neighbourly deeds in the village.

For some tribal reason, childless couples are constantly asked why they have no children or, more discreetly, whether they miss, or mind, the lack of them. Trevor was asked such a question during a television interview with Daniel Farson, who writes '. . . including the sadness of not having children. Some people thought I should *not* have pressed him on this, but he answered well.' Daniel Farson is far from being a thumbscrew type interviewer and is highly admiring of Trevor Howard. His letter ends: 'Ironically, it would be easier to write about him if he was not such a loveable man. Bastards are better copy.' So it can be assumed that Trevor did not express sadness about his childless state, under duress.

Helen has regrets – she regrets not having grandchildren! But that is all. When they were first married, they had careers to build in the post-war era and felt it was too soon to have children. Much later, there came a time when they decided to start a family. 'But it was really too late or just wasn't going to happen. We never sat down and actually discussed it, which seems odd now.'

Trevor probably does have some regrets, but it would be impossible to gauge their depth. Helen is quite sure that, given a family, she would have had to accept the major responsibility for their upbringing and well-being; she would have been permanent Mummy and Trevor would have been occasional Daddy – except with boys, when they grew old enough to play cricket. Helen knows that, outside his work, Trevor doesn't accept responsibilities in daily life, and this can be seen to be true. With children, Helen's own career would have died, she would have been unable to follow her husband around the world and – she can't be sure but who can? – she is reasonably certain that children would have driven them apart rather than kept them together. In essence, it would have been a choice between motherhood and marriage. Helen preferred to protect the latter. She feels that, had they had children, they would not be together now.

The most Trevor says, with an odd little smile, is: 'It's the women who decide these things, isn't it?'

Nevertheless, Trevor has made his contribution to posterity. In May 1983 he started the funding of a Martin Hardcastle Scholarship at Clifton College. With Helen, he visited Clifton to meet the present headmaster, Stewart Andrews, and to see his old friend, Martin Hardcastle.

At that time Stewart Andrew's suggested that part of Trevor's funding should go to create a Trevor Howard Award to be associated with the School Theatre. This was agreed and the Award was first given in June 1985 for direction during a House Drama Festival.

The academic Scholarship has also been supported by Tom Dover, the present Housemaster of School House – a position formerly held by Martin Hardcastle. Mr Dover organizes The Clifton Wine Offer, whereby a lorry-load of wine is purchased in France and resold. Formerly the profits went to some good cause outside the school, now they go towards the Scholarship – forming an apt association for a fund associated with Trevor Howard.

The Martin Hardcastle Scholarship was awarded for the first

time in May 1985 to a pupil of thirteen years of age for academic prowess. This will endure for the final five years of the pupil's term at the school and will next be awarded in 1990. When Trevor first created this fund Martin Hardcastle was overwhelmed by the idea of a Scholarship in his name. This marvellous man held the view that he had never been much of a scholar himself. That was his modest view and he may have been right but there is no doubt that he has always been an outstanding humanist.

According to Helen, Trevor has not changed one iota in all the years she has known him. For all the razzmatazz of stardom, he has retained the same standards, the same principles, the same indifference to wealth, the same reluctance to 'make character' to further his career and the same courtesy to one and all – regardless of social standing. He has always remembered Helen's birthday and their wedding anniversary, but has rarely chosen to celebrate either on the exact day. Let any celebration be a surprise, an adventure, not forced or automatic sentimentality.

In their early days Helen remembers accusing Trevor of being totally unromantic, whereupon he would mime the lovelorn swain, down on one knee with hands clasped dramatically to heart. He played it so far over the top that Helen could only rock with laughter. He used none of the usual ploys of courtship and reference to the giving or sending of flowers causes him to wince as though struck, 'Oh God, I never did any of *that!*'

From the very beginning Helen has been absolutely sure that nothing and nobody could separate them – so for the biggest role and the longest run of his life Trevor Howard *did* get his girl.

Le Rouret
1986

Awards

1958 *The Key*, British Film Academy, Best Actor.

1963 *The Invincible Mr Disraeli*, The National Academy of Television Arts and Sciences Emmy, Best Actor.

1965 *Eagle in a Cage*, The National Academy of Television Arts and Sciences, Nomination.

(Undated) *The Taming of the Shrew*, American Shakespearean Festival 7th Annual Shakespeare Award for Recording Presentations, for the role of Petruchio.

1960 *Sons and Lovers*, American Academy Awards, Nomination for Best Actor.

1960 *Sons and Lovers*, Hollywood Foreign Press Association, Nomination for Best Actor.

1975 *The Count of Monte Cristo*, The National Academy of Television Arts and Sciences, Nomination.

1982 *Light Years Away*, Evening Standard Award, Best Actor.

FILMS

Year	Title	Role	Director
1944	*The Way Ahead*	Naval Officer	Carol Reed
1945	*The Way to the Stars*	S/L Carter	Anthony Asquith
1945	*Brief Encounter*	Alec Harvey	David Lean
1945	*I See a Dark Stranger*	Lt. David Bayne	Frank Launder
1946	*Green for Danger*	Dr Barney Barnes	Sidney Gilliat
1947	*So Well Remembered*	Dr Whiteside	Edward Dmytryk
1947	*They Made Me a Fugitive*	Clem Morgan	Alberto Cavalcanti
1949	*The Passionate Friends*	Steven Stratton	David Lean
1949	*The Third Man*	Maj. Galloway	Carol Reed
1950	*The Golden Salamander*	David Redfern	Ronald Neame
1950	*Odette*	Capt. Peter Churchill	Herbert Wilcox
1950	*The Clouded Yellow*	David Somers	Ralph Thomas
1951	*An Outcast of the Islands*	Peter Willems	Carol Reed
1952	*The Gift Horse*	Lt.-Com. Hugh Fraser	Compton Bennett

Year	Title	Character	Director
1953	*The Heart of the Matter*	Harry Scobie	George More O'Ferrall
1953	*The Stranger's Hand*	Maj. Court	Mario Soldati
1954	*The Lovers of Lisbon*	Harry Lewis	Henri Vermeuil
1955	*Cockleshell Heroes*	Capt. Thompson	Jose Ferrer
1956	*Run for the Sun*	Browne	Roy Boulting
1956	*Around the World in Eighty Days*	Flanagan	Mkchael Anderson
			Kevin McClory
1957	*Manuela*	James Prothero	Guy Hamilton
1957	*Interpol*	Frank McNally	John Gilling
1958	*The Key*	Chris Ford	Carol Reed
1958	*The Roots of Heaven*	Morel	John Huston
1959	*Moment of Danger*	John Bain	Laslo Benedek
1960	*Sons and Lovers*	Walter Morel	Jack Cardiff
1962	*Mutiny on the Bounty*	Capt. Bligh	Lewis Milestone
1962	*The Lion*	John Bullitt	Jack Cardiff
1964	*The Man in the Middle*	Maj. Kensington	Guy Hamilton
1964	*Father Goose*	Frank Houghton	Ralph Nelson
1965	*Operation Crossbow*	Prof. Lindemann	Michael Anderson
1965	*Von Ryan's Express*	Maj. Eric Fincham	Mark Robson
1965	*The Saboteur, Code Name Morituri*	Col. Statter	Bernhard Wicki
1965	*The Liquidator*	Col. Mostyn	Jack Cardiff
1965	*The Poppy is Also a Flower*	Agent Lincoln	Terence Young

1967	Triple Cross	Civilian	Terence Young
1967	The Long Duel	Freddy Young	Ken Annakin
1967	Pretty Polly	Robert Young	Guy Green
1968	The Charge of the Light Brigade	Lord Cardigan	Tony Richardson
1969	The Battle of Britain	AVM Keith Parke	Guy Hamilton
1969	Twinky	Grandfather	Richard Donner
1971	Ryan's Daughter	Father Collins	David Lean
1971	Catch Me a Spy	Sir Trevor Dawson	Dick Clement
1971	The Night Visitor	Police Inspector	Laslo Benedek
1971	Mary Queen of Scots	William Cecil, Lord Burghley	Charles Jarrott
1971	Ludwig	Richard Wagner	Luchino Visconti
1972	The Offence	Cartwright	Sidney Lumet
1972	Pope Joan	Pope Leo	Michael Anderson
1973	A Doll's House	Dr Rank	Joseph Losey
1973	Craze	Superintendent Bellamy	Freddie Francis
1974	Eleven Harrowhouse	Clyde Massey	Aram Avakian
1974	Persecution	Paul Bellamy	Don Chaffey
1975	Conduct Unbecoming	Col. Benjamin Strang	Michael Anderson
1975	Hennessy	Rice	Don Sharp
1975	Death in the Sun	Johannes	Jurgen Goslar
1975	The Bawdy Adventures of Tom Jones	Squire Western	Cliff Owen
1976	Aces High	Lt. Col. Silkin	Jack Gold

Year	Film	Character	Director
1976	*Eliza Fraser*	Capt. Foster Fyans	Tim Burstall
1977	*Slavers*	Alec MacKenzie	Jurgen Goslar
1977	*The Last Remake of Beau Geste*	Sir Hector	Marty Feldman
1978	*Stevie*	The Man	Robert Enders
1978	*Superman*	1st Elder	Richard Donner
1979	*Meteor*	Sir Michael Hughes	Ronald Neame
1979	*The Missionary*	Lord Ames	Richard Loncraine
1979	*Hurricane*		Jan Troell
1980	*The Sea Wolves*	Jack Cartwright	Andrew V. McLaglen
1980	*Sir Henry at Rawlinson End*	Sir Henry Rawlinson	Steve Roberts
1980	*The Windwalker*	Windwalker	Kieth Merrill
1981	*Light Years Away*	Yoshka Poliakoff	Alain Tanner
1982	*Gandhi*	Judge Broomfield	Richard Attenborough
1983	*Sword of the Valiant*		Stephen Weekes
1984	*Dust*	Le Père	Marion Hansel
1985	*Foreign Body*	Dr Stirrup	Ronald Neame

With the exception of the years 1984 and 1985 all dates given are those of general release.

THEATRE

Year	Play	Character	Theatre	Producer
1934	Revolt in a Reformatory	2nd Boy	The Gate Theatre	Peter Godfrey
1934	The Drums Begin	Schwenck	The Embassy Theatre	John Fernald
1934	Androcles and the Lion	Slave	Winter Garden Theatre	Robert Atkins
1934	The Faithful	Sagisaka	Westminster Theatre	Norman Page
1934	Alien Corn	Harry Conway	Westminster Theatre	Beatrice Wilson
1935	The Rivals	Jack Absolute	Q Theatre	Dennis Roberts
1935	Crime and Punishment	Dmitri Coachman	Embassy Theatre	John Fernald
1935	Aren't We All?	Hon. Willie Tatham	Royal Court Theatre	Harrison Culff
1935	Justice	Walter How Wooder	Playhouse	Leon M. Lion
1935	The Skin Game	Charles Hornblower	Playhouse	Leon M. Lion
1935	A Family Man	Journalist	Playhouse	Leon M. Lion
1935	Lady Patricia	William O'Farrell	Westminster Theatre	John Wyse

Year	Play	Role	Theatre	Director
1935	*Legend of Yesterday*	Fred Johnson	Aldwych Theatre	
1935	*Timon of Athens*	Lucullus	Westminster Theatre	
1936			Stratford Memorial Theatre Company	Harold French
1936	*French Without Tears*	Kenneth Lake (Babe)	Criterion Theatre	
1937	*Waters of Jordan*	Bryan Elliott	Arts Theatre	
1938	*A Star Comes Home*	Ronnie Dent	Arts Theatre	
1943	*On Life's Sunny Side*	Joachim Bris	Arts Theatre	
1939			Stratford Memorial Theatre Company	
1939			Colchester Repertory Company	
1940			White Rose Players, Harrogate	
1943	*The Recruiting Officer*	Captain Plume	Arts Theatre	Alec Clunes
1944	*A Soldier for Christmas*	Ronald Vines	Wyndhams Theatre	Norman Marshall
1944	*Anna Christie*	Mat Burke	Arts Theatre	Judith Furse
1947	*The Taming of The Shrew*	Petruchio	New Theatre	John Burrell
1953	*The Devil's General*	General Harras	Savoy Theatre	John Fernald
1954	*The Cherry Orchard*	Lopahin	Lyric Theatre, Hammersmith	John Gielgud
1962	*Two Stars for Comfort.*	Sam Turner	Garrick Theatre	Michael Elliott
1964	*The Father*	The Captain	Piccadilly	Casper Wrede
1974	*The Waltz of the Toreadors*	General St-Pé	Haymarket Theatre	Peter Dews
1976	*The Scenario*	d'Anthac	Royal Alexandra, Toronto	Stuart Burge

TELEVISION

Date	Title	Role	Director
US 1954	*Tonight at 8.30*	Alec Harvey	Otto Preminger
US 1954	*The Flower of Pride*		Franklyn Schaefner
US	*Deception*		
GB	*Reunion in Vienna*		Cyril Coke
GB/US 1962	*Hedda Gabler*	Lovborg	Alex Segal
US 1963	*The Invincible Mr Disraeli*	Disraeli	George Schaefer
US 1965	*Eagle in a Cage*	Napoleon	George Schaefer
US 1973	*Catholics*	The Abbot	Jack Gold
US 1975	*The Count of Monte Cristo*	Old Man	
GB 1978	*Scorpion Tales (Easterman)*	Detective Inspector	David Reid
US 1979	*Night Flight*	Rivière	Desmond Davis
GB 1979	*The Shillingbury Blowers*	Old Saltie	Val Guest
GB 1980	*Staying On*	Tusker	Silvio Narizzano
US 1980	*Windwalker*	Windwalker	Kieth Merrill

INDEX